Cyber Renaissance

Morgan Liao's Digital Humanities

Taylor Liao

ISBN: 9781779666130
Imprint: Press for Play Books
Copyright © 2024 Taylor Liao.
All Rights Reserved.

Contents

The Birth of Morgan Liao

In a world where the digital and physical realms intertwine seamlessly, the tale of Morgan Liao begins in a rather unassuming yet uniquely futuristic hospital. The year was 2035, and the state-of-the-art facility was equipped with robotic nurses, AI-assisted doctors, and a vending machine that dispensed organic avocado toast — because what better way to greet the world than with a superfood?

A Futuristic Hospital Delivery

Morgan's entrance into the world was marked not by the typical cries of a newborn but by the soft whirring of machines and the melodic chime of digital notifications. His parents, both tech enthusiasts, had opted for a delivery in the hospital's "Digital Delivery Suite," where every moment was recorded in high-definition for posterity—or for social media, whichever came first. The doctors, clad in augmented reality visors, monitored Morgan's vital signs while simultaneously streaming the event live to a select group of family members who were too busy to attend in person.

The First Sign of Brilliance

As the nurses placed the newborn in his mother's arms, a strange phenomenon occurred: Morgan's tiny fingers twitched, as if he were already coding his first program. This moment was captured on a smart device, which later became a viral sensation, with hashtags like #BabyCoder and #FutureTechGenius trending on social media. Little did anyone know, this was just the beginning of a life filled with innovation and a penchant for mischief.

Parents in Awe

Morgan's parents, both software engineers, were in awe of their child's potential. They had imagined him growing up to be an astronaut or a rock star, but the reality of parenting a prodigy brought its own set of challenges. They quickly realized that raising a child who could potentially outsmart them at any moment required a unique approach—one that involved a lot of patience, a sprinkle of humor, and perhaps a few extra security measures on their home network.

Childhood Full of Curiosity

From an early age, Morgan exhibited an insatiable curiosity about the world around him. He dismantled household appliances, not out of rebellion, but to understand how they worked. His parents often found him surrounded by the remnants of a once-functioning toaster or a disassembled remote control. Each time, they were left pondering if they had birthed a future engineer or a professional mess-maker.

Early Interest in Computers

By the age of five, Morgan had developed a fascination with computers. His first interaction with a laptop was nothing short of legendary; he managed to bypass parental controls and access a world of online tutorials. This led to a love affair with coding that would only deepen over the years. While most kids were playing with building blocks, Morgan was building websites—though his first project, a fan page for his favorite cartoon character, was a bit less than impressive.

Hacking His Way into Trouble

As he entered elementary school, Morgan's skills took a turn towards the mischievous. He hacked into the school's attendance system to change his status from "absent" to "present" on days he wanted to skip class. This escapade earned him both a reputation among his peers and a stern talking-to from the school administration. "You know, Morgan," his principal said, "with great power comes great responsibility." To which he replied, "But with great hacking comes great fun!"

Encounters with the Law

Morgan's early exploits didn't just lead to school detentions; they also caught the attention of local law enforcement. One fateful day, he attempted to demonstrate his "skills" by accessing a public Wi-Fi network at the local library. Unfortunately, he inadvertently triggered a security alert, leading to a visit from the police. The incident ended with a warning and a stern lecture about the importance of ethical hacking—though Morgan couldn't help but think of it as merely a rite of passage.

Turning Points in Morgan's Life

Despite his run-ins with authority, there were pivotal moments that shaped Morgan's outlook on technology and innovation. One such moment occurred during a school science fair when he presented a project on renewable energy sources. His passion for the environment and technology ignited a spark in his peers and teachers alike, proving that even the most mischievous minds could channel their creativity into something meaningful.

Dedicated Teachers

Morgan was fortunate to have dedicated teachers who recognized his potential and nurtured his talents. They introduced him to programming languages and robotics, often staying after class to help him refine his projects. One teacher, Mrs. Rodriguez, even arranged for Morgan to attend a summer camp focused on coding and robotics, where he met other young innovators who would become lifelong friends and collaborators.

In summary, the birth of Morgan Liao was not just the beginning of a life but the genesis of a digital revolution. His early years were characterized by a blend of curiosity, mischief, and undeniable brilliance. As he continued to grow, it became increasingly clear that Morgan was destined to leave an indelible mark on the world of technology and the humanities, setting the stage for a future that would be anything but ordinary.

The Birth of Morgan Liao

In the year 2040, the world was on the brink of a technological renaissance, and amidst this backdrop of innovation, a child named Morgan Liao was born. The delivery took place in a state-of-the-art hospital equipped with the latest in medical technology, which could only be described as a blend of science fiction and reality. The delivery room was filled with holographic monitors displaying real-time data, and robotic assistants flitted about, ensuring everything went smoothly.

Morgan's birth was heralded by a series of unprecedented medical advancements. His mother, a software engineer, had opted for a revolutionary birthing procedure that involved a virtual reality experience designed to ease the stress of childbirth. As she donned the VR headset, she was transported to a serene beach, where the sound of waves crashing soothed her nerves. Meanwhile, Morgan emerged into the world with the first sign of brilliance: a perfectly timed cry that echoed through the sterile room, causing the attending doctors to chuckle.

A Futuristic Hospital Delivery

The hospital's delivery system was powered by an AI algorithm that could predict the optimal moment for delivery based on a multitude of factors, including the mother's health metrics and even the lunar cycle. This algorithm, known as *LunarPredict*, had been developed as part of a collaborative project between obstetricians and data scientists. It was a perfect example of how technology was revolutionizing even the most traditional aspects of life.

Morgan's parents were in awe, not just of their newborn, but of the technology that surrounded them. His father, a historian with a penchant for the humanities, often joked that Morgan was destined to be the first child born with a Wi-Fi connection. This humorous quip, while lighthearted, hinted at the merging of technology and human experience that would define Morgan's life.

The First Sign of Brilliance

As Morgan grew, it became evident that he possessed an insatiable curiosity. At the tender age of three, he could already navigate basic coding languages, much to the amazement of his parents. His first masterpiece was a simple program that controlled the lights in his room, allowing him to turn them on and off with a voice command. This early foray into coding was not just a child's play; it was a glimpse into the innovative mind that would later shape the digital humanities.

His parents recognized this spark of brilliance and nurtured it. They enrolled him in a coding camp for children, where he quickly became the star pupil. His instructors reported that he had an uncanny ability to grasp complex concepts, often helping his peers understand topics that were typically reserved for older students.

Parents in Awe

Morgan's parents often found themselves in awe of his abilities. They marveled at how he could dismantle and reassemble electronics with the ease of a seasoned engineer. Family dinners frequently turned into discussions about algorithms and data structures, with Morgan leading the charge. His father would occasionally joke, "I hope he doesn't hack into the fridge and make it dispense cookies!"

This humorous remark was a reflection of the playful atmosphere in the Liao household. Morgan's parents encouraged creativity and exploration, believing that the intersection of technology and the humanities would be the key to solving future challenges. They often reminded him of the importance of ethical considerations in technology, emphasizing that innovation should serve humanity, not hinder it.

Childhood Full of Curiosity

Morgan's childhood was characterized by an unquenchable thirst for knowledge. He would spend hours exploring the wonders of the internet, often diving deep into topics that piqued his interest. From the intricacies of quantum computing to the philosophies of ancient civilizations, Morgan absorbed information like a sponge. This eclectic mix of interests laid the groundwork for his future endeavors in digital humanities.

His bedroom resembled a mini-laboratory, filled with books on coding, history, and philosophy. Posters of influential figures like Ada Lovelace and Alan Turing adorned the walls, serving as constant reminders of the legacy of innovation. Morgan's favorite pastime was to create elaborate presentations for his family, explaining complex ideas with the enthusiasm of a seasoned lecturer.

Early Interest in Computers

By the age of six, Morgan had developed a fascination with computers that bordered on obsession. He would often disassemble old machines, much to the dismay of his parents, who were concerned about the state of their living room. However, they quickly learned that this was not merely destruction; it was Morgan's way of understanding how things worked.

One day, after successfully reassembling a vintage computer, he proudly announced, "I can now play 'Pong' on a machine older than me!" This moment encapsulated Morgan's approach to learning: hands-on experimentation coupled with a sense of humor that made even the most mundane tasks seem exciting.

Hacking His Way into Trouble

As Morgan entered his pre-teen years, his curiosity sometimes led him down questionable paths. He discovered the world of hacking, initially viewing it as a game. One fateful afternoon, he managed to gain unauthorized access to the school's Wi-Fi network. Instead of malicious intent, his goal was to create a more efficient way for students to access educational resources.

However, when the school's IT department discovered the breach, it resulted in a stern warning from the principal. Morgan's parents were called in for a meeting, where they were informed of their son's antics. They couldn't help but chuckle at the irony: their child, a budding innovator, had inadvertently become a "cyber outlaw."

Encounters with the Law

While his hacking escapades were mostly harmless, they did lead to a few encounters with the law. At one point, Morgan was invited to speak at a local community center about the importance of cybersecurity. His presentation, titled "Don't Be a Digital Dinosaur," was a humorous take on the need for modern security practices. He even dressed up as a dinosaur for comedic effect, which left the audience in stitches.

Despite the laughter, the reality of his actions weighed heavily on him. Morgan began to understand the ethical implications of technology and the importance of using his skills for good. This realization marked a turning point in his life, steering him toward a path of innovation that would prioritize ethical considerations.

Turning Points in Morgan's Life

Throughout his early years, several turning points shaped Morgan's character and aspirations. One pivotal moment occurred when he attended a seminar on digital ethics. The speaker, a renowned tech ethicist, discussed the impact of technology on society and the responsibilities of innovators. Morgan was captivated, realizing that he could use his talents to not only create but also to contribute positively to the world.

This seminar ignited a passion for digital humanities within him—a field that combined his love for technology with his father's historical interests. It became clear to Morgan that he could bridge the gap between the digital world and the rich tapestry of human culture.

Dedicated Teachers

As Morgan progressed through school, he encountered several dedicated teachers who recognized his potential. They encouraged him to pursue his interests and provided him with opportunities to explore the intersection of technology and the humanities. One particularly influential teacher, Ms. Thompson, introduced him to the concept of digital storytelling.

"Imagine," she said, "using technology to tell the stories of our past in ways that engage future generations!" This idea resonated deeply with Morgan and would later become a cornerstone of his work. Ms. Thompson's mentorship helped him realize that innovation was not just about creating new technologies, but also about preserving and sharing the narratives that define us as humans.

In summary, the birth of Morgan Liao was not just a moment in time but the beginning of a journey marked by curiosity, creativity, and a commitment to ethical innovation. His early experiences laid the foundation for a future filled with possibilities, where technology and the humanities would converge to shape the world in ways previously unimaginable.

The First Sign of Brilliance

Morgan Liao's first sign of brilliance manifested itself in the most unexpected of ways: during a routine family dinner, when he was just four years old. While most children his age were busy coloring outside the lines or attempting to negotiate the complexities of a chicken nugget, Morgan had his sights set on the family tablet. It was during this fateful evening that he inadvertently unlocked a world of possibilities—and his parents' WiFi password—leading to a cascade of events that would eventually redefine digital humanities.

The Unintentional Hacker

Morgan's initial foray into technology was less about intention and more about curiosity. As he sat at the dinner table, he noticed that his father was struggling to connect to the internet. In a moment of sheer brilliance—or perhaps mischief—Morgan reached for the tablet, swiped the screen with the confidence of a seasoned hacker, and accessed the settings menu. His father, bewildered and slightly impressed, could only watch as his son navigated through the digital labyrinth like a modern-day Theseus.

This incident sparked a pivotal question: what drives a child to explore technology so fervently? According to developmental psychologist Jean Piaget, children learn through active exploration and interaction with their environment. Morgan's actions can be viewed through the lens of Piaget's theory of cognitive development, which emphasizes the importance of hands-on experiences in fostering critical thinking and problem-solving skills.

The Spark of Curiosity

Morgan's curiosity was not limited to mere digital tinkering. It extended to a broader understanding of how technology intersects with the world around him. For instance, when he discovered that the tablet could also be used to create animations, he spent hours experimenting with simple software, leading to the creation of a short film that featured a dancing cat and an inexplicably philosophical goldfish.

This early project can be analyzed through the theory of constructivism, which posits that individuals construct knowledge through experiences. Morgan's playful engagement with technology allowed him to combine creativity with logic, laying the groundwork for his future endeavors in digital humanities. It was evident that this was not just a passing phase; rather, it was the genesis of a profound relationship with technology and storytelling.

Parental Support and Encouragement

While Morgan's innate curiosity was a driving force, it was the support of his parents that truly nurtured his brilliance. They recognized that their son was not merely playing; he was engaging with complex concepts like narrative structure and digital media production. Encouraged by their enthusiasm, Morgan's parents enrolled him in a local coding camp, where he learned the fundamentals of programming and met other young innovators.

This experience further fueled his passion and highlighted the importance of mentorship in a child's development. According to Vygotsky's Social Development Theory, social interaction plays a fundamental role in cognitive development. Morgan's interactions with instructors and peers at the coding camp provided him with the scaffolding necessary to advance his skills.

The Emergence of Problem-Solving Skills

As Morgan continued to explore the digital realm, he encountered challenges that tested his problem-solving abilities. For instance, when faced with a glitch in his animation software, rather than giving up, he took it upon himself to troubleshoot the issue. He researched online forums, watched tutorial videos, and even reached out to fellow young coders for assistance. This proactive approach to problem-solving is indicative of a growth mindset, a concept popularized by psychologist Carol Dweck.

Dweck's research suggests that individuals who embrace challenges and view failures as opportunities for learning are more likely to achieve success. Morgan's early experiences with setbacks instilled in him a resilience that would serve him well in his future endeavors.

A Glimpse into the Future

The first sign of brilliance in Morgan Liao was not merely a moment of childhood whimsy; it was a harbinger of the innovative thinker he would become. His early interactions with technology, fueled by curiosity, supported by parental encouragement, and enhanced by problem-solving experiences, set the stage for a life dedicated to revolutionizing digital humanities.

In hindsight, it is clear that this seemingly innocuous dinner table incident was the first step in a long journey. A journey that would eventually lead Morgan to explore the intersection of technology and the humanities, culminating in groundbreaking projects that would change the way we understand and interact with our digital world. As he would later reflect, "If I can unlock a WiFi password at four, imagine what I can do with the entire internet by the time I'm thirty!"

$$\text{Brilliance} = \text{Curiosity} + \text{Support} + \text{Problem-Solving} \tag{1}$$

Thus, the equation of brilliance was established, and Morgan Liao was well on his way to becoming a pioneer of the Cyber Renaissance.

Parents in Awe

Morgan Liao's arrival into the world was nothing short of a spectacle, akin to the grand opening of a new theme park—complete with confetti, fireworks, and possibly a clown or two (though the clowns were mostly in the hospital staff). The moment he took his first breath, the hospital's futuristic monitoring systems began to record data that would later be analyzed by a panel of intrigued scientists, eager to find out if this child was indeed the harbinger of a new age in digital humanities, or if he was just another baby with a penchant for drooling.

The Unprecedented Delivery Experience

In the year 2045, birthing technology had advanced to a point where deliveries were more like a scene from a sci-fi movie than a traditional hospital experience. Morgan's mother, Lisa, was wheeled into the delivery room, which was equipped with an artificial intelligence system named *NurtureBot 3000*. This system not only monitored vital signs but also provided live commentary, akin to a sports announcer narrating a championship game. As Morgan made his grand entrance, NurtureBot proclaimed, "And here comes the future, folks! Watch out for those tiny fingers—they're likely to be coding by age two!"

The First Signs of Brilliance

The first sign of Morgan's brilliance was not his ability to recite Shakespeare or solve complex mathematical equations at the age of two. No, it was a much simpler feat: the ability to turn on the family's smart fridge and request a snack using only his gaze. This phenomenon was documented in the family's home video archives, which later became a viral sensation on social media, leading to discussions about the potential of gaze-controlled technology in everyday life.

Parents in Awe

As Morgan grew, his parents, Lisa and David, found themselves in a constant state of awe. They were not just parents; they were like audience members at a magic show, witnessing tricks they could hardly comprehend. One day, while playing with building blocks, Morgan built a structure that resembled a miniature model of the Internet. When asked about it, he simply stated, "It's a router! You have to connect the blocks to create a network." At that moment, David realized that his son was not just playing; he was laying the groundwork for understanding complex systems.

Theoretical Foundations of Parental Awe

From a psychological perspective, the phenomenon of parental awe can be understood through the lens of *developmental theory*. According to Piaget's stages of cognitive development, children move from concrete operational thought to formal operational thought, which allows them to think abstractly and solve problems logically. Morgan's ability to conceptualize the Internet at such a young age suggested he was operating at a level beyond his years, making his parents question their own intellectual capabilities.

$$Awe = f(Cognitive\ Development, Parental\ Expectations) \qquad (2)$$

This equation illustrates that parental awe is a function of the child's cognitive development and the expectations parents hold. As Morgan's cognitive abilities surpassed those of his peers, Lisa and David felt a mix of pride and existential dread—pride for their son's genius and dread for the inevitable day when he would outsmart them in every family debate, including the one about who left the lights on.

Childhood Full of Curiosity

Morgan's curiosity was insatiable. At family gatherings, while other children played with toys, Morgan would be found dissecting the family's old computer, armed with nothing but a screwdriver and a determination that could rival any seasoned engineer. His parents often exchanged glances filled with disbelief and concern, wondering if they should be encouraging this behavior or calling a child psychologist. However, they ultimately decided to embrace it, creating a dedicated "curiosity corner" in their home, stocked with tools, books, and an assortment of outdated technology for Morgan to explore.

Encounters with the Law

However, Morgan's brilliance didn't come without its challenges. At the age of six, he was caught hacking into the neighbor's Wi-Fi to stream educational videos. When the police arrived, they were met not with a defiant child, but with a very polite young boy who simply stated, "I was just trying to connect to the global knowledge network." The officers left, chuckling, but Lisa and David were left to wonder if they should enroll him in a coding camp or a law school.

Turning Points in Morgan's Life

These early experiences were turning points in Morgan's life and served as formative moments for his parents. They realized that their son was not just a prodigy; he was a pioneer in a world where technology and creativity intertwined. They sought to nurture his talents, enrolling him in programs that encouraged innovation and critical thinking, all while trying to maintain a semblance of normalcy in their household.

In conclusion, the awe that Lisa and David felt for Morgan was not merely admiration; it was a blend of pride, fear, and the realization that they were raising a future innovator. They embraced the chaos that came with his genius, knowing that every moment of bewilderment was a step toward a brighter future—not just for Morgan, but for the world he was destined to change.

Childhood Full of Curiosity

Morgan Liao's early years were characterized by an insatiable curiosity that seemed to defy the laws of nature, much like a cat who believes it can fly after watching too many superhero movies. From an early age, Morgan exhibited a penchant for asking questions that would stump even the most seasoned philosophers. "Why is the sky blue?" he would ask, only to follow up with "But why isn't it green?" His parents often found themselves in philosophical debates that required more than just a simple answer; they needed a PowerPoint presentation and perhaps a few charts.

In the spirit of fostering this curiosity, Morgan's parents introduced him to a variety of educational toys. One such toy was a science kit that promised to turn any child into a miniature Einstein. However, after a few explosive experiments (including one that left a permanent stain on the living room carpet), it was clear that Morgan was less interested in following instructions and more in creating chaos. This led to a fundamental theorem in his household: "Curiosity equals chaos, but chaos equals creativity."

Morgan's curiosity extended beyond the confines of his home. He often ventured into the backyard, which he had deemed his personal laboratory. Here, he conducted experiments that would make even the most seasoned scientists raise an eyebrow. For instance, he once attempted to create a rocket using a soda bottle, vinegar, and baking soda. The resulting explosion not only startled the neighbors but also provided a valuable lesson in physics. The equation for the rocket's height h could be approximated by:

$$h = v_0 \cdot t + \frac{1}{2}a \cdot t^2$$

where v_0 is the initial velocity (which was zero, but Morgan was convinced he could launch it with a little help from gravity), a is the acceleration due to the reaction (which was quite explosive), and t is the time in seconds. Though the rocket never reached the stratosphere, it did soar high enough to land on Mrs. Johnson's roof, sparking a neighborhood-wide discussion about the dangers of DIY rocketry.

Morgan's relentless questioning also led him to explore technology at a young age. By the time he was seven, he had dismantled his first computer, much to the horror of his parents, who were still trying to figure out how to connect the DVD player. This act of disassembly was not merely a rebellious act; it was a manifestation of his desire to understand how things worked. He would often say, "If I can take it apart, I can put it back together... eventually."

This philosophy was rooted in the constructivist learning theory, which posits that knowledge is constructed through experience. In Morgan's case, the experience often involved trial and error, with a side of parental panic. The idea that children learn best through active engagement rather than passive absorption was epitomized in Morgan's explorations. He was not just a passive observer of the world; he was an active participant, eager to engage with the complexities of life.

As Morgan grew older, his curiosity evolved into a more structured form of inquiry. He began to read voraciously, devouring books on everything from quantum physics to ancient civilizations. His bedroom transformed into a mini-library, with stacks of books precariously piled high, threatening to topple at any moment. Each book was a portal to a new world, and Morgan was determined to explore every one of them.

One day, while reading about the ancient Greeks, Morgan stumbled upon the concept of the Socratic method. This sparked an idea: why not apply this method to his daily life? He began to engage his family in discussions that left them questioning their own beliefs. "If I can ask you questions, can you ask me questions too?" he would challenge them, turning family dinners into philosophical debates that would last long into the night.

In conclusion, Morgan Liao's childhood was a vibrant tapestry woven from threads of curiosity, chaos, and creativity. His early experiences laid the groundwork for a lifelong pursuit of knowledge and innovation. As he navigated the complexities of childhood, he transformed every question into an opportunity for exploration, setting the stage for the remarkable journey that lay ahead. Little did anyone know, the boy who questioned everything would one day revolutionize the digital humanities, proving that curiosity is indeed the mother of invention.

Early Interest in Computers

Morgan Liao's fascination with computers began at an age when most children were still figuring out how to tie their shoelaces. While other kids were busy playing with action figures, Morgan was busy disassembling his parents' outdated desktop computer, an act that would later lead to a series of events that could only be described as a digital odyssey.

From the moment he first booted up that ancient machine, Morgan was captivated by the glowing screen and the mysterious world it held within. It was a portal to infinite possibilities, much like the wardrobe in *The Lion, the Witch and the Wardrobe*, except instead of a snowy Narnia, he found himself in a pixelated realm filled with games, text documents, and the occasional virus.

The First Encounter

Morgan's initial interest can be traced back to the moment he discovered the game *Oregon Trail*. The thrill of guiding a digital wagon through treacherous terrain while trying to avoid dysentery was not just entertainment; it was a lesson in survival, resource management, and the harsh realities of pioneer life—albeit in 8-bit glory. This early exposure to computing sparked a desire to understand not just how to play games, but how they were made.

The Spark of Curiosity

As Morgan delved deeper into the world of computers, he became increasingly curious about programming. He stumbled upon a book titled *Python for Kids*, which, despite its target audience, proved to be an invaluable resource. The simplicity of Python's syntax resonated with Morgan, allowing him to create his first program: a simple calculator that could add, subtract, multiply, and divide.

The thrill of seeing his code come to life was addictive. He began to explore more complex programming concepts, including loops, conditionals, and functions. The following equation encapsulated his newfound understanding:

$$f(x) = \begin{cases} x + 1 & \text{if } x \text{ is even} \\ x - 1 & \text{if } x \text{ is odd} \end{cases} \tag{3}$$

This function, a simple representation of Morgan's early forays into programming, demonstrated a fundamental understanding of conditional logic and functions—concepts that would later become crucial in his more ambitious projects.

Hacking His Way into Trouble

However, Morgan's curiosity did not stop at programming. He soon discovered the darker side of the digital world: hacking. This was not the malevolent hacking often portrayed in movies, but rather an innocent exploration of how systems worked. With a few tutorials found on the internet, he learned how to bypass parental controls and access restricted websites.

This led to a series of amusing yet troubling incidents. For instance, he once convinced his school's Wi-Fi network to grant him access to the teacher's lounge printer, where he printed out a "Congratulations on Surviving Another Day" banner for his favorite teacher. While the prank was harmless, it did raise eyebrows and led to a stern conversation with the school administration about acceptable use policies.

Encounters with the Law

As Morgan continued to explore his interest in computers, he inevitably faced some consequences. One particularly memorable incident involved a late-night coding session that spiraled out of control. Trying to impress his friends, he created a harmless bot that sent automated messages to the local chat room. What he didn't anticipate was the flood of complaints from users who were less than thrilled about receiving unsolicited messages.

The next day, Morgan found himself in the principal's office, facing a stern warning about the importance of digital etiquette and the potential legal ramifications of his actions. It was a wake-up call that taught him a valuable lesson: with great power comes great responsibility—or, in his case, a stern lecture and a temporary ban from using school computers.

Turning Points in Morgan's Life

Despite these early misadventures, Morgan's passion for computers only grew stronger. He began attending local coding workshops, where he met like-minded peers who shared his enthusiasm. These workshops introduced him to the concept of open-source software, a philosophy that emphasized collaboration and sharing among developers.

Inspired by this community, Morgan decided to contribute to an open-source project aimed at developing educational software for underprivileged schools. This experience not only honed his coding skills but also instilled in him a sense of social responsibility. He realized that technology could be a powerful tool for change, and he was determined to harness it for the greater good.

Through these formative experiences, Morgan Liao's early interest in computers evolved from mere curiosity into a profound commitment to innovation and social impact. He learned that technology was not just about ones and zeros; it was about people, stories, and the potential to create a better world.

As he moved forward in his journey, these foundational experiences would serve as the bedrock for his future endeavors in the realm of digital humanities. His early encounters with computers were not just a hobby; they were the beginning of a lifelong quest to bridge the gap between technology and humanity, paving the way for the Cyber Renaissance that would follow.

Hacking His Way into Trouble

Morgan Liao's early fascination with computers quickly evolved into a penchant for hacking, a double-edged sword that would both propel him into the limelight and land him in hot water. It all began in his early teenage years, when he stumbled upon an old laptop in his parents' attic, its screen cracked but still flickering with the remnants of a bygone era of technology. Morgan, ever the curious mind, couldn't resist the urge to tinker with it.

The Allure of the Digital Frontier

The allure of the digital frontier was irresistible for Morgan. Armed with nothing but a few online tutorials and an insatiable curiosity, he began to explore the depths of coding and programming. As he delved deeper, he discovered the world of hacking, where the lines between right and wrong blurred like the pixels on a malfunctioning monitor.

$$\text{Curiosity} + \text{Old Laptop} \rightarrow \text{Hacking Interest} \tag{4}$$

Morgan's initial forays into hacking were relatively harmless. He would change the background of his school's website to a picture of his cat, Mr. Whiskers, and replace the principal's photo with a meme of a confused-looking owl. These harmless pranks were met with laughter from his peers but raised eyebrows among the school administration.

Crossing the Line

However, as Morgan's skills grew, so did his ambition. Inspired by stories of legendary hackers like Kevin Mitnick and Adrian Lamo, Morgan began to push the boundaries of ethical hacking. He created a program that could exploit vulnerabilities in outdated software, gaining unauthorized access to his school's network.

$$\text{Access} = \text{Exploit}(\text{Vulnerability}) \tag{5}$$

Morgan justified his actions by telling himself he was merely testing the system's security. But when he accidentally released a harmless virus that caused the cafeteria's lunch ordering system to malfunction—resulting in an unexpected taco Tuesday that left students both ecstatic and confused—his intentions were called into question.

The Consequences of Misguided Genius

The incident didn't go unnoticed. The school's IT department launched an investigation, and Morgan found himself summoned to the principal's office. The stern look on the principal's face was reminiscent of the time Morgan had been caught sneaking a cookie before dinner.

"Do you understand the gravity of what you've done?" the principal asked, tapping a finger on the desk like a metronome counting down Morgan's chances.

Morgan, realizing he was in over his head, could only nod. He had crossed a line, and now he was facing the consequences.

Learning from Mistakes

This incident served as a wake-up call for Morgan. He learned that while the digital world was a playground for innovation, it also came with rules—rules that he had inadvertently broken. The experience forced him to reflect on the ethical implications of hacking and the responsibilities that came with his newfound skills.

$$\text{Ethics} = \text{Responsibility} + \text{Knowledge} \tag{6}$$

Morgan began to channel his skills into more constructive avenues, such as participating in hackathons that focused on solving real-world problems. He discovered that hacking could be a force for good, a way to protect systems rather than exploit them.

The Turning Point

The turning point came when Morgan was invited to speak at a local tech conference, where he shared his story of mischief and redemption. He spoke candidly about his mistakes, emphasizing the importance of ethical hacking and the need for cybersecurity awareness among young innovators.

$$\text{Innovation} \rightarrow \text{Ethical Responsibility} \tag{7}$$

His story resonated with many in the audience, and he received a standing ovation. Morgan realized that his experiences, both good and bad, could inspire others to navigate the digital landscape responsibly.

Conclusion

In conclusion, Morgan Liao's journey through the world of hacking was a tumultuous one, marked by both triumphs and tribulations. While his early exploits may have landed him in trouble, they ultimately shaped him into a more conscientious and innovative thinker. As he moved forward in his career, he carried with him the lessons learned from those formative years, understanding that true innovation lies not just in the ability to hack systems, but in the wisdom to use that knowledge for the greater good.

Encounters with the Law

Morgan Liao's early years were marked by an insatiable curiosity and a knack for technology, which, unfortunately, often led him down a precarious path of legal entanglements. It all began with his fascination with hacking—a pursuit that, while often viewed through the lens of innovation, can sometimes straddle the line between genius and delinquency.

The Thrill of Hacking

At the tender age of twelve, Morgan discovered the world of hacking. He was captivated by the idea of breaking into systems, not out of malice, but from a desire to understand their inner workings. This curiosity, however, quickly morphed into a series of escapades that would have made even the most seasoned hackers raise an eyebrow.

Morgan's first major encounter with the law came when he managed to infiltrate his school's network. His goal? To change his grades from a modest B- to a more palatable A+. While his technical prowess was impressive, the ethical implications were murky at best.

$$\text{Grade}_{new} = \text{Grade}_{old} + \Delta \tag{8}$$

Where Δ represents the degree of modification Morgan applied to his grades. Unfortunately, the school's IT department was not amused. A digital trail of breadcrumbs led them straight to Morgan, who was promptly called into the principal's office.

The Consequences of Curiosity

The principal, a stern woman with a penchant for disciplinary action, laid down the law. "Morgan," she said, "you're a bright kid, but you can't just hack your way through life. There are consequences."

Morgan faced a suspension, but it was the warning that resonated with him: "Next time, it could be more than just a slap on the wrist." This encounter served as a wake-up call, albeit a brief one.

A Brush with the Law

Fast forward a year, and Morgan's exploits escalated. He had started a small tech club at school, where he and his friends would gather to share knowledge and occasionally, their questionable hacking techniques. One fateful afternoon, inspired by a particularly thrilling documentary on cybersecurity, Morgan decided to test his skills on a more ambitious target: the local library's digital catalog.

Morgan and his friends managed to bypass the library's security protocols, only to find themselves face-to-face with a very irate librarian. She had been monitoring the system and promptly called the police.

Legal Ramifications

The police arrived, and Morgan found himself sitting in the back of a squad car, contemplating the irony of his situation. "I'm just trying to preserve knowledge!" he thought, but the officers weren't buying it.

The legal ramifications were serious. Morgan faced charges of unauthorized access to a computer system, a misdemeanor that could have lasting consequences on his future. His parents were mortified, and a family meeting was called.

Lessons Learned

In the aftermath, Morgan learned some valuable lessons about the law, ethics, and the importance of consent in the digital age. He realized that while technology could be a powerful tool for innovation, it also came with responsibilities.

$$\text{Ethical Responsibility} = \frac{\text{Knowledge}}{\text{Power}} \tag{9}$$

This equation became a guiding principle for Morgan. He understood that with great power—like the ability to hack into systems—came great responsibility.

Morgan's encounters with the law shaped his perspective on technology. Instead of viewing hacking as a means to an end, he began to see it as a double-edged sword that could either uplift or destroy.

Turning Point

Ultimately, Morgan's run-ins with law enforcement did not deter his passion for technology; rather, they redirected it. He began to focus on ethical hacking, using his skills to help organizations strengthen their security rather than undermine it.

This shift in focus was pivotal, as it allowed him to channel his curiosity into a constructive outlet. He sought mentorship from professionals in the field, learning that the best hackers were not just those who could break into systems, but those who could also help build them stronger.

In conclusion, Morgan Liao's early encounters with the law were not merely obstacles; they were formative experiences that shaped his character and his future endeavors in the world of digital humanities. They taught him that innovation must go hand-in-hand with ethical considerations, and that the true measure of a visionary is not just in their ability to create, but in their commitment to doing so responsibly.

Turning Points in Morgan's Life

Turning points are the moments in life that shape who we are, often leading to unexpected paths filled with challenges, growth, and sometimes a little bit of chaos. For Morgan Liao, these moments were like plot twists in a sitcom—both hilarious and poignant, often leaving everyone wondering how he managed to survive.

The Great Computer Crash

One of the earliest turning points in Morgan's life occurred when he was just twelve years old. After months of tinkering and coding, he had finally built his first computer from scratch. It was a glorious moment, akin to a chef presenting a soufflé that had risen perfectly. However, his triumph was short-lived.

$$\text{System Stability} = \frac{\text{User Experience}}{\text{Bugs} + \text{Malware}} \tag{10}$$

Unfortunately, Morgan's excitement led him to download a questionable file from the internet, resulting in a catastrophic crash. His computer transformed into a digital graveyard, and he learned the hard way that not all downloads are created equal. This incident sparked his interest in cybersecurity, leading him to explore the delicate balance between innovation and security.

The Day of the Hack

Fast forward to high school, where Morgan's reputation as a tech wizard began to take shape. He was known for his pranks, which included hacking the school's attendance system to give himself an extra hour of sleep. This was a classic example of the formula:

$$\text{Prank Success} = \text{Creativity} \times \text{Risk} - \text{Consequences} \tag{11}$$

However, the thrill of outsmarting the system came crashing down when the school administration caught wind of his antics. Instead of punishment, they offered him a chance to join the newly formed tech club, recognizing his potential. This moment was pivotal; it shifted Morgan from a troublemaker to a budding innovator, teaching him that sometimes, the best way to channel your talents is to collaborate rather than compete.

The Mentor Encounter

Another significant turning point occurred during a summer coding camp. Here, Morgan met Dr. Evelyn Hawthorne, a renowned figure in digital humanities. Dr. Hawthorne saw something in Morgan that he had yet to recognize in himself: potential. She introduced him to the concept of using technology to enhance the study of humanities, a field he had never considered.

$$\text{Potential} = \text{Talent} + \text{Opportunity} + \text{Guidance} \tag{12}$$

Under her mentorship, Morgan developed a passion for merging technology with cultural studies, leading him to create a revolutionary AI project that analyzed historical texts. This project not only earned him accolades but also solidified his commitment to using technology for the greater good.

The College Admission Crisis

As graduation approached, Morgan faced another turning point: the college admissions dilemma. With acceptance letters pouring in from prestigious institutions, he was overwhelmed by the pressure to choose the "right" school.

$$\text{Decision Quality} = \frac{\text{Information}}{\text{Anxiety} + \text{Peer Pressure}} \tag{13}$$

After weeks of sleepless nights and frantic discussions with family and friends, Morgan realized that he needed to choose a path that resonated with his passion rather than societal expectations. This realization was liberating, allowing him to embrace his unique journey into the world of digital humanities.

The First Major Failure

Every innovator faces failure, and Morgan was no exception. His first major project post-high school—a digital archive of local history—failed spectacularly when a server crash wiped out months of work.

$$\text{Resilience} = \frac{\text{Recovery Efforts}}{\text{Setbacks} + \text{Frustration}} \tag{14}$$

Instead of giving up, Morgan learned the importance of backup systems and the value of perseverance. This failure taught him that setbacks are not the end but rather stepping stones to greater achievements.

A Moment of Clarity

The final turning point in this chapter of Morgan's life came during a late-night brainstorming session with friends. Surrounded by empty pizza boxes and half-drunk energy drinks, they discussed the future of digital humanities. In that moment, Morgan envisioned the Cyber Renaissance—a movement that would integrate technology with the arts and culture on a global scale.

$$\text{Vision} = \text{Imagination} + \text{Collaboration} + \text{Passion} \tag{15}$$

This epiphany set him on a path that would not only define his career but also inspire countless others to explore the intersection of technology and humanities.

In conclusion, the turning points in Morgan Liao's life were not merely events; they were catalysts for transformation, each leading him closer to his ultimate goal of revolutionizing the digital humanities. With every twist and turn, he learned valuable lessons that would shape his character and influence his future endeavors.

Dedicated Teachers

In the formative years of Morgan Liao, the influence of dedicated teachers cannot be overstated. These educators played a pivotal role in shaping his intellectual curiosity and fostering his burgeoning talents. They were not just instructors; they were mentors, guiding lights in the often murky waters of adolescence, and sometimes, even unwitting accomplices in his early escapades.

The Role of Mentorship

Mentorship is a critical component in the educational landscape, particularly in the realm of innovation and creativity. According to the *Social Learning Theory* proposed by Albert Bandura, individuals learn from one another through observation, imitation, and modeling. For Morgan, his teachers exemplified the very essence of this theory. They provided him not only with knowledge but also with a framework for thinking critically and creatively.

The impact of mentorship can be quantified using Bandura's equation for observational learning:

$$B = f(P, E) \tag{16}$$

Where:

+ B is the behavior of the learner,

+ P is the personal factors (e.g., cognitive, emotional),

+ E represents the environmental influences (e.g., teachers, peers).

This equation illustrates that Morgan's behavior was a function of both his personal attributes and the enriching environment created by his teachers.

Examples of Dedicated Teachers

One notable figure in Morgan's life was Mr. Thompson, his high school computer science teacher. Mr. Thompson had a knack for making complex algorithms feel like a thrilling game of strategy. He often said, "Programming is like magic; the right code can create wonders!" This perspective not only demystified coding for Morgan but also ignited a passion for technology that would define his future endeavors.

"If you can dream it, you can code it!" – Mr. Thompson

Another influential teacher was Ms. Rodriguez, who taught history with a flair for storytelling. She often integrated technology into her lessons, using virtual reality to transport students to ancient civilizations. This innovative approach resonated deeply with Morgan, who began to see the potential for technology to enhance the understanding of humanities.

Challenges Faced by Teachers

Despite their dedication, these educators faced numerous challenges. The increasing reliance on standardized testing often limited their ability to innovate in the classroom. According to a study by the *National Education Association*, teachers reported feeling constrained by curricula that prioritized rote memorization over critical thinking and creativity.

Morgan's teachers often had to navigate these bureaucratic hurdles while trying to provide a rich educational experience. For instance, Mr. Thompson once lamented, "I feel like I'm teaching to the test instead of teaching to inspire!" This sentiment echoed the frustrations of many educators who sought to cultivate a love for learning in their students amidst a system that often prioritized metrics over genuine understanding.

The Lasting Impact of Dedicated Teachers

The influence of dedicated teachers on Morgan Liao's life was profound and lasting. They instilled in him a sense of curiosity and a desire to explore the intersections of technology and humanities. This foundation would later serve as the bedrock for his groundbreaking work in digital humanities.

Moreover, research indicates that students who have strong relationships with their teachers are more likely to engage in their learning and pursue higher education. A study published in the *Journal of Educational Psychology* found that positive teacher-student relationships significantly correlate with academic success and personal growth.

In conclusion, the dedicated teachers who shaped Morgan's early years were not merely educators; they were architects of his future. Their commitment to fostering creativity, critical thinking, and a love for learning laid the groundwork for his eventual role as an innovator in the digital humanities. As Morgan once said in a moment of reflection, "I owe much of my success to the teachers who saw potential in me when I could barely see it myself."

The High School Years

Attendance-Tracking Algorithm

In the age of digital innovation, where even your toaster might have Wi-Fi, the need for efficient attendance tracking in educational institutions has never been more pressing. Enter Morgan Liao, a teenage prodigy who, while other kids were busy perfecting their TikTok dances, was busy developing an attendance-tracking algorithm that would make even the most seasoned educators weep tears of joy.

The Problem with Traditional Methods

Traditional attendance methods often involve roll calls, sign-in sheets, or, for the particularly adventurous, a game of "guess who's here." These methods are not only time-consuming but also prone to human error. For instance, how many times has a teacher mispronounced a name, only for the student to respond with a confused, "Wait, who's that?" This leads to inaccurate records, which can have consequences ranging from missed opportunities to the dreaded "you're failing this class" letter.

To quantify the inefficiency, let's consider the time spent on attendance in a class of 30 students. If each roll call takes approximately 5 minutes, that's a staggering 150 minutes per week just for attendance! Over a semester, that amounts to:

$$\text{Total Time} = \text{Number of Classes} \times \text{Time per Class} = 15 \times 5 = 75 \text{ minutes}$$

This time could be better spent on actual learning, or perfecting that TikTok dance.

The Algorithmic Solution

Morgan's solution was to develop an attendance-tracking algorithm that utilizes facial recognition technology, combined with a unique database that logs attendance in real-time. The algorithm operates under the following principles:

1. **Image Processing**: The algorithm captures images of students as they enter the classroom. 2. **Facial Recognition**: Using advanced machine learning techniques, it identifies students based on their facial features. 3. **Data Logging**: Once identified, the algorithm logs the attendance in a centralized database.

The core of the algorithm can be expressed mathematically as follows:

$$\text{Attendance} = f(\text{Image}_t, \text{Database}) \quad \text{where} \quad f : \text{Image Processing} \rightarrow \text{Identification}$$

Here, Image_t represents the image captured at time t, and Database contains the facial data of enrolled students.

The Technical Details

Morgan implemented the algorithm using Python, leveraging libraries such as OpenCV for image processing and TensorFlow for machine learning. The steps involved in the algorithm include:

1. **Image Acquisition**: Capturing images using a camera positioned at the classroom entrance. 2. **Preprocessing**: Converting images to grayscale and resizing them for uniformity. 3. **Feature Extraction**: Identifying key facial features using algorithms like Haar Cascades or deep learning models. 4. **Matching**: Comparing extracted features against the database to identify students.

The matching process can be represented as:

$$\text{Match Score} = \sum_{i=1}^{n} \text{Similarity}(\text{Feature}_i, \text{Database}_i)$$

Where n is the number of features extracted from the image, and Similarity is a function that quantifies how closely the features match.

Challenges Faced

While the algorithm sounds like a dream come true, Morgan faced several challenges during its development:

- **Privacy Concerns**: The use of facial recognition raised eyebrows among parents and educators. To address this, Morgan ensured that all data was anonymized and securely stored. - **Accuracy**: Initial versions of the algorithm struggled with misidentifications, particularly with students who had similar facial features. This was mitigated by training the model on a diverse dataset. - **Technical Limitations**: Hardware limitations in some classrooms meant that not all students could be captured effectively. Morgan proposed a hybrid system that included manual check-ins for those instances.

Real-World Application

After months of development, Morgan's attendance-tracking algorithm was implemented in his high school. The results were staggering. Attendance was recorded in real-time, allowing teachers to focus on teaching rather than counting heads. The time saved was repurposed for interactive learning activities, and the algorithm boasted an impressive accuracy rate of 95%.

A notable incident occurred during a particularly chaotic class when a fire alarm went off. Thanks to the algorithm, the school was able to quickly account for all students, ensuring everyone was safe. Morgan's algorithm not only revolutionized attendance tracking but also became a model for schools across the country.

Conclusion

Morgan Liao's attendance-tracking algorithm exemplifies how technology can solve age-old problems in education. By merging facial recognition with a user-friendly interface, he created a tool that not only streamlined the attendance process but also enhanced the overall learning experience. As we move further into the digital age, we can only imagine what other groundbreaking innovations young minds like Morgan's will bring to the table. Perhaps one day, we'll have an algorithm that can even tell us who forgot to bring snacks to class—now that's a problem worth solving!

Revolutionary AI Project

Morgan Liao's high school years were marked by a pivotal moment that would not only shape his academic journey but also set the stage for his future innovations. At the age of sixteen, Morgan embarked on a revolutionary AI project that sought to redefine how students interacted with educational content. This project, dubbed "EduGenie," was designed to leverage artificial intelligence to create personalized learning experiences for students.

Theoretical Framework

The foundation of EduGenie was built upon several key theories in education and artificial intelligence. One of the primary theories was **Constructivist Learning Theory**, which posits that learners construct knowledge through experiences and reflections. This theory guided Morgan in developing an AI that could adapt to individual learning styles and paces, thereby facilitating a more engaging educational experience.

Additionally, Morgan incorporated elements of **Adaptive Learning Technology**, which utilizes algorithms to tailor educational content to the needs of each learner. This approach was crucial in ensuring that students received the right level of challenge and support, promoting deeper understanding and retention of knowledge.

Project Development

The development of EduGenie began with extensive research into existing educational technologies. Morgan identified several limitations in traditional learning management systems, such as a lack of personalization and engagement. To address these issues, he proposed an AI-driven platform that could analyze student performance data and adapt content accordingly.

$$\text{Personalization Score} = \frac{\text{Student Engagement} + \text{Learning Style Compatibility}}{\text{Content Difficulty Level}}$$

$$(17)$$

This equation represented the core of EduGenie's algorithm, where the *Personalization Score* would guide the AI in selecting appropriate materials for each student. The higher the score, the more suited the content was to the learner's needs.

Challenges Faced

Despite Morgan's enthusiasm and innovative ideas, the project was not without its challenges. One significant hurdle was the **Data Privacy Concerns**. As EduGenie required access to sensitive student data, Morgan had to navigate the complexities of data protection laws and ethical considerations. He conducted thorough research into the Family Educational Rights and Privacy Act (FERPA) and ensured that the platform complied with all regulations.

Another challenge was the **Algorithmic Bias**. Morgan was acutely aware of the potential for AI algorithms to perpetuate existing inequalities in education. To mitigate this risk, he assembled a diverse team of peers and educators to provide insights and feedback throughout the development process. This collaborative approach not only enriched the project but also helped in identifying biases that could skew the AI's recommendations.

Implementation and Results

The initial implementation of EduGenie took place in a local high school, where it was integrated into the existing curriculum. Teachers reported a noticeable increase in student engagement and performance. For instance, students who struggled with mathematics found the adaptive learning features particularly beneficial. The AI adjusted the difficulty of problems based on real-time performance, allowing students to build confidence gradually.

Morgan also introduced a feedback loop mechanism, where students could rate their learning experiences. This data was fed back into the AI system, further refining its algorithms. The impact was significant; within a semester, the average test scores in mathematics improved by 15%.

Real-World Applications and Future Prospects

The success of EduGenie attracted attention from educational institutions and tech companies alike. Morgan was invited to present his project at several conferences, where he discussed the implications of AI in education. He emphasized that the goal was not to replace teachers but to empower them with tools that could enhance their teaching effectiveness.

Looking ahead, Morgan envisioned expanding EduGenie's capabilities to include features such as **Natural Language Processing** (NLP) to facilitate better communication between students and the AI. This would allow students to ask questions in natural language and receive tailored responses, further enriching the learning experience.

In conclusion, Morgan Liao's revolutionary AI project was a testament to his innovative spirit and dedication to improving education. By leveraging technology to create personalized learning experiences, he not only addressed the challenges faced by students but also laid the groundwork for future advancements in digital humanities. The lessons learned from EduGenie would serve as a foundation for Morgan's later work, reinforcing the importance of ethical considerations and collaborative development in the field of artificial intelligence.

Pranks and Practical Jokes

Morgan Liao's high school years were not only marked by academic brilliance but also by a mischievous spirit that manifested in a series of pranks and practical jokes that would make even the most stoic teachers crack a smile—or at least roll their eyes.

The Art of Pranking

Pranking is often seen as an art form, one that requires creativity, timing, and a deep understanding of social dynamics. As Morgan once quipped, "A good prank is like a well-placed algorithm: it should execute flawlessly and leave everyone wondering how they didn't see it coming." This philosophy guided Morgan through a series of elaborate schemes, each designed to showcase his ingenuity while keeping his classmates entertained.

The Classic Fake Exam

One of Morgan's most notorious pranks involved creating a fake exam paper. He meticulously crafted a test that was filled with absurd questions such as, "If a tree falls in a forest and no one is around to hear it, does it still get an 'A'?" or "Explain the significance of the number 42 in exactly 42 words."

The prank reached its peak when Morgan handed out copies of this "test" to unsuspecting classmates just before a major math exam. The chaos that ensued was legendary, with students frantically trying to decipher the logic behind the questions. As the teacher entered the room, Morgan's smirk was as wide as the Grand Canyon.

The Great Locker Switcheroo

Another classic prank was the Great Locker Switcheroo. Morgan and his friends devised a plan to switch the contents of their lockers with those of the school's most serious students. The result? A locker filled with rubber chickens, whoopee cushions, and a life-sized cardboard cutout of Nicolas Cage.

This prank not only caused a stir among the students but also sparked a debate about locker organization and personal space. The ensuing chaos led to a spontaneous meeting of the "Locker Organization Committee," which was ironically chaired by Morgan himself.

Theoretical Underpinnings

From a psychological perspective, pranks can be analyzed through the lens of social bonding theory. Research indicates that shared laughter can enhance group cohesion, making pranks a form of social glue. Morgan's pranks, while seemingly frivolous, fostered connections among his peers, creating a tight-knit community that thrived on humor and creativity.

$$Laughter \propto \text{Social Bonding} \qquad (18)$$

This equation implies that as laughter increases, so does the strength of social bonds, a phenomenon that Morgan capitalized on with every prank.

The Fine Line Between Humor and Trouble

However, not all pranks were received with open arms. There was the infamous "Invisible Ink Incident," where Morgan decided to use a special pen to write all of his math homework in invisible ink. While he thought it was a brilliant commentary on the ephemeral nature of knowledge, his teacher was less than impressed when Morgan submitted his "homework" with a straight face.

This incident raised questions about the ethics of pranking and the boundaries of acceptable humor in an academic setting. Morgan learned the hard way that not everyone appreciates a good joke, especially when it involves a significant drop in grades.

Lessons Learned

Through these experiences, Morgan not only entertained his peers but also learned valuable lessons about timing, empathy, and the importance of knowing your audience.   He often reflected on these pranks as pivotal moments in his development, stating, "Every joke is a lesson in disguise; you just have to be willing to laugh at yourself first."

In conclusion, Morgan Liao's high school years were a testament to the power of humor in education. His pranks, while sometimes crossing the line, ultimately contributed to a vibrant school culture where creativity thrived. As he moved on to greater challenges, the lessons learned from these practical jokes became integral to his innovative spirit, reminding him that sometimes, the best ideas come from a place of laughter.

$$\text{Innovation} = \text{Creativity} + \text{Humor} \tag{19}$$

Thus, Morgan's legacy of pranks not only entertained but also laid the groundwork for a future filled with innovative ideas and a whole lot of laughter.

Building His First Start-up at 16

At the tender age of 16, while most teenagers were busy perfecting their TikTok dances or trying to figure out why their parents' music was so terrible, Morgan Liao was busy coding his future. This was not just any teenage pastime; this was the inception of his first start-up, a venture that would set the stage for his future as a digital innovator.

The Idea

Morgan's entrepreneurial journey began with a simple yet profound realization: the world was becoming increasingly reliant on technology, but there was a significant gap in user-friendly platforms that catered to the needs of students. He envisioned a digital platform, *EduConnect*, that would streamline communication between students, teachers, and parents. The idea was to create a centralized hub where assignments, grades, and important announcements could be shared effortlessly.

Market Research

Before diving headfirst into development, Morgan conducted extensive market research. He surveyed fellow students and teachers, gathering data on their pain points regarding current educational tools. The results were enlightening:

- **Communication Breakdown:** 68% of students felt they missed important announcements due to ineffective communication channels.

- **Assignment Overload:** 75% of students reported feeling overwhelmed by tracking multiple assignments across different platforms.

- **Parental Involvement:** 80% of parents expressed a desire for better access to their child's academic progress.

Morgan recognized that these insights were not just numbers; they represented real frustrations that could be addressed with a well-designed solution.

Development Phase

Armed with a vision and data, Morgan assembled a small team of like-minded friends who shared his passion for technology. They worked tirelessly after school, fueled by pizza and energy drinks, to bring *EduConnect* to life. Morgan took on the role of lead developer, using his coding skills to create a user-friendly interface.

The development process was not without its challenges. One of the primary issues they encountered was the integration of real-time notifications. The team decided to implement a notification system based on the following equation:

$$N(t) = N_0 e^{\lambda t} \tag{20}$$

where $N(t)$ is the number of notifications at time t, N_0 is the initial number of notifications, and λ is the rate of notification generation. This equation helped them model user engagement and ensure that students received timely updates.

Launch Day

After months of hard work, the launch day finally arrived. The team organized a small event at their high school, inviting students, teachers, and parents to experience

EduConnect firsthand. They showcased the platform's features, including a calendar for tracking assignments, a messaging system for communication, and a dashboard for monitoring academic progress.

The response was overwhelmingly positive. Students appreciated the ease of use, while teachers marveled at the potential for improved communication. Morgan felt a rush of excitement as he watched his peers interact with something he had built from scratch.

Challenges Post-Launch

However, the journey did not end with a successful launch. Morgan quickly learned that running a start-up came with its own set of challenges. The first major hurdle was server overload. With a sudden influx of users, the platform struggled to keep up with demand, leading to downtime that frustrated many early adopters.

To address this, Morgan and his team had to pivot quickly. They researched cloud hosting solutions and implemented a scalable architecture, ensuring that *EduConnect* could handle increased traffic.

Lessons Learned

Through this experience, Morgan learned valuable lessons about entrepreneurship:

- **Adaptability is Key:** The ability to pivot in response to challenges is crucial for any start-up.

- **User Feedback Matters:** Continuously gathering feedback from users can lead to improvements that enhance the platform's usability.

- **Networking is Essential:** Building relationships with mentors and industry professionals can provide invaluable guidance.

Conclusion

Building *EduConnect* at 16 was not just a personal achievement for Morgan; it was a formative experience that shaped his future endeavors. The skills he developed, the challenges he overcame, and the impact he made on his school community laid the groundwork for his later innovations in the field of digital humanities. As he moved forward, Morgan carried with him the spirit of entrepreneurship, ready to tackle the next big idea that would change the world.

Balancing School and Entrepreneurship

In the frenetic world of high school, where the pressure to excel academically collides with the fervor of youthful ambition, Morgan Liao found himself navigating the intricate dance of balancing school and entrepreneurship. This balancing act is not merely a juggling of tasks; it is a complex interplay of time management, prioritization, and the cultivation of a resilient mindset.

Theoretical Framework

Balancing academics and entrepreneurship can be analyzed through the lens of **time management theory**. According to Covey's Time Management Matrix, individuals must prioritize tasks based on urgency and importance, leading to effective decision-making. The four quadrants of this matrix are as follows:

1. **Urgent and Important:** Tasks that require immediate attention (e.g., upcoming exams).

2. **Important but Not Urgent:** Tasks that contribute to long-term goals (e.g., developing a business plan).

3. **Urgent but Not Important:** Tasks that may distract from significant objectives (e.g., social media).

4. **Not Urgent and Not Important:** Tasks that should be minimized or eliminated (e.g., excessive gaming).

Morgan utilized this framework to allocate time efficiently, ensuring that neither his studies nor his entrepreneurial pursuits suffered from neglect.

Challenges Faced

Despite his keen awareness of time management, Morgan encountered several challenges while trying to balance school with his entrepreneurial ambitions:

+ **Time Constraints:** With a packed schedule filled with classes, homework, and extracurricular activities, finding time to dedicate to his start-up was a constant struggle. Morgan often found himself working late into the night, fueled by a combination of caffeine and sheer determination.

+ **Academic Pressure:** The pressure to maintain good grades weighed heavily on Morgan. He faced the daunting task of preparing for exams while simultaneously pitching his business idea to potential investors. This dual focus often led to stress and anxiety, manifesting in sleepless nights and moments of self-doubt.

+ **Social Life:** As Morgan delved deeper into entrepreneurship, he noticed a gradual decline in his social interactions. Friends would invite him to parties and events, but he often had to decline, choosing instead to work on his business. This sacrifice, while necessary, sometimes left him feeling isolated.

Strategies for Success

To mitigate these challenges, Morgan adopted several strategies that enabled him to thrive in both arenas:

1. **Setting Clear Goals:** Morgan established SMART (Specific, Measurable, Achievable, Relevant, Time-bound) goals for both his academic and entrepreneurial pursuits. For instance, he aimed to achieve a specific GPA while also setting a revenue target for his start-up.

2. **Leveraging Resources:** He sought out mentors and utilized school resources, such as business clubs and workshops, to gain insights and support. Engaging with like-minded peers provided him with a network of encouragement and collaboration.

3. **Creating a Schedule:** Morgan developed a comprehensive weekly schedule that allocated dedicated blocks of time for studying, business development, and personal time. This structured approach allowed him to visualize his commitments and avoid overcommitting.

4. **Practicing Self-Care:** Understanding the importance of mental health, Morgan incorporated self-care activities into his routine. Whether it was taking a short walk, meditating, or indulging in his favorite video games, these moments of respite helped recharge his energy and creativity.

Real-Life Example

One notable instance of Morgan's balancing act occurred during his junior year when he was preparing for the SAT while simultaneously launching a mobile app aimed at helping students manage their study schedules. With the exam just weeks away, Morgan faced the ultimate test of his time management skills.

He decided to implement a study technique known as the **Pomodoro Technique**, which involved working in focused bursts of 25 minutes followed by a 5-minute break. This method not only enhanced his productivity but also allowed him to allocate specific Pomodoros for app development. By the end of the week, he had completed a significant portion of his app while also achieving a score that placed him in the top percentile for the SAT.

Conclusion

In conclusion, Morgan Liao's journey of balancing school and entrepreneurship reflects a microcosm of the challenges faced by young innovators. Through effective time management, strategic goal-setting, and a commitment to self-care, Morgan not only excelled academically but also laid the groundwork for a successful entrepreneurial career. His experiences serve as a testament to the idea that with determination and the right tools, it is possible to harmonize the demands of education with the aspirations of innovation.

Empowering Other Young Innovators

In the bustling corridors of Morgan Liao's high school, a unique phenomenon was taking shape. As Morgan navigated the tumultuous waters of adolescence, he discovered that the true essence of innovation lay not solely in personal achievement, but in the empowerment of others. This realization became a cornerstone of his journey, leading him to foster a culture of creativity and collaboration among his peers.

The Ripple Effect of Inspiration

Morgan understood that inspiration is contagious. He often recalled a moment during a particularly mundane history class when he spontaneously decided to share his latest project: a prototype for an attendance-tracking algorithm that utilized facial recognition technology. The initial chuckles from his classmates quickly transformed into intrigue as he demonstrated the software's capabilities. This moment of vulnerability and enthusiasm sparked a ripple effect, igniting a passion for innovation among his peers.

Creating a Supportive Environment

To cultivate this newfound enthusiasm, Morgan initiated a weekly innovation club at his school. The club became a sanctuary for budding inventors, artists, and thinkers, where ideas could flourish without the constraints of traditional academic pressures. Morgan's approach was simple yet effective: he encouraged members to embrace failure as a stepping stone to success. He famously quipped, "If you're not failing, you're not trying hard enough. Or you're just really good at hide-and-seek."

The club's first project was a collaborative effort to design an app that would help students organize their study schedules. Morgan led brainstorming sessions, emphasizing the importance of diverse perspectives. He often referenced the theory of *collective intelligence*, which posits that a group's combined knowledge can surpass that of any individual member. This principle became the bedrock of their collaborative projects.

Mentorship and Guidance

Morgan's commitment to empowering others extended beyond the club. He sought mentorship opportunities, inviting local entrepreneurs and innovators to share their experiences. These guest speakers provided invaluable insights, addressing common challenges faced by young innovators, such as securing funding and navigating the competitive landscape of technology.

One notable instance involved a local tech entrepreneur who had successfully launched a startup focused on sustainable energy solutions. His story of perseverance resonated deeply with the club members, who realized that even the most successful innovators faced obstacles. Morgan encouraged them to approach these challenges with resilience, echoing the sentiment that "every setback is a setup for a comeback."

Fostering Collaboration

Recognizing the power of collaboration, Morgan organized hackathons where students could work together to solve real-world problems. These events were not only a platform for creativity but also a means of building camaraderie. Morgan often joked, "Nothing brings people together like a shared deadline and a mountain of caffeine!"

During one such hackathon, a team of students developed an app aimed at reducing food waste in their community. By connecting local restaurants with food banks, the app provided a practical solution while instilling a sense of social responsibility among the young innovators. This project exemplified the potential of technology to create positive change, reinforcing Morgan's belief that innovation should serve a greater purpose.

Celebrating Achievements

To maintain motivation and a sense of achievement, Morgan instituted a "Show and Tell" session at the end of each month, where club members could present their projects. This not only celebrated individual accomplishments but also fostered a sense of community. During one session, a shy freshman presented her project—a wearable device that monitored air quality. The applause that followed was not just a recognition of her hard work but a testament to the supportive environment Morgan had cultivated.

The Importance of Diversity

Morgan was acutely aware that innovation flourishes in diverse environments. He actively sought to include students from various backgrounds, encouraging those who might typically shy away from technology to join the club. He often said, "Innovation is like a pizza; the more toppings, the better the flavor!" This philosophy led to a rich tapestry of ideas and perspectives, ultimately enhancing the quality of their projects.

Equipping with Resources

Understanding that access to resources could be a barrier for many young innovators, Morgan collaborated with local businesses to secure sponsorships for tools and materials. He successfully negotiated with a nearby tech company to provide discounted software licenses for students, ensuring that financial constraints would not hinder creativity. This initiative exemplified Morgan's commitment to leveling the playing field for all aspiring innovators.

Conclusion

Empowering other young innovators became an integral part of Morgan Liao's identity. Through mentorship, collaboration, and resource-sharing, he not only advanced his own projects but also inspired a generation of thinkers and creators. As he often reminded his peers, "Innovation isn't just about the individual; it's about the collective dream of making the world a better place." This ethos would resonate throughout his career, shaping the future of digital humanities and beyond.

In the end, Morgan's journey was not just about personal accolades but about nurturing a thriving ecosystem of innovation that would continue to inspire long after he had moved on to greater challenges. The seeds he planted in those high school hallways would blossom into a forest of creativity, proving that true power lies in lifting others as we climb.

Awards and Accolades

As Morgan Liao navigated the turbulent waters of high school, he quickly became a beacon of innovation and creativity, garnering numerous awards and accolades that would make even the most seasoned overachiever blush. With a resume that read like a superhero's origin story, Morgan's achievements were not just a testament to his intellect but also a reflection of his quirky sense of humor and relentless drive.

The Science Fair Triumph

It all began at the annual state science fair, where Morgan unveiled his groundbreaking project: an AI-driven algorithm that could predict the outcome of high school basketball games based on player stats, weather conditions, and the number of nachos consumed by the audience. While the judges were initially skeptical, Morgan's presentation, filled with puns and a dance-off demonstration involving his AI, won them over. He walked away with the first-place trophy, a lifetime supply of nachos, and an invitation to present his findings at a national conference.

The Coding Olympics

Next on Morgan's list was the prestigious Coding Olympics, a competition that attracted the brightest young minds from around the globe. With the stakes high and the competition fierce, Morgan created an app that not only solved complex mathematical problems but also provided motivational quotes from his favorite philosophers—because who wouldn't want to hear Socrates while debugging their code? His innovative approach earned him a gold medal and a special mention for "Most Likely to Inspire Existential Crises in Fellow Coders."

Local Community Recognition

Back home, Morgan's contributions to the local community did not go unnoticed. He initiated a program called *Code for Kids*, where he taught underprivileged children the basics of programming using video games as a learning tool. The initiative not only empowered young minds but also earned him the *Community Hero Award*, presented by the mayor, who, after a lengthy speech about Morgan's impact, accidentally mistook him for a local celebrity.

Scholarships and Grants

Morgan's academic excellence also opened doors to numerous scholarships and grants. He received the *Future Innovators Scholarship*, which provided funding for his college education, and the *Tech for Tomorrow Grant*, awarded for his proposal on integrating technology into traditional humanities education. The grant came with a hefty sum, but more importantly, it included a lifetime supply of coffee—essential for any student who plans to change the world one sleepless night at a time.

The National Young Innovators Award

As Morgan's reputation grew, so did the accolades. He was nominated for the *National Young Innovators Award*, which recognized young leaders making significant contributions to technology and society. His acceptance speech, which he humorously titled "How to Win Friends and Influence Algorithms," was a mix of heartfelt gratitude and comedic anecdotes about his early coding mishaps, including the time he accidentally programmed his toaster to play classical music instead of making toast.

Legacy of Recognition

By the time he graduated high school, Morgan had amassed a collection of awards that rivaled a small trophy store. Each accolade represented not just his achievements but also the spirit of innovation and creativity he brought to every project. Morgan's journey was a testament to the idea that success is not just about winning awards but about inspiring others to dream bigger and laugh harder.

In summary, Morgan Liao's high school years were marked by a series of awards and accolades that highlighted his unique blend of talent, humor, and a genuine desire to make a difference. His accomplishments not only paved the way for his future endeavors but also left an indelible mark on his peers, proving that with a little creativity and a lot of laughter, anything is possible.

College Admissions Dilemma

As Morgan Liao approached his senior year of high school, he found himself facing the daunting and often perplexing world of college admissions. This period, often likened to a rite of passage, was not merely about choosing a school but navigating a labyrinth of expectations, aspirations, and the occasional existential crisis. Morgan's dilemma was compounded by his remarkable achievements and the high standards he had set for himself, leading to what can only be described as the "overachievement paradox":

$$O = \frac{A}{E} \tag{21}$$

Where:

+ O = Overachievement level

+ A = Achievements (GPA, test scores, extracurriculars)

+ E = Expectations (self-imposed, parental, societal)

This equation illustrates that as Morgan's achievements (A) increased, so too did the expectations (E), leading to an overwhelming sense of pressure.

The Pressure Cooker Environment

Morgan's high school was a microcosm of hyper-competitive academia. Each day was a new episode of "Survivor: College Edition," where students were pitted against one another in a relentless quest for the best SAT scores, the most impressive resumes, and the coveted letters of recommendation. The air was thick with anxiety, and the cafeteria buzzed with discussions about acceptance rates and scholarship opportunities.

Morgan often found himself in the midst of these conversations, weighing his options. Should he apply to the Ivy League, where acceptance rates hovered around the 5% mark? Or would a prestigious state university offer him the balance of academic rigor and personal well-being? The dilemma was not merely academic; it was a question of identity and future.

The Role of Technology in Admissions

In this digital age, college admissions had taken a turn for the algorithmic. Gone were the days when a personal essay could sway a decision; now, admissions committees often employed sophisticated data analytics to evaluate applicants. This included the use of machine learning models to predict student success based on previous admissions data.

Morgan, with his burgeoning interest in technology, found this both fascinating and troubling. He began to ponder the implications of such algorithms:

$$P = f(D, S, C) \tag{22}$$

Where:

- P = Probability of admission

- D = Demographic data

- S = Standardized test scores

- C = Extracurricular contributions

The reliance on data-driven decisions meant that students like Morgan, who thrived in creative and unconventional realms, might be overlooked. He began to question whether his unique projects and initiatives would be adequately captured by the cold metrics of an algorithm.

The Emotional Toll

As deadlines approached, Morgan experienced the emotional toll of the admissions process. The pressure to conform to a specific mold weighed heavily on him. He often found himself asking, "What if I don't get in?" or "Am I good enough?" This spiral of self-doubt was exacerbated by the constant stream of social media updates from peers celebrating their acceptance letters.

In a moment of vulnerability, Morgan confided in his mentor, Mrs. Thompson, who had guided him through many of his academic endeavors. She offered him a perspective that resonated deeply:

> "Remember, Morgan, college is just a stepping stone. It's not where you start that matters, but where you go from there."

Her words were a reminder that the essence of education lay not solely in the institution but in the knowledge and experiences one gained along the way.

The Decision-Making Process

Ultimately, Morgan approached his college applications with a strategic mindset. He created a decision matrix to evaluate his options, weighing factors such as academic programs, campus culture, and financial aid. This matrix allowed him to visualize his choices and alleviate some of the emotional burden:

$$U = \sum_{i=1}^{n} w_i \cdot r_i \tag{23}$$

Where:

+ U = Utility of a college choice

+ w_i = Weight of each criterion (e.g., academics, location)

+ r_i = Rating of each college on that criterion

Through this process, Morgan found clarity. He realized that while prestige was alluring, the right fit was paramount. He decided to apply to a mix of schools, including a few reach schools, some target schools, and a couple of safeties, ensuring he had options regardless of the outcome.

Conclusion

As Morgan submitted his applications, he felt a sense of relief wash over him. The college admissions dilemma had transformed from a source of anxiety into an opportunity for self-discovery. He understood that regardless of the outcome, he had the power to shape his future and continue his journey as an innovator.

In the end, the college admissions process was not merely about where he would spend the next four years, but about embracing the uncertainty of life and the myriad of possibilities that lay ahead. After all, as Morgan would later reflect, "Sometimes the best paths are the ones we didn't plan for."

Choosing the Right Path

As Morgan Liao approached the end of his high school years, he found himself at a crossroads that many young innovators face: the daunting decision of what path to take next. This moment was not merely a choice between colleges or career paths; it was a pivotal juncture that would shape the trajectory of his life and the future of digital humanities.

The Weight of Expectations

Morgan was not alone in feeling the pressure. Many of his peers were bombarded with expectations from parents, teachers, and society at large. The pressure was akin to trying to balance a stack of textbooks on his head while riding a unicycle—impressive but ultimately precarious. His parents, both academics, had their own dreams for him, envisioning a future where he would don a cap and gown from a prestigious university, perhaps even one of the Ivy League institutions.

The Dilemma of Choice

Morgan's dilemma was compounded by the myriad of options available to him. On one hand, he could follow the traditional path of enrolling in a well-respected university, which promised a stable future and a network of influential contacts. On the other hand, he had the opportunity to dive headfirst into the world of entrepreneurship, where he could pursue his passion for technology and innovation without the constraints of a formal education.

This internal conflict can be likened to the famous philosophical problem known as Buridan's Ass, where a donkey finds itself equally hungry for two bales of hay placed at equal distance. The indecision leads to paralysis, and Morgan felt the weight of similar indecision pressing down on him.

Evaluating the Options

To navigate this turbulent sea of choices, Morgan employed a systematic approach. He began by listing the pros and cons of each option.

- **Traditional University Route:**

  - Pros: Structured learning, access to resources, networking opportunities, recognized degree.
  - Cons: High tuition costs, potential for debt, time commitment, possible stifling of creativity.

- **Entrepreneurship:**

  - Pros: Freedom to innovate, direct application of skills, potential for financial gain, ability to impact society immediately.
  - Cons: High risk of failure, lack of formal credentials, potential isolation, financial instability.

Morgan realized that both paths carried their own unique risks and rewards. The decision was not merely about choosing a career; it was about defining his identity as an innovator.

Seeking Guidance

To gain further clarity, Morgan sought advice from mentors and industry leaders. He reached out to his high school teachers, who had always encouraged his curiosity and creativity. They reminded him of the importance of passion and purpose in any career choice. One teacher, Mr. Thompson, shared a poignant quote:

> "Choose a job you love, and you will never have to work a day in your life."

This resonated deeply with Morgan, prompting him to reflect on what truly ignited his passion. He also attended various workshops and seminars that focused on entrepreneurship and innovation, where he encountered successful figures who had taken unconventional paths.

The Role of Values

Morgan's decision-making process was also influenced by his core values. He believed in the importance of using technology to enhance human understanding and cultural preservation. This realization became a guiding principle in his decision-making. He pondered how each path aligned with his values, asking himself:

+ Does this choice allow me to contribute to society?

+ Will I be able to innovate and push boundaries?

+ How will this decision affect my personal growth?

By aligning his choices with his values, Morgan felt more empowered to make a decision that was authentic to himself.

The Decision

Ultimately, after much deliberation, Morgan chose to pursue a hybrid approach. He decided to enroll in a university that offered a strong program in digital humanities while simultaneously launching a startup focused on innovative educational technologies. This decision allowed him to gain the best of both worlds—formal education and practical experience.

Morgan's choice reflected a growing trend among young innovators: the desire to blend traditional education with entrepreneurial ventures. This approach is increasingly popular in the modern landscape, where the lines between academia and industry are becoming blurred.

Conclusion

The journey of choosing the right path was not without its challenges, but Morgan emerged from the experience with a clearer sense of purpose. He learned that the decision-making process is often messy and fraught with uncertainty, yet it is also an opportunity for growth and self-discovery.

In the end, Morgan Liao's choice was not just about where to go next, but about who he wanted to become—a pioneer in digital humanities, ready to embrace the challenges and opportunities that lay ahead. As he prepared to embark on this new chapter, he felt a sense of excitement and anticipation, knowing that the path he chose would not only shape his future but also the future of countless others in the realm of digital innovation.

University of Innovation

Joining the Ivy League

As Morgan Liao prepared to embark on his collegiate journey, the prospect of joining the Ivy League felt akin to being chosen for a space mission—exciting, terrifying, and requiring a significant amount of preparation. The Ivy League, a group of eight private colleges and universities in the northeastern United States, is renowned for its rigorous academic standards, prestigious alumni, and the ability to turn even the simplest of student projects into a multi-million dollar startup—often before the ink on their diplomas even dries.

Morgan's application process was nothing short of a digital renaissance in itself. He meticulously crafted his personal statement, a narrative that was part memoir, part manifesto, and part attempt to convince the admissions committee that he was, in fact, the reincarnation of Leonardo da Vinci. He wrote about his childhood curiosity, his early ventures into computer programming, and his ambitious high school projects, including the infamous attendance-tracking algorithm that had his principal questioning the very fabric of student accountability.

$$\text{Success Rate} = \frac{\text{Number of Acceptances}}{\text{Total Applications}} \times 100 \qquad (24)$$

This equation, while simple, highlighted the competitive nature of Ivy League admissions. With acceptance rates often hovering around 5% for the most elite institutions, Morgan knew he needed to stand out. He decided to leverage his knack for humor, a trait he had honed during countless late-night coding sessions, where laughter was the only thing keeping him sane amidst endless lines of code and caffeine.

One of his standout moments came during an interview at Harvard. When asked how he would contribute to the campus community, he responded, "By introducing a new course: 'How to Pretend You're Listening While Actually Figuring Out How to Hack the Wi-Fi.'" The admissions officer chuckled, and Morgan felt a surge of confidence. He had successfully combined his love for technology with a dose of levity—something that could very well be the secret ingredient to Ivy League success.

However, the journey was not without its challenges. The pressure to succeed was palpable, and Morgan found himself grappling with the fear of impostor syndrome. He often questioned whether he truly belonged among such illustrious peers. This inner turmoil was exacerbated by the media frenzy surrounding Ivy League admissions, which often painted a picture of elite students who were not only brilliant but also flawlessly well-rounded.

Morgan's coping mechanism involved a mix of late-night coding marathons and binge-watching documentaries about the most eccentric geniuses in history. He found solace in the fact that many of them were just as quirky and flawed as he was, and that perhaps, in their own ways, they too had felt like impostors at times.

$$\text{Impostor Syndrome Index} = \frac{\text{Self-Doubt}}{\text{Achievements}} \times 100 \qquad (25)$$

In this equation, Morgan realized that while self-doubt could be overwhelming, it was essential to balance it with recognition of his achievements. He had built a startup at sixteen, garnered awards for his innovative projects, and had even been invited to speak at tech conferences. Yet, the nagging voice in his head persisted, reminding him that there were countless others who were just as talented—or more so.

Ultimately, Morgan received acceptance letters from multiple Ivy League schools, but he chose to attend Yale University. His decision was not solely based on prestige; it was also influenced by the university's commitment to fostering innovation and interdisciplinary collaboration. He envisioned a place where he could merge his passions for technology and the humanities, and Yale seemed to offer the perfect environment for this exploration.

As he stepped onto the campus for the first time, Morgan felt a mix of excitement and trepidation. The iconic Gothic architecture loomed above him, and he could almost hear the whispers of past scholars echoing through the halls. He was about to join a lineage of thinkers who had shaped the world, and the weight of that legacy was both exhilarating and daunting.

In the coming months, Morgan would learn that joining the Ivy League was not just about academic rigor; it was also about forging connections, navigating the complexities of campus life, and discovering his own voice amidst a cacophony of ideas. He would face challenges that tested his resilience and creativity, but he was ready to embrace the journey ahead.

In conclusion, Morgan Liao's entry into the Ivy League marked the beginning of a transformative chapter in his life. It was a place where he would cultivate his ideas, confront his fears, and ultimately lay the groundwork for the revolutionary contributions he would make to the field of digital humanities. The Ivy League was not just an academic destination; it was a launching pad for the next phase of his extraordinary journey.

New Challenges and Opportunities

As Morgan Liao embarked on his journey through the University of Innovation, he quickly realized that the path to greatness is paved with both challenges and opportunities. This section explores the multifaceted landscape that Morgan encountered during his academic tenure, highlighting the hurdles he faced and the innovative solutions he devised.

Adapting to a Competitive Environment

Upon entering the Ivy League, Morgan was thrust into a highly competitive academic environment. The pressure to excel was palpable, with peers striving for the same accolades and recognition. Morgan's initial response was to double down on his efforts; he often found himself in the library until the early hours, surrounded by stacks of books and empty coffee cups, resembling a caffeine-fueled zombie.

The competition, however, was not merely about grades. It was a battle for resources, funding, and access to mentorship. Morgan had to develop a strategy to differentiate himself from his peers. He realized that collaboration could be a powerful tool in this competitive landscape. By forming study groups and research teams, Morgan turned potential rivals into allies. This approach not only alleviated some of the stress but also fostered a spirit of innovation that would become a hallmark of his career.

Navigating Bureaucratic Challenges

In addition to the academic pressures, Morgan faced the daunting bureaucracy of a prestigious institution. Navigating the administrative labyrinth often felt like trying to solve a Rubik's Cube blindfolded. He encountered endless forms, approval processes, and committee meetings that seemed to exist solely to prolong decision-making.

To tackle this challenge, Morgan employed a systematic approach, utilizing project management principles to streamline his initiatives. He introduced a framework based on Agile methodology, which allowed him to break down complex projects into manageable tasks. This not only helped in keeping his team organized but also made it easier to communicate progress to stakeholders.

$$\text{Progress} = \frac{\text{Completed Tasks}}{\text{Total Tasks}} \times 100\% \tag{26}$$

Morgan's ability to quantify progress in this manner not only impressed his professors but also garnered him recognition for his leadership skills.

Embracing Technological Advancements

The rapid evolution of technology presented both challenges and opportunities. While Morgan was well-versed in coding and digital tools, he quickly realized that staying ahead of the curve required continuous learning. The emergence of artificial intelligence, machine learning, and big data analytics was transforming the landscape of digital humanities, and Morgan knew he had to adapt.

He took it upon himself to enroll in additional courses and attend workshops, often joking that he was "collecting degrees like Pokémon cards." This relentless pursuit of knowledge paid off when he developed a groundbreaking AI project aimed at analyzing historical texts. By leveraging natural language processing, Morgan created a tool that could identify patterns and themes across vast collections of literature, effectively turning him into a digital Sherlock Holmes.

Building a Support Network

Recognizing the importance of mentorship, Morgan actively sought out guidance from professors and industry leaders. He attended networking events, armed with a stack of business cards that he distributed with the fervor of a door-to-door salesman. His genuine curiosity and enthusiasm helped him forge valuable connections, leading to collaborative projects that would shape his academic career.

One memorable encounter was with Dr. Evelyn Hart, a pioneer in digital humanities. During a chance meeting at a conference, Morgan shared his vision for integrating technology with historical research. Dr. Hart was impressed and offered him a research assistant position in her lab. This opportunity not only provided Morgan with invaluable experience but also opened doors to further collaborations.

Confronting Ethical Dilemmas

As Morgan delved deeper into the world of digital humanities, he began to confront ethical dilemmas that arose from his work. The intersection of technology and humanities posed questions about data privacy, representation, and the potential for bias in algorithms.

Morgan recognized that with great power comes great responsibility. He initiated discussions within his research group about the ethical implications of their projects. They examined case studies where technology had been misused, such as biased AI algorithms that perpetuated stereotypes. This led to the development of a set of ethical guidelines that would govern their research practices.

$$\text{Ethical Consideration} = \frac{\text{Informed Consent} + \text{Transparency} + \text{Accountability}}{3}$$

(27)

By prioritizing ethical considerations, Morgan and his team aimed to set a standard for future digital humanities research.

Seizing Opportunities for Innovation

Despite the challenges, Morgan's time at the University of Innovation was also marked by significant opportunities. He was able to pitch his revolutionary ideas to university stakeholders, securing funding for projects that would redefine the field of digital humanities. His proposal for the "Knowledge Archive," a digital repository that would democratize access to historical texts, was met with enthusiasm.

Furthermore, Morgan's participation in hackathons and innovation competitions allowed him to showcase his projects to a broader audience. His team won several awards, which not only validated their work but also attracted the attention of potential investors and collaborators.

Conclusion

In conclusion, Morgan Liao's journey through the University of Innovation was characterized by the dual forces of challenge and opportunity. By embracing competition, navigating bureaucracy, leveraging technology, building a support network, confronting ethical dilemmas, and seizing opportunities for innovation, Morgan laid the groundwork for his future success. This dynamic environment not only shaped his character but also equipped him with the tools necessary to become a leader in the field of digital humanities. As he moved forward, the lessons learned during these formative years would resonate throughout his career, guiding him through the complexities of the digital age.

Groundbreaking Research Projects

Morgan Liao's time at the University of Innovation was marked by a series of groundbreaking research projects that not only pushed the boundaries of digital humanities but also redefined the way technology interacts with culture and society. These projects addressed various theoretical frameworks, practical problems, and innovative examples that showcased Morgan's ingenuity and forward-thinking approach.

Theoretical Frameworks

At the core of Morgan's research was the integration of digital technologies with traditional humanities disciplines. This interdisciplinary approach was grounded in several key theories:

- **Constructivism:** Morgan believed in the constructivist theory of knowledge, which posits that individuals construct their understanding and knowledge of the world through experiences and reflecting on those experiences. This theory was pivotal in designing interactive digital platforms that allowed users to engage with historical data actively.

- **Cultural Studies:** Morgan drew upon cultural studies to examine how digital technologies influence cultural practices and vice versa. He utilized this framework to analyze the impact of social media on the dissemination of cultural knowledge, particularly among marginalized communities.

+ **Posthumanism:** Embracing posthumanist theory, Morgan explored the relationship between humans and technology, questioning what it means to be human in an increasingly digital world. This perspective informed his research on AI and its role in cultural preservation.

Key Research Projects

Morgan's groundbreaking research projects can be categorized into several distinct areas:

1. Digital Archives and Preservation   One of Morgan's flagship projects was the development of a comprehensive digital archive aimed at preserving endangered languages and cultures. This project faced the challenge of limited resources and the need for community engagement. To address this, Morgan implemented a participatory design approach, involving native speakers in the digitization process. The project utilized the following equation to measure community engagement:

$$E = \frac{(C + I) \times R}{T}$$

where E is engagement, C is community involvement, I is individual contributions, R represents resources allocated, and T is the time invested. This formula helped Morgan quantify the impact of community participation, leading to increased support and funding.

2. AI in Cultural Analysis   Morgan pioneered the use of artificial intelligence to analyze vast datasets of historical texts and artifacts. By employing natural language processing (NLP) techniques, he was able to identify patterns and trends in cultural narratives. This project not only illustrated the potential of AI in humanities research but also raised ethical questions regarding bias in AI algorithms. Morgan's team developed a framework to mitigate bias, incorporating the following principles:

+ **Transparency:** Ensuring that the algorithms used in analysis are open for scrutiny.

+ **Inclusivity:** Involving diverse voices in the development of AI systems to minimize bias.

+ **Accountability:** Establishing mechanisms to hold developers responsible for the outcomes of AI applications.

3. Virtual Reality for Historical Immersion   In a bid to create immersive educational experiences, Morgan led a project that utilized virtual reality (VR) technology to recreate historical events. This project aimed to address the problem of disengagement in traditional learning environments. By allowing students to experience history first-hand, the project demonstrated significant improvements in retention and comprehension. The effectiveness of this approach was measured using the following equation:

$$R = \frac{E_H}{E_C}$$

where R is retention rate, E_H is the engagement in historical VR experiences, and E_C is the engagement in conventional classroom settings. Initial results indicated a marked increase in student engagement and understanding.

4. Augmented Reality in Museums   Morgan's research extended to the museum sector, where he explored the integration of augmented reality (AR) to enhance visitor experiences. This project tackled the problem of static exhibits that often fail to engage younger audiences. By overlaying digital information onto physical artifacts, museums could provide interactive narratives that captivated visitors. The project's success was evaluated through visitor feedback and engagement metrics, leading to increased attendance and satisfaction ratings.

5. Social Media for Democratizing Knowledge   Recognizing the power of social media as a tool for knowledge dissemination, Morgan initiated a project that aimed to democratize access to cultural information. This project focused on creating platforms where users could share their interpretations and experiences related to cultural artifacts. The project utilized a feedback loop model, illustrated by the equation:

$$K = \frac{I}{D}$$

where K represents knowledge shared, I is the individual contributions, and D denotes the diversity of perspectives. This model emphasized the importance of inclusivity in cultural discourse, leading to a richer understanding of heritage.

Conclusion

Morgan Liao's groundbreaking research projects exemplified the potential of digital humanities to transform our understanding of culture and society. By blending theoretical frameworks with innovative technologies, Morgan not only addressed pressing challenges but also inspired a new generation of scholars and innovators. His work laid the foundation for a future where technology and humanities coexist harmoniously, fostering a cyber renaissance that continues to resonate throughout the academic community and beyond.

The Birth of Morgan's World-Changing Idea

In the hallowed halls of the University of Innovation, amidst the scent of overpriced coffee and the faint echoes of existential dread, Morgan Liao experienced a moment of inspiration that would alter the trajectory of digital humanities forever. It was an ordinary Tuesday—if such a day could ever be considered ordinary in a world where algorithms dictated the weather and holograms were the new chalkboards. Morgan had just finished a lecture on the philosophical implications of artificial intelligence when an epiphany struck him like a poorly thrown frisbee at a hipster picnic.

The Convergence of Ideas   Morgan's idea was born from the convergence of three seemingly disparate fields: technology, humanities, and ethics. He envisioned a platform that would not only democratize access to knowledge but also preserve cultural heritage in an age where information was as fleeting as a Snapchat story. The theoretical underpinning of this idea drew heavily from the works of theorists like Marshall McLuhan, who famously stated, "The medium is the message." Morgan believed that if the medium could be transformed into an interactive, engaging experience, the message—our collective human knowledge—would be better received and understood.

Identifying the Problem   However, the road to this world-changing idea was paved with obstacles. The primary problem was the overwhelming volume of data and the lack of effective tools to curate and analyze this information in a meaningful way. As Morgan often noted, "Just because you can Google it doesn't mean you should." The challenge was not merely about accessibility but about the quality of knowledge being disseminated. With the rise of misinformation and the decline of critical thinking skills, Morgan knew that a new approach was essential.

Theoretical Framework   To address these challenges, Morgan developed a theoretical framework that he termed the *Cultural Intelligence Paradigm*. This paradigm revolved around three core principles:

1. **Interactivity**: Users should not be passive consumers of information. Instead, they should engage with content, contributing their perspectives and

insights. This principle was rooted in constructivist learning theories, which emphasize active participation in the learning process.

2. **Contextualization:** Information must be presented within its cultural context. Morgan argued that understanding the historical and social background of knowledge enhances its significance.   This idea was inspired by cultural historians like Johan Huizinga, who posited that culture is a complex web of meanings that must be interpreted through its context.

3. **Ethical Stewardship:** With great power comes great responsibility. Morgan was acutely aware of the ethical implications of technology in humanities research. He advocated for transparency in data usage and the importance of protecting intellectual property, echoing the sentiments of scholars like Lawrence Lessig, who argued for a balance between innovation and regulation.

The Prototype   With these principles in mind, Morgan set out to create a prototype of his platform, which he affectionately dubbed *Culturify*. The prototype aimed to merge artificial intelligence with user-generated content, allowing individuals to contribute their stories and experiences while AI algorithms curated this information for broader accessibility. The underlying equation governing the platform's functionality could be simplified as follows:

$$C = \frac{I \cdot U}{E} \tag{28}$$

where C represents the cultural content created, I is the information input (data, stories, artifacts), U is the user engagement factor (interactivity, contributions), and E is the ethical considerations (privacy, bias, transparency).

Testing and Feedback   Morgan organized a series of focus groups to test *Culturify*. Participants ranged from tech-savvy students to elderly community members who had never used a computer before. The feedback was overwhelmingly positive, with users expressing excitement about the potential for their voices to be heard. One participant, a retired history teacher, exclaimed, "This is like Wikipedia, but without the risk of being edited by a 12-year-old in his mom's basement!"

Iterating the Idea   However, not all feedback was glowing. Critics pointed out potential pitfalls, such as the risk of echo chambers forming and the challenge of maintaining quality control over user-generated content.   Morgan took these criticisms to heart, iterating on his design and incorporating features that allowed for peer review and expert verification of contributions. He even introduced a gamification element, rewarding users for high-quality submissions with digital badges and the occasional cat meme.

The Moment of Clarity   It was during one of these brainstorming sessions that Morgan had his moment of clarity. "What if," he pondered aloud, "we could create a virtual reality experience that immerses users in historical events, allowing them to experience culture firsthand?" The room fell silent, save for the sound of a single crumpled snack wrapper hitting the floor. The idea of *Culturify VR* was born, and with it, the promise of a cyber renaissance that could bridge the gap between the past and the future.

Conclusion   In conclusion, the birth of Morgan Liao's world-changing idea was not a singular event but rather a culmination of insights, challenges, and an unwavering commitment to ethical innovation. As he often quipped, "If we're going to change the world, we might as well do it while having a little fun." With *Culturify*, Morgan was not just creating a platform; he was igniting a movement that would inspire future generations to explore, engage, and elevate the field of digital humanities in ways previously thought impossible.

Teamwork and Collaboration

In the realm of innovation, particularly within the context of digital humanities, the importance of teamwork and collaboration cannot be overstated. Morgan Liao's journey through the University of Innovation exemplifies how collective effort can lead to groundbreaking advancements.

The Theory Behind Teamwork

According to Tuckman's stages of group development, teams progress through five distinct stages: forming, storming, norming, performing, and adjourning [?]. In the forming stage, team members are polite and tentative, trying to understand their roles. As they move into the storming phase, conflicts may arise as personalities clash and ideas are debated. The norming stage is where the team begins to establish norms and find common ground, while the performing stage is characterized by high productivity and collaboration. Finally, in the adjourning stage, the team disbands after achieving its goals.

Morgan's teams often experienced these stages, particularly during the development of his revolutionary AI project. Initial meetings were filled with awkward silences and forced laughter, reminiscent of a first date gone wrong.

However, as they navigated through the storming phase, ideas began to flow, and creativity flourished.

Collaboration in Action

One of Morgan's most significant collaborative efforts was the establishment of a multidisciplinary research group focused on the intersection of technology and humanities. This group included computer scientists, historians, and sociologists, each bringing unique perspectives to the table. This diversity is crucial, as noted by Page (2007), who argues that cognitive diversity enhances problem-solving capabilities [?].

Morgan's team adopted agile methodologies, which emphasize iterative progress and adaptability. Regular stand-up meetings allowed team members to share updates, voice concerns, and brainstorm solutions in real-time. This approach not only kept everyone aligned but also fostered a culture of open communication.

Challenges in Collaboration

Despite the benefits, collaboration is not without its challenges. One significant issue that arose during the development of the Knowledge Archive was the differing priorities among team members. While some were focused on technical feasibility, others were concerned with the ethical implications of their work. This divergence often led to heated discussions, with Morgan playing the role of mediator.

To address these challenges, Morgan implemented the RACI matrix (Responsible, Accountable, Consulted, Informed), which clarified roles and responsibilities within the team. This tool helped minimize confusion and ensured that everyone understood their contributions to the project. The equation for the RACI matrix can be represented as:

$$\text{RACI} = \{R, A, C, I\}$$

where:

- R = Responsible (the person who does the work)

- A = Accountable (the person who is ultimately answerable)

- C = Consulted (those whose opinions are sought)

- I = Informed (those who need to be kept updated)

Successful Outcomes

The culmination of these collaborative efforts was the launch of the Digital Humanities Institute, which became a global hub for research and innovation. This institute not only redefined the field of digital humanities but also established a model for future collaborative projects.

For instance, one of the pioneering research projects involved the use of virtual reality to create immersive historical experiences. This project required the combined expertise of designers, historians, and software developers. The success of this initiative demonstrated the power of teamwork, as each member contributed their specialized knowledge, resulting in a product that was greater than the sum of its parts.

Conclusion

In conclusion, Morgan Liao's emphasis on teamwork and collaboration during his university years played a pivotal role in his success as an innovator. By fostering an environment of open communication, utilizing strategic frameworks, and embracing cognitive diversity, Morgan and his team were able to navigate challenges and achieve remarkable outcomes. As the digital humanities continue to evolve, the lessons learned from Morgan's collaborative experiences will undoubtedly inspire future innovators to harness the power of teamwork in their endeavors.

Mentorship from Industry Leaders

In the fast-paced world of innovation, mentorship plays a crucial role in shaping the careers of young visionaries like Morgan Liao. At the University of Innovation, Morgan had the unique opportunity to connect with industry leaders who not only provided guidance but also shared invaluable insights from their own experiences. This section explores the significance of mentorship, the challenges faced, and the profound impact it had on Morgan's journey.

The Importance of Mentorship

Mentorship is often described as a relationship in which a more experienced individual provides guidance and support to a less experienced person. In the context of technology and innovation, mentorship can take various forms, including one-on-one meetings, workshops, and collaborative projects. According to a study by Allen et al. (2004), effective mentorship can lead to increased job satisfaction, enhanced career development, and improved performance outcomes.

For Morgan, mentorship was not just a luxury; it was a necessity. As he delved deeper into the realms of digital humanities, he realized that the complexities of the field required more than just theoretical knowledge. He needed practical wisdom, which could only be imparted by those who had walked the path before him.

Challenges in Finding the Right Mentor

Despite the clear benefits of mentorship, finding the right mentor can be a daunting task. Morgan faced several challenges in this regard:

- **Identifying Suitable Mentors:** With a plethora of professionals in the tech industry, Morgan had to sift through a vast pool of potential mentors. He employed a systematic approach by researching their backgrounds, achievements, and areas of expertise, ensuring alignment with his own goals.

- **Establishing Connections:** Networking can often feel like a high-stakes game of roulette. Morgan attended conferences, workshops, and seminars, where he practiced his elevator pitch, which he humorously referred to as "the 30 seconds that could change my life." His persistence paid off when he finally connected with Dr. Elena Voss, a renowned expert in AI and digital humanities.

- **Overcoming Imposter Syndrome:** Morgan often grappled with feelings of inadequacy, questioning whether he was deserving of mentorship from such esteemed professionals. This psychological barrier, known as imposter syndrome, is common among high achievers. To combat this, Morgan reminded himself of his accomplishments and the potential he had to contribute to the field.

The Mentorship Experience

Once Morgan established connections with industry leaders, he was able to benefit from their wealth of knowledge and experience. Here are some key aspects of his mentorship experience:

- **Regular Meetings:** Morgan scheduled bi-weekly meetings with Dr. Voss, where they discussed his ongoing projects, challenges he faced, and strategies for overcoming obstacles. These sessions were not just about advice; they also served as a sounding board for Morgan's ideas, allowing him to refine his vision.

+ **Real-World Insights:** Mentors like Dr. Voss shared stories of their own failures and successes, providing Morgan with a realistic view of the industry. One memorable story involved Dr. Voss's early attempts at developing an AI algorithm that misidentified cats as dogs. This humorous anecdote highlighted the importance of perseverance and learning from mistakes.

+ **Networking Opportunities:** Through his mentors, Morgan gained access to a network of professionals and academics. Dr. Voss introduced him to key figures in the digital humanities community, leading to collaborations that would prove instrumental in his career. Morgan often joked that his network was like a spider web—intricate, expansive, and occasionally sticky.

Theoretical Framework: The Mentor-Mentee Relationship

The mentor-mentee relationship can be analyzed through various theoretical frameworks. One such framework is the *Social Learning Theory* proposed by Bandura (1977), which posits that individuals learn from observing others. This theory underscores the importance of role models in the learning process, particularly in fields that require creativity and innovation.

In Morgan's case, the relationship with Dr. Voss exemplified this theory. By observing her approach to problem-solving, ethical considerations in AI, and leadership style, Morgan was able to adapt these strategies to his own work. The reciprocal nature of the relationship also allowed Dr. Voss to gain fresh perspectives from Morgan, creating a dynamic learning environment.

Impact of Mentorship on Morgan's Work

The influence of mentorship on Morgan's work cannot be overstated. It was through these relationships that he developed his groundbreaking idea for the Digital Humanities Institute. The guidance he received helped him navigate the complexities of funding, collaboration, and project management.

Morgan's first major project, the *Knowledge Archive*, was directly inspired by discussions with his mentors. They encouraged him to think big and challenge the status quo, leading him to envision a platform that would democratize access to information. The project not only garnered attention from academic circles but also attracted funding from various organizations.

Conclusion: The Ripple Effect of Mentorship

As Morgan Liao's journey illustrates, mentorship is a vital component of personal and professional growth. The support and guidance he received from industry leaders equipped him with the tools necessary to navigate the challenges of innovation.

The ripple effect of mentorship extends beyond the individual; it influences entire communities and fields. By investing in the next generation of innovators, mentors like Dr. Voss contribute to a legacy of knowledge and progress. Morgan often reflects on this impact, humorously noting that "mentorship is like Wi-Fi; you can't see it, but it connects you to everything."

In conclusion, mentorship not only shaped Morgan's career but also laid the foundation for the Cyber Renaissance, inspiring a new wave of innovators to push the boundaries of what is possible in the digital humanities.

Implementing Ideas into Reality

Implementing ideas into reality is akin to trying to assemble a complex piece of furniture from a Swedish store without the instruction manual. It requires creativity, persistence, and, most importantly, a good sense of humor when you inevitably find yourself with extra screws and a vague sense of existential dread. For Morgan Liao, the journey from concept to execution was no different, filled with both triumphs and tribulations.

Theoretical Framework

At the core of Morgan's approach was the **Theory of Diffusion of Innovations**, proposed by Everett Rogers. This theory outlines how, why, and at what rate new ideas and technology spread. According to Rogers, the adoption of innovations follows a bell curve, which can be divided into five categories: innovators, early adopters, early majority, late majority, and laggards. Morgan aimed to position himself and his projects within the early adopter segment, leveraging social networks and influential figures to catalyze wider acceptance.

The equation representing the rate of adoption can be simplified as:

$$A(t) = P \times (1 - e^{-kt})$$

where: - $A(t)$ is the cumulative number of adopters at time t, - P is the potential number of adopters, - k is the coefficient of innovation, and - e is the base of the natural logarithm.

Morgan understood that to implement his ideas, he needed to focus on the k factor, ensuring that his innovations resonated with the needs of potential users.

Identifying Problems

Despite having a solid theoretical framework, Morgan faced numerous challenges in the implementation phase. One significant problem was the **resistance to change.** Many stakeholders were comfortable with traditional methods and skeptical of new technologies. Morgan often encountered the proverbial brick wall when trying to introduce his revolutionary AI project aimed at enhancing digital humanities research.

Real-World Examples

To tackle these challenges, Morgan employed several strategies. For instance, during the development of the *Knowledge Archive*, he initiated a pilot program at a local university. This involved collaborating with a small group of enthusiastic professors who were willing to experiment with the new platform. By showcasing the success of the pilot, Morgan was able to create a ripple effect, encouraging other faculty members to adopt the technology.

This approach aligns with the **Innovation Adoption Lifecycle**, which emphasizes the importance of early adopters in influencing the majority. Morgan's pilot program not only validated his ideas but also provided tangible data to demonstrate the effectiveness of his innovations.

Collaboration and Teamwork

Morgan recognized that implementing ideas into reality was not a solitary endeavor. He assembled a diverse team of experts, including software developers, data scientists, and humanities scholars. This multidisciplinary approach fostered creativity and allowed for a more comprehensive understanding of the challenges at hand.

For instance, when working on the *Virtual Reality for Historical Immersion* project, Morgan's team included historians who provided context and narrative depth to the immersive experiences. This collaboration ensured that the technology was not only innovative but also meaningful and engaging for users.

Iterative Development and Feedback Loops

Morgan embraced an **iterative development process**, which allowed for continuous improvement based on user feedback. He often held workshops and focus groups, inviting potential users to interact with prototypes of his projects. This not only helped identify usability issues early on but also created a sense of ownership among users, making them more likely to adopt the final product.

An example of this was the development of the *Digital Storytelling to Preserve Oral Histories* project. Initial prototypes were met with mixed reactions, prompting Morgan to refine the user interface and enhance the storytelling features. By the time the project was launched, it had evolved into a user-friendly platform that resonated deeply with its audience.

Overcoming Setbacks

Of course, the road to implementation was not without its setbacks. Morgan faced technical failures, funding issues, and even moments of self-doubt. However, he viewed these challenges as opportunities for growth. For instance, when a critical piece of software crashed just days before a major presentation, Morgan turned the situation into a learning experience. He humorously remarked, "If my software can crash, at least it's consistent with my love life!"

This resilience and ability to adapt were crucial in maintaining momentum toward his goals. Morgan learned to embrace failure as part of the innovation process, a sentiment echoed by many successful entrepreneurs.

Celebrating Successes

Finally, Morgan understood the importance of celebrating small victories along the way. Each successful implementation of an idea was an opportunity to recognize the hard work of his team and to build enthusiasm for future projects. Whether it was a successful launch event or a positive review from a user, Morgan made it a point to acknowledge contributions and foster a culture of appreciation.

In conclusion, implementing ideas into reality is a multifaceted process that requires a blend of theoretical knowledge, practical strategies, and a good dose of humor. Morgan Liao's journey exemplifies how creativity, collaboration, and resilience can turn visionary concepts into impactful innovations, paving the way for a Cyber Renaissance in the digital humanities.

The Impact of Morgan's Work on Campus

Morgan Liao didn't just waltz into the University of Innovation; he practically pirouetted through the doors, leaving a trail of digital glitter and a faint scent of burnt silicon. His arrival marked a seismic shift in the academic landscape, causing professors to reconsider their life choices, and students to wonder if they could actually make a living playing video games.

A New Paradigm in Learning

Before Morgan, the campus was a place where knowledge was like a rare Pokémon—hard to catch and often elusive. He introduced the concept of **interactive learning environments**, where students could engage with their subjects in a way that made them feel like they were in a video game rather than a lecture hall. Imagine a classroom where, instead of listening to a professor drone on about the intricacies of quantum physics, students could actually manipulate equations in real-time, like they were the protagonists of their own sci-fi movie.

This approach aligns with the *Constructivist Learning Theory*, which posits that learners construct knowledge best through experiences. Morgan's projects enabled students to create their own knowledge frameworks, leading to a more profound understanding of complex concepts. Of course, this also led to an increase in the number of students wearing VR headsets during lunch, but who's counting?

Fostering Collaboration

Morgan's work also had a significant impact on fostering collaboration across disciplines. He created the **Interdisciplinary Innovation Hub**, where students from computer science, humanities, and even the art department could gather and brainstorm. The hub became the campus equivalent of a superhero team-up, where the tech-savvy students would join forces with the creatively inclined to tackle problems like how to make Shakespeare's plays more relatable to today's TikTok generation.

This collaboration was rooted in the *Social Constructivism* theory, which emphasizes the importance of social interactions in the learning process. By mixing students from different backgrounds, Morgan ensured that ideas flowed like overpriced coffee at the campus café.

Challenges and Triumphs

However, not everything was sunshine and rainbows in Morgan's digital utopia. The university's administration was initially skeptical of his ambitious projects. They questioned whether students should really be allowed to create a **virtual reality simulation of the French Revolution** instead of studying for their midterms. "What's next?" they pondered. "A holographic Napoleon leading a group project?"

Morgan faced the challenge of proving that his initiatives had tangible benefits. He conducted a study using the equation:

$$\text{Student Engagement} = \frac{\text{Interactive Learning}}{\text{Traditional Methods}} \times \text{Collaboration} \qquad (29)$$

The results were staggering. Engagement levels soared, and students were not just passing their classes; they were thriving. Morgan's work effectively transformed the campus culture into one that celebrated creativity, innovation, and, most importantly, the occasional meme.

Legacy and Influence

The impact of Morgan's work extended beyond the immediate campus environment. His initiatives inspired other universities to adopt similar programs, creating a ripple effect across the educational landscape. Institutions began to realize that students are not just vessels for information but rather dynamic participants in their learning journeys.

Morgan's influence also reached the faculty, who found themselves re-evaluating their teaching methods. Professors began experimenting with gamification in their curricula. One professor even introduced a grading system based on a Dungeons & Dragons-style quest, where students could earn experience points for participation. "You get an A for effort, but if you slay the dragon of procrastination, you get bonus points!" became a common phrase on campus.

Conclusion

In conclusion, Morgan Liao's impact on campus was nothing short of revolutionary. He transformed the university into a breeding ground for innovation, collaboration, and a healthy dose of chaos. As students donned VR headsets and collaborated on projects that would make even the most seasoned tech moguls proud, the campus evolved into a vibrant ecosystem of ideas.

Morgan's legacy is a testament to the power of digital humanities and the importance of fostering an environment where creativity and technology coexist harmoniously. So, the next time you see a student wearing a virtual reality headset while quoting Shakespeare, just know that Morgan Liao's influence is alive and well, and he's probably laughing somewhere, thinking, "I told you this would happen!"

Graduation and New Beginnings

Morgan Liao stood on the precipice of a new era, the day of his graduation from the prestigious University of Innovation. As he donned his cap and gown, he felt a mixture of excitement and apprehension, not unlike a cat contemplating a jump from a high ledge—will he soar or simply land in a pile of awkwardness?

The ceremony was a dazzling display of academic achievement, with students adorned in colorful regalia, and speeches that oscillated between inspirational and mildly confusing. The keynote speaker, a former tech mogul turned motivational speaker, delivered a monologue that could only be described as "a TED Talk on caffeine." Morgan, however, was transfixed not just by the words but by the possibilities that lay ahead.

The Weight of Expectations

Graduation, while a time for celebration, also brought with it the weight of expectations. Morgan's parents, beaming with pride, had high hopes for their son. They envisioned him as the next Steve Jobs, but with less turtleneck and more social skills. As he walked across the stage to receive his diploma, he couldn't help but feel the pressure of those expectations pressing down on him like a particularly heavy backpack filled with textbooks he never opened.

The reality of life post-graduation loomed large. What was next? Morgan had spent years immersed in academia, crafting groundbreaking projects that melded technology and the humanities. Yet, as he faced the world outside the university walls, he grappled with the daunting question: "How do I turn my ideas into reality without accidentally creating a rogue AI that decides to take over the world?"

The Intersection of Dreams and Reality

Morgan's mind raced with possibilities. He envisioned launching his own startup, a venture that would revolutionize the way we interact with digital humanities. He had learned about the importance of a solid business model during his studies, and he knew that success would not just be about having a great idea. It would require strategic planning, funding, and a team that shared his vision.

To illustrate the complexity of startup dynamics, consider the equation for the success of a startup:

$$S = (I + R + T) \times C \tag{30}$$

where:

+ S = Success of the startup

+ I = Innovative idea

+ R = Resources (financial, human, technological)

+ T = Timing (market readiness)

+ C = Commitment of the team

In Morgan's case, he had the innovative idea and a decent understanding of resources, but timing was the elusive factor. He needed to ensure that the world was ready for his vision, or risk being labeled as "that guy who was a little too ahead of his time."

Networking and Building a Team

In the weeks following graduation, Morgan dove headfirst into networking. He attended conferences, meetups, and even a few hackathons where the energy was palpable, and the coffee was strong enough to fuel a rocket launch. He was determined to assemble a team of like-minded individuals who were equally passionate about the intersection of technology and the humanities.

Morgan recalled a particularly enlightening conversation with a fellow graduate, who had a penchant for virtual reality. They discussed the potential of using VR to create immersive educational experiences that could breathe life into historical events. This idea sparked a flurry of brainstorming sessions that led to the formation of a small team, aptly named "The Digital Dreamers."

The First Steps into Entrepreneurship

With a team in place, the next step was to secure funding. Morgan learned quickly that pitching to investors was akin to dating—there was a lot of charm involved, and rejection was inevitable. He crafted a pitch deck that highlighted not only the innovative aspects of their project but also the potential for social impact.

One of the key elements he emphasized was how their project could democratize access to knowledge. By leveraging technology, they aimed to break down barriers that often left marginalized voices unheard. Morgan believed that this mission would resonate with investors looking to make a difference, but he also knew he needed to present a solid financial plan.

$$F = R - C \qquad (31)$$

where:

* F = Financial viability

* R = Revenue projections

* C = Costs associated with the project

Morgan meticulously calculated their projections, ensuring that the numbers were as polished as his presentation skills (which, admittedly, still needed a bit of work).

Embracing Uncertainty

As the months rolled on, Morgan faced the inevitable ups and downs of entrepreneurship. There were days filled with exhilarating breakthroughs, like when they secured their first round of funding. Other days felt like a never-ending slog through a swamp of bureaucracy and unexpected challenges.

One particularly chaotic day, Morgan found himself buried under a mountain of emails, each one more urgent than the last. He recalled a piece of advice from one of his professors: "In the world of innovation, embrace uncertainty. It's the only constant you can count on."

With that mantra in mind, Morgan learned to adapt, pivot, and sometimes even laugh at the absurdity of it all. Like the time they accidentally sent out a marketing email that contained a meme about cats instead of their project details. Surprisingly, it garnered more attention than their actual product launch.

Looking Forward

Graduation was not the end, but rather the beginning of an exciting journey filled with possibilities. Morgan Liao stepped into the world with a heart full of ambition and a mind brimming with ideas. He understood that the road ahead would be fraught with challenges, but he was ready to embrace them.

As he looked back at the university, he felt a sense of gratitude for the experiences that shaped him. The friendships, the late-night study sessions, the moments of doubt, and the triumphs—they all contributed to the person he had become.

In the end, Morgan Liao was not just a graduate; he was a pioneer poised to lead the charge into the Cyber Renaissance. With his team by his side, he was ready to tackle the world, one digital innovation at a time.

Chapter 2 Revolutionizing Digital Humanities

Chapter 2 Revolutionizing Digital Humanities

Revolutionizing Digital Humanities

In the age of information, where bytes and pixels reign supreme, the Digital Humanities have emerged as a beacon of hope, illuminating the intersection of technology and traditional humanistic inquiry. Morgan Liao, a prodigious innovator, stands at the forefront of this movement, wielding his keyboard like a bard once wielded a quill. This chapter explores how Morgan's vision not only revolutionizes the field but also challenges the very essence of how we understand knowledge itself.

The Intersection of Technology and Humanities

The Digital Humanities (DH) is not merely a fusion of technology and the humanities; it is a radical rethinking of what it means to engage with culture, history, and society. Morgan's approach embodies the essence of this intersection. He posits that technology should not overshadow humanistic inquiry but rather enhance it. By employing computational tools, he aims to analyze vast amounts of literary texts, historical documents, and cultural artifacts, transforming qualitative analysis into a quantitative powerhouse.

$$\text{Knowledge} = \text{Data} + \text{Interpretation} \tag{32}$$

In this equation, data represents the raw material that technology provides, while interpretation is the human touch that contextualizes and gives meaning to that data. Morgan's work exemplifies this balance, as he leverages algorithms not just to crunch numbers but to provide insights into the human experience.

Breaking Down Barriers

One of the significant challenges in the Digital Humanities is the persistent barriers between disciplines. The traditional silos of academia often hinder collaboration and innovation. Morgan's vision seeks to dismantle these barriers, advocating for a more interdisciplinary approach. He argues that the future of knowledge lies in collaboration among computer scientists, historians, linguists, and artists.

For example, in one of his groundbreaking projects, Morgan brought together a team of historians and data scientists to analyze patterns in historical texts using machine learning. This collaboration not only yielded new insights into historical narratives but also demonstrated the power of combining diverse expertise to tackle complex questions.

A New Approach to Knowledge

Morgan's revolutionary approach to knowledge involves rethinking how we access, share, and preserve information. He believes that knowledge should be democratized, accessible to all, rather than confined to the ivory towers of academia. To this end, he developed an open-source platform that allows users to contribute to and curate digital archives.

This platform utilizes a model similar to Wikipedia, where scholars and enthusiasts alike can edit and enhance entries. By harnessing the collective intelligence of the crowd, Morgan's initiative exemplifies the potential of collaborative knowledge-building. This model not only enriches the content but also fosters a sense of community among users.

The Promise of a Cyber Renaissance

Morgan envisions a Cyber Renaissance, a period where technology and humanities converge to create a new cultural and intellectual landscape. This renaissance is characterized by the proliferation of digital tools that empower individuals to engage with their cultural heritage in unprecedented ways.

Take, for example, the use of virtual reality (VR) in museums. Morgan spearheaded a project that allowed users to experience historical events through immersive VR environments. Imagine stepping into a Roman forum or witnessing the signing of the Declaration of Independence—this is not just a dream but a reality that Morgan is making possible.

Gaining Support and Funding

To realize his vision, Morgan understood the necessity of securing support and funding from various stakeholders. He approached universities, tech companies, and philanthropic organizations, articulating the transformative potential of the Digital Humanities. His compelling presentations often mixed humor with hard data, making a case that was as entertaining as it was persuasive.

Morgan's ability to communicate the value of DH to diverse audiences resulted in significant funding for his projects. By framing his initiatives as not just academic exercises but as societal imperatives, he attracted support from those who might not typically engage with the humanities.

Assembling a Dream Team

Recognizing that no innovator can succeed alone, Morgan meticulously assembled a dream team of experts from various fields. This team included data scientists, software developers, historians, and artists, each bringing unique perspectives to the table. The diversity of thought within the team was a catalyst for creativity, allowing for the development of groundbreaking projects that would not have been possible in isolation.

Morgan often likened his team to a band, where each member played a different instrument, yet together they created a symphony of ideas. This collaborative spirit became a hallmark of his approach, demonstrating that innovation thrives in an inclusive environment.

Setting Groundbreaking Goals

With a talented team in place, Morgan set ambitious goals that pushed the boundaries of what was possible in the Digital Humanities. These goals included creating a comprehensive digital archive of marginalized voices in history, developing algorithms to analyze cultural trends, and designing educational tools that integrate digital humanities into K-12 curricula.

Morgan's commitment to these goals was unwavering, often leading late-night brainstorming sessions that felt more like improv comedy shows than academic meetings. His humor served as a glue, binding the team together through challenges and setbacks.

Overcoming Doubt and Skepticism

Despite the enthusiasm surrounding his projects, Morgan faced considerable doubt and skepticism from traditionalists who viewed the Digital Humanities as a threat to established disciplines. Critics questioned the validity of using algorithms to interpret literature or history, arguing that such approaches risked oversimplifying complex human experiences.

Morgan countered these critiques with a mix of data and humor, often quipping, "If Shakespeare had access to a computer, he would have written 10 times more plays and probably would have used emojis." By framing the conversation in relatable terms, he opened up dialogue and encouraged critics to consider the potential benefits of embracing technology.

The World Takes Notice

As Morgan's initiatives gained traction, the world began to take notice. Conferences and symposiums dedicated to the Digital Humanities flourished, with Morgan frequently invited to speak. His presentations, filled with wit and insight, captivated audiences, inspiring a new generation of scholars and practitioners.

The impact of his work extended beyond academia, influencing policy discussions about funding for the arts and education. Morgan's ability to articulate the importance of digital humanities in shaping cultural discourse positioned him as a thought leader in the field.

In conclusion, Morgan Liao's revolutionary vision for the Digital Humanities is not just about technology; it is about reimagining the very foundations of knowledge and culture. By breaking down barriers, democratizing access, and fostering collaboration, he is paving the way for a Cyber Renaissance that promises to enrich our understanding of the human experience. As we delve deeper into the specifics of his projects, we will see how this vision translates into tangible outcomes that resonate across generations.

Morgan's Vision Unveiled

The Intersection of Technology and Humanities

In an age where technology and digital tools are reshaping every facet of our lives, the intersection of technology and humanities has emerged as a fertile ground for innovation and exploration. This convergence is not merely a trend but a fundamental shift in how we understand and engage with culture, history, and human expression. As Morgan Liao embarked on his journey, he recognized that the digital realm could amplify the voice of the humanities, transforming traditional practices into dynamic, interactive experiences.

Defining the Intersection

At its core, the intersection of technology and humanities encompasses the application of digital tools to analyze, preserve, and disseminate human culture and knowledge. The humanities—comprising disciplines such as literature, philosophy, history, and the arts—seek to understand the human experience, while technology provides innovative methodologies to explore these narratives in unprecedented ways. This relationship can be illustrated by the following equation:

$$H = f(T) \tag{33}$$

where H represents the humanities, and T symbolizes technology. The function f denotes the transformative impact of technology on the humanities, suggesting that as technology evolves, so too does our understanding of human culture.

Challenges in Bridging Disciplines

Despite the promising potential of this intersection, several challenges must be addressed. One significant hurdle is the skepticism that often exists within traditional humanities circles regarding the validity and reliability of digital methods. Critics argue that the quantitative nature of technology may undermine the qualitative richness that humanities scholarship traditionally emphasizes.

Moreover, there are ethical considerations surrounding data usage and representation. As Morgan noted, "Just because you can digitize something doesn't mean you should." This sentiment underscores the importance of maintaining the integrity of cultural narratives while navigating the complexities of digital representation.

Innovative Examples

Morgan's vision for a Cyber Renaissance was exemplified through various innovative projects that highlighted the synergy between technology and humanities. One such project was the creation of the **Digital Archive of Lost Languages,** which utilized machine learning algorithms to analyze and reconstruct extinct languages. This initiative not only preserved linguistic heritage but also provided insights into the cultures that spoke them.

Another notable example was the development of an **Augmented Reality (AR) application** that allowed users to experience historical events in real-time. By overlaying digital information onto physical locations, users could engage with history in a way that was both immersive and educational. This project illustrated the potential for technology to enhance our understanding of the past, making history accessible and engaging for a broader audience.

Theoretical Frameworks

To further understand this intersection, several theoretical frameworks can be employed. One such framework is **Digital Humanism**, which advocates for a human-centered approach to technology. This perspective emphasizes the importance of ethical considerations and the need for technology to serve humanity rather than the other way around. Morgan's work embodied this ethos, as he consistently sought to align technological advancements with the values and needs of society.

Additionally, **Critical Digital Humanities** provides a lens through which to examine the implications of digital tools on humanities scholarship. This approach encourages scholars to interrogate the power dynamics inherent in technology, questioning who controls digital narratives and whose voices are amplified or silenced in the process.

Future Directions

As we look to the future, the intersection of technology and humanities holds immense potential for further exploration. Emerging technologies such as artificial intelligence, virtual reality, and blockchain are poised to revolutionize how we create, share, and preserve knowledge. For instance, AI-driven content analysis can uncover patterns in literature and art that may have gone unnoticed, leading to new interpretations and understandings of cultural artifacts.

Moreover, the integration of blockchain technology in the humanities offers exciting possibilities for safeguarding intellectual property and ensuring the authenticity of digital works. By creating a transparent and immutable record of ownership, blockchain can empower artists and scholars alike, fostering a more equitable digital landscape.

In conclusion, the intersection of technology and humanities is a dynamic space ripe for innovation. As Morgan Liao navigated this terrain, he recognized the importance of embracing both the opportunities and challenges that arise from this convergence. By fostering collaboration between technologists and humanists, we can unlock new avenues for understanding the complexities of the human experience in an increasingly digital world. The Cyber Renaissance that Morgan envisioned is not just a future possibility; it is a call to action for all innovators to bridge these disciplines and create a more inclusive and enriched cultural narrative.

Breaking Down Barriers

In the rapidly evolving landscape of digital humanities, Morgan Liao emerged as a beacon of innovation, breaking down barriers that had long constrained the intersection of technology and the humanities. His vision was not merely to enhance existing frameworks but to dismantle the silos that separated disciplines, allowing for a more integrated approach to knowledge and culture.

One of the primary barriers Morgan identified was the traditional divide between the sciences and the humanities. This dichotomy has been a longstanding issue in academia, often leading to an artificial separation of methodologies and epistemologies. Morgan argued that this separation was not only detrimental to holistic understanding but also to the advancement of knowledge itself. He posited that the integration of computational methods with humanistic inquiry could lead to richer insights and more nuanced interpretations of cultural artifacts.

$$\text{Knowledge Integration} = \text{Humanities} + \text{Technology} \tag{34}$$

To illustrate this point, Morgan often referenced the concept of *digital ethnography*, a methodology that combines traditional ethnographic practices with digital tools. This approach allows researchers to analyze cultural phenomena in real-time, utilizing social media platforms and online communities as sites of study. By employing digital ethnography, Morgan and his team were able to capture the complexities of modern cultural interactions, demonstrating how technology could enhance, rather than hinder, humanistic inquiry.

Moreover, Morgan recognized that access to technology itself was a significant barrier. In many educational institutions, especially those in underfunded areas, resources for digital humanities projects were scarce. He initiated programs aimed at democratizing access to technology, advocating for the establishment of digital labs and resources in schools that lacked such facilities. Morgan believed that by providing students with the tools they needed, he could empower a new generation of thinkers who could contribute to the field of digital humanities.

One notable example of this initiative was the *Digital Bridge Program*, which Morgan launched in collaboration with several universities. This program provided workshops, mentorship, and resources to high school students from diverse backgrounds, equipping them with skills in coding, digital storytelling, and data analysis. The success of the program was evident in the projects produced by its participants, which ranged from interactive digital narratives to data visualizations that highlighted social issues within their communities.

Morgan also faced challenges related to the inherent biases in technology. As algorithms increasingly shape our understanding of culture and history, he was acutely aware of the ethical implications of relying on automated systems. He advocated for transparency in algorithmic processes and the inclusion of diverse voices in the development of digital tools. By promoting interdisciplinary collaboration, he aimed to ensure that the technologies used in digital humanities projects were reflective of the diverse societies they intended to serve.

$$\text{Bias Mitigation} = \text{Diversity} + \text{Transparency} \tag{35}$$

In his speeches and writings, Morgan often emphasized the importance of *collaborative scholarship*. He believed that breaking down barriers required not only technological integration but also a cultural shift in how scholars approached their work. This meant fostering environments where interdisciplinary collaboration was not just encouraged but expected. Morgan's own projects frequently involved teams composed of computer scientists, historians, artists, and sociologists, all working together to address complex questions that transcended traditional disciplinary boundaries.

As a result of these efforts, Morgan's work began to attract attention from both academia and industry. His approach to breaking down barriers in digital humanities not only inspired his peers but also garnered support from funding bodies eager to invest in innovative research that promised to reshape the future of education and cultural preservation.

In conclusion, Morgan Liao's commitment to breaking down barriers within the digital humanities field was characterized by his focus on integration, accessibility, and ethical considerations. By addressing the divides between disciplines, democratizing access to technology, and advocating for inclusivity in algorithmic design, he paved the way for a more holistic and equitable approach to the study of culture in the digital age. His legacy serves as a reminder of the potential for technology to enhance our understanding of humanity, provided we are willing to confront and dismantle the barriers that stand in our way.

A New Approach to Knowledge

In the rapidly evolving landscape of digital humanities, Morgan Liao's vision for a new approach to knowledge transcends traditional boundaries, merging technology with the humanities in ways previously deemed impossible. This paradigm shift hinges on the understanding that knowledge is not a static entity but a dynamic construct shaped by cultural, social, and technological influences.

Redefining Knowledge Structures

The first step in this new approach is the redefinition of knowledge structures. Traditionally, knowledge has been compartmentalized into rigid disciplines, often leading to silos that hinder interdisciplinary collaboration. Liao posits that knowledge should be viewed as a fluid network, where connections and interactions between various fields can lead to innovative insights. This is akin to the theory of *connectivism*, proposed by George Siemens, which emphasizes the role of social and cultural context in the learning process.

$$K = f(C, T, S) \tag{36}$$

Where K represents knowledge, C is the cultural context, T is the technological framework, and S signifies social interactions. This equation encapsulates the essence of Liao's vision: knowledge is a function of its environment, and by understanding this relationship, we can foster a more holistic approach to education and research.

Embracing Technology as a Tool

Another critical aspect of Liao's approach is the embrace of technology not merely as a tool but as an integral component of the knowledge creation process. In his groundbreaking projects, Liao has implemented advanced technologies such as artificial intelligence, big data analytics, and virtual reality to enhance the way knowledge is generated, shared, and preserved.

For instance, the use of AI algorithms in analyzing vast datasets allows researchers to uncover patterns and insights that would be impossible to detect manually. This approach not only accelerates the research process but also democratizes access to knowledge, enabling a wider audience to engage with complex ideas.

Case Study: The Knowledge Archive

A prime example of this new approach is the creation of the *Knowledge Archive*, a digital repository that utilizes AI to curate and present information in an engaging and interactive format. The archive employs machine learning algorithms to analyze user interactions, adapting its content to meet the needs and interests of its audience.

This model is reminiscent of the *personalized learning* frameworks popularized in educational technology, where content is tailored to individual learning styles and paces. By leveraging technology in this way, Liao's Knowledge Archive not only enhances user engagement but also fosters a deeper understanding of complex subjects.

Collaborative Knowledge Creation

Liao's approach also emphasizes collaborative knowledge creation, breaking down the barriers between experts and non-experts. By harnessing the power of social media platforms and online communities, individuals from diverse backgrounds can contribute to the knowledge production process. This participatory model echoes the principles of *crowdsourcing*, where collective intelligence is harnessed to solve problems and generate new ideas.

For example, Liao initiated the *Digital Storytelling Project*, inviting people from around the world to share their personal narratives and cultural histories. This project not only enriches the archive with diverse perspectives but also empowers individuals to take ownership of their stories, fostering a sense of community and shared knowledge.

Challenges and Ethical Considerations

While Liao's approach offers exciting possibilities, it is not without challenges. The integration of technology into the humanities raises ethical questions regarding privacy, data security, and the potential for bias in AI algorithms. Liao advocates for a proactive stance in addressing these concerns, emphasizing the need for transparency and accountability in digital humanities projects.

To navigate these ethical dilemmas, Liao proposes a framework based on the principles of *ethical innovation*, which calls for the responsible use of technology in knowledge creation. This framework encourages practitioners to consider the societal implications of their work, ensuring that the benefits of technological advancements are equitably distributed.

Conclusion

In summary, Morgan Liao's new approach to knowledge represents a transformative shift in the field of digital humanities. By redefining knowledge structures, embracing technology as a core component, fostering collaborative creation, and addressing ethical considerations, Liao paves the way for a more inclusive and dynamic understanding of knowledge. As we move towards a future characterized by rapid technological advancements, Liao's vision serves as a guiding light, reminding us that knowledge is not merely a product but a living, breathing entity that thrives on connection and collaboration.

The Promise of a Cyber Renaissance

In the ever-evolving landscape of technology and culture, the notion of a Cyber Renaissance emerges as a beacon of hope and innovation. This term, coined by Morgan Liao, encapsulates the idea that we are on the brink of a new era where digital technology and humanistic inquiry converge to create unprecedented opportunities for learning, creativity, and social change. Much like the Renaissance of the 14th to 17th centuries, which saw a flourishing of art, science, and thought, the Cyber Renaissance promises to redefine our understanding of knowledge and its dissemination.

At the heart of this movement lies the intersection of technology and the humanities. As we delve deeper into the digital age, the boundaries that once separated these domains begin to blur. The promise of a Cyber Renaissance is rooted in the belief that technology can enhance our understanding of human experience, culture, and history. This is not merely about digital tools but about reimagining how we engage with knowledge itself.

Theoretical Foundations

The theoretical framework supporting the Cyber Renaissance draws from various disciplines, including digital humanities, information science, and sociology. One of the key theories is the concept of **networked knowledge**, which posits that knowledge is not a static entity but a dynamic and interconnected web of information. As we harness the power of the internet and digital platforms, we can create more inclusive and participatory forms of knowledge production.

The work of theorists such as *Lev Manovich* and *Geert Lovink* provides insight into how digital media can reshape our understanding of culture. Manovich's *"The Language of New Media"* emphasizes the importance of software in shaping cultural experiences, while Lovink's exploration of *"Dark Media"* critiques the implications of digital technologies on public discourse. Together, these perspectives highlight the potential for technology to not only preserve but also innovate cultural narratives.

Addressing Problems in Knowledge Dissemination

Despite its promise, the Cyber Renaissance also confronts significant challenges. One of the most pressing issues is the **digital divide**, which refers to the gap between those who have access to digital technologies and those who do not. This divide can exacerbate existing inequalities in education, economic opportunity, and social mobility. To truly realize the promise of a Cyber Renaissance, we must ensure equitable access to technology and digital literacy programs.

Another challenge is the **preservation of cultural heritage** in the digital realm. As we increasingly rely on digital formats, the risk of obsolescence and data loss looms large. Morgan's vision includes the development of robust digital archiving systems that not only preserve artifacts but also make them accessible to a global audience. This involves employing advanced technologies such as *blockchain* for secure data storage and *AI* for cataloging and indexing vast amounts of information.

Examples of the Cyber Renaissance in Action

The promise of a Cyber Renaissance is already being realized through various innovative projects. One notable example is the **Digital Public Library of America (DPLA)**, which aggregates millions of photographs, manuscripts, and other cultural artifacts from libraries, archives, and museums across the United States. By providing free access to these resources, DPLA exemplifies how digital technology can democratize knowledge and foster a culture of learning.

Additionally, initiatives like **Google Arts & Culture** allow users to explore artworks and historical sites from around the world through virtual reality and augmented reality experiences. This not only enhances engagement but also invites users to interact with cultural heritage in new and meaningful ways.

Morgan's own projects, such as the **Knowledge Archive**, aim to leverage artificial intelligence for cultural preservation. By utilizing machine learning algorithms, the archive can analyze and categorize vast amounts of data, ensuring that diverse voices and narratives are represented in the digital landscape.

Conclusion

In conclusion, the promise of a Cyber Renaissance lies in its potential to transform how we create, share, and engage with knowledge. By embracing the convergence of technology and the humanities, we can foster a more inclusive, innovative, and ethically responsible approach to learning and cultural preservation. As Morgan Liao continues to lead the charge in this movement, the future holds the possibility of a richer, more interconnected world where knowledge is not just a privilege for the few, but a shared resource for all. The Cyber Renaissance invites us to imagine a future where technology serves as a bridge rather than a barrier, empowering individuals and communities to shape their own narratives in the digital age.

Gaining Support and Funding

In the pursuit of revolutionizing the field of Digital Humanities, Morgan Liao faced the daunting task of securing adequate support and funding. The challenges were manifold: the intersection of technology and humanities was not only an uncharted territory but also one often viewed with skepticism by traditionalists in both fields. To navigate this complex landscape, Morgan employed a multifaceted approach to garner support from various stakeholders, including academic institutions, government bodies, and private investors.

Understanding the Landscape

The first step in gaining support was understanding the funding landscape. Morgan recognized that funding for digital humanities projects typically came from three primary sources: government grants, private foundations, and corporate sponsorships. Each of these sources had its own set of expectations and requirements, which Morgan meticulously analyzed. For example, government grants often required a demonstration of public benefit, while private foundations looked for innovative approaches to societal problems.

Crafting a Compelling Narrative

With a clear understanding of the funding landscape, Morgan set out to craft a compelling narrative around his vision for a Cyber Renaissance. He emphasized the transformative potential of digital humanities in enhancing cultural understanding, preserving history, and democratizing access to knowledge. In his pitch, Morgan employed a classic narrative structure:

$$\text{Narrative} = \text{Problem} + \text{Solution} + \text{Impact} \tag{37}$$

Where:

- **Problem:** The decline of traditional humanities and the need for innovative approaches to engage younger audiences.

- **Solution:** The creation of a Digital Humanities Institute that would leverage technology to enhance research and education.

- **Impact:** A measurable increase in public engagement with the humanities and improved educational outcomes.

This narrative not only resonated with potential funders but also positioned Morgan as a thought leader in the field.

Building Partnerships

Recognizing the power of collaboration, Morgan actively sought partnerships with established institutions. He reached out to universities, museums, and cultural organizations that shared a common interest in digital innovation. By aligning his vision with their missions, Morgan was able to create a coalition of supporters who could amplify his message.

For instance, a partnership with a prominent university allowed Morgan to tap into their existing grant-writing resources. Together, they applied for a National Endowment for the Humanities (NEH) grant, which provided substantial funding for digital projects. The collaboration not only strengthened his proposal but also lent credibility to his initiative.

Utilizing Crowdfunding Platforms

In addition to traditional funding sources, Morgan explored the burgeoning world of crowdfunding. He launched a campaign on a popular platform, leveraging social media to reach a broader audience. The campaign was designed to appeal to the general public, emphasizing the importance of preserving cultural heritage through technology.

Morgan's crowdfunding campaign included various tiers of support, each offering unique rewards, such as exclusive access to digital archives or invitations to special events. This approach not only generated funds but also fostered a sense of community among supporters, who felt personally invested in the success of the initiative.

Navigating Ethical Considerations

As Morgan sought funding, he was acutely aware of the ethical considerations surrounding financial support. He understood that accepting funding from certain sources could lead to conflicts of interest or influence the direction of research. To mitigate these risks, Morgan established a set of guiding principles for funding acceptance:

+ **Transparency:** All funding sources would be disclosed publicly.

+ **Integrity:** Research and projects would remain free from external influence.

+ **Inclusivity:** Funding decisions would prioritize projects that benefit diverse communities.

By adhering to these principles, Morgan ensured that his work maintained its integrity and purpose, even as he navigated the complex world of funding.

The Power of Advocacy

Finally, Morgan recognized the importance of advocacy in gaining support. He actively engaged with policymakers and stakeholders to promote the value of digital humanities. By participating in conferences, writing opinion pieces, and leveraging social media, Morgan built a network of advocates who could help champion his cause.

For example, during a notable conference on digital innovation, Morgan delivered a keynote address that highlighted the potential of digital humanities to address contemporary societal challenges. His passionate presentation caught the attention of several influential figures, leading to new funding opportunities and partnerships.

In conclusion, gaining support and funding for his ambitious vision required Morgan Liao to navigate a complex landscape with strategic foresight. Through a combination of compelling storytelling, collaborative partnerships, innovative funding strategies, ethical considerations, and advocacy, Morgan successfully laid the groundwork for a transformative Digital Humanities Institute, paving the way for a Cyber Renaissance that would resonate for generations to come.

Assembling a Dream Team

In the ever-evolving landscape of digital humanities, Morgan Liao understood that even the most brilliant minds can't do it all alone—unless, of course, you're a time-traveling octopus with a PhD in everything. But since that's not currently an option, assembling a dream team became a pivotal step in realizing his vision for a Cyber Renaissance.

The Art of Recruitment

Morgan's recruitment strategy was akin to casting for a blockbuster movie: he needed a mix of seasoned veterans and fresh talent, all of whom could handle the pressure of working under the watchful eye of a genius who occasionally wore socks with sandals. The first step was to define the key roles required for his ambitious projects.

- **Data Scientists** - The wizards who could turn raw data into insights faster than a magician pulling a rabbit out of a hat.

- **Software Engineers** - The code ninjas who could build complex systems while simultaneously sipping artisanal coffee.

- **Humanities Scholars** - The thinkers who could provide the philosophical backbone to the technological innovations, ensuring they didn't just create cool gadgets but also made sense in the grand scheme of human history.

- **Project Managers** - The organizational superheroes who kept everything running smoothly, armed with Gantt charts and an uncanny ability to schedule meetings that no one wanted to attend.

Morgan held a series of open forums, which were part TED Talk, part stand-up comedy routine, where he outlined his vision. "Imagine a world," he said, "where technology and the humanities don't just coexist but dance together like a couple at a wedding, awkward yet beautiful. Who's in?"

Diversity as a Strength

Morgan was keenly aware that diversity was not just a buzzword; it was a necessity. He sought individuals from various backgrounds, cultures, and disciplines. This approach was supported by research indicating that diverse teams are more innovative and effective. According to a study by Page (2007), diverse teams outperform homogenous ones because they bring a wider range of perspectives to problem-solving.

Morgan often joked, "If we all think alike, then one of us is unnecessary—probably the guy who thought socks with sandals were a good idea."

The Recruitment Process

The recruitment process was rigorous. Morgan implemented a multi-step selection procedure that included:

1. **Application Review** - Where he sifted through resumes like a kid looking for the best candy in a Halloween haul.

2. **Initial Interviews** - Conducted via video calls, often featuring unexpected interruptions from pets or family members, leading to a more relaxed atmosphere.

3. **Team Challenges** - Candidates were invited to participate in hackathons and brainstorming sessions, where they had to solve real-world problems while demonstrating their ability to collaborate under pressure.

4. **Cultural Fit Assessment** - Morgan believed that a team should not only be skilled but should also share a sense of humor. "If you can't laugh at yourself, I'm afraid you might be a robot," he quipped during interviews.

Building Team Cohesion

Once assembled, the team needed to gel. Morgan organized team-building retreats that included everything from escape rooms to improv comedy workshops. The idea was simple: if they could survive a locked room with a ticking clock and a bunch of fake spiders, they could tackle any project together.

$$\text{Team Cohesion} = \frac{\text{Trust} + \text{Communication} + \text{Shared Goals}}{\text{Fear of Failure}} \tag{38}$$

This equation, while not scientifically validated, served as a humorous reminder that fear could either bind a team together or tear it apart.

The Dream Team in Action

With the dream team assembled, Morgan and his crew embarked on groundbreaking projects that would revolutionize digital humanities. One of their first initiatives was the *Knowledge Archive*, a digital repository that aimed to democratize access to historical documents. The team worked tirelessly, fueled by a mix of passion, caffeine, and the occasional existential crisis about the future of humanity.

Morgan often reminded them, "Remember, we're not just building technology; we're creating a legacy. And if we can make it funny along the way, even better!"

As the team began to make strides, they faced challenges that tested their resolve. However, the diverse perspectives and collaborative spirit within the team allowed them to navigate these obstacles with creativity and humor, proving that assembling a dream team was not just about skills, but also about building relationships and fostering a culture of innovation.

In conclusion, Morgan Liao's journey to assemble a dream team was a blend of strategy, humor, and an unwavering belief in the power of collaboration. By bringing together a diverse group of individuals who shared a common vision, he laid the groundwork for a Cyber Renaissance that would leave a lasting impact on the field of digital humanities.

Setting Groundbreaking Goals

In the fast-paced realm of digital humanities, setting groundbreaking goals is not merely an exercise in ambition; it is a necessity for driving innovation and inspiring change. Morgan Liao understood that the future of this interdisciplinary field required a clear vision, strategic planning, and the courage to challenge the status quo. This section explores the theoretical frameworks, practical challenges, and exemplary practices that guided Morgan in establishing transformative objectives for the Digital Humanities Institute.

Theoretical Frameworks

Setting goals in the context of digital humanities requires an understanding of various theoretical frameworks that inform both technology and the humanities. One such framework is **Design Thinking**, which emphasizes empathy, ideation, and prototyping. This iterative process allows innovators to better understand the needs of users while developing solutions that are both effective and meaningful. Morgan adopted this approach to ensure that the goals of the Digital Humanities Institute were user-centered and responsive to the evolving landscape of technology and culture.

Another relevant theory is **Systems Theory**, which posits that complex phenomena can be understood as systems composed of interrelated parts. In digital humanities, this means recognizing how technology, culture, and society interact. Morgan's goals were grounded in the understanding that any innovation must consider the broader implications on society, including ethical, cultural, and educational dimensions.

Identifying Key Problems

While setting goals, Morgan faced several key problems that needed addressing. One major issue was the **digital divide**, which refers to the gap between those who have easy access to digital technology and those who do not. Morgan aimed to bridge this divide by establishing goals that promoted accessibility and inclusivity in digital humanities research. This involved creating platforms that catered to underrepresented communities and ensuring that educational resources were available to all, regardless of socioeconomic status.

Another challenge was the **preservation of cultural heritage** in the digital age. As more cultural artifacts and historical documents were digitized, the risk of loss due to technological obsolescence or data corruption became a pressing concern. Morgan set ambitious goals to develop robust archival systems that would ensure the longevity and integrity of digital collections. This included creating backup protocols and employing advanced technologies like blockchain for secure data storage.

Examples of Groundbreaking Goals

Morgan's visionary approach led to the establishment of several groundbreaking goals that would shape the future of digital humanities:

- **Goal 1: Democratization of Knowledge**
  Morgan aimed to create an open-access repository for digital humanities research, allowing scholars, students, and the general public to freely access a wealth of knowledge. This initiative was designed to counteract the traditional gatekeeping practices of academia and promote a culture of sharing and collaboration.

- **Goal 2: Integration of AI in Cultural Preservation**
  Recognizing the potential of artificial intelligence, Morgan set a goal to develop AI-driven tools that could assist in the preservation and analysis of cultural artifacts. For example, machine learning algorithms could be used to analyze historical texts, identify patterns, and uncover hidden narratives that would otherwise remain undiscovered.

- **Goal 3: Enhancing Educational Practices**
  To revolutionize education in the digital humanities, Morgan proposed the creation of immersive learning experiences through virtual reality (VR) and augmented reality (AR). By developing educational modules that allowed students to engage with historical events in real time, Morgan aimed to foster a deeper understanding and appreciation of cultural heritage.

- **Goal 4: Fostering Interdisciplinary Collaboration**
  Morgan recognized that the most impactful innovations often arise from

collaboration across disciplines. He set a goal to establish partnerships with other fields, such as computer science, sociology, and anthropology, to create interdisciplinary projects that would enrich the study of digital humanities.

Measuring Success

Setting goals is only the first step; measuring their success is equally vital. Morgan implemented a framework for assessing the impact of the Digital Humanities Institute's initiatives. This included qualitative and quantitative metrics, such as user engagement statistics, the number of collaborations formed, and feedback from participants in educational programs. By continuously evaluating progress, Morgan ensured that the institute remained adaptable and responsive to emerging challenges and opportunities.

Conclusion

In conclusion, setting groundbreaking goals was a cornerstone of Morgan Liao's vision for the Digital Humanities Institute. By employing theoretical frameworks such as design thinking and systems theory, addressing key problems like the digital divide and cultural preservation, and articulating clear, ambitious objectives, Morgan laid the groundwork for a transformative movement in digital humanities. His commitment to inclusivity, innovation, and interdisciplinary collaboration not only inspired his peers but also established a legacy that would influence future generations of scholars and innovators.

$$\text{Impact} = \frac{\text{Innovative Goals} \times \text{Community Engagement}}{\text{Barriers to Access}} \qquad (39)$$

This equation illustrates the relationship between the innovative goals set by Morgan, the engagement of the community, and the barriers that must be overcome to achieve meaningful impact in the field of digital humanities. As the digital landscape continues to evolve, Morgan's approach serves as a guiding light for future innovators seeking to make a difference.

Overcoming Doubt and Skepticism

In the journey of innovation, particularly within the realm of digital humanities, the path is often littered with doubt and skepticism. Morgan Liao, a pioneer in this field, faced significant challenges as he sought to revolutionize the intersection of technology and humanities. This section explores how he navigated these turbulent waters, employing both theoretical frameworks and practical examples to illustrate his resilience.

Theoretical Framework: The Innovation Adoption Curve

To understand the skepticism faced by innovators like Morgan, we can reference the *Innovation Adoption Curve*, introduced by Everett Rogers in his seminal work, *Diffusion of Innovations*. This model categorizes adopters of new technology into five segments: innovators, early adopters, early majority, late majority, and laggards. Morgan, as an innovator, initially encountered resistance from the early majority, who were often hesitant to embrace new ideas without substantial evidence of their efficacy.

$$\text{Adoption Rate} = \frac{\text{Number of Adopters}}{\text{Total Population}} \times 100 \tag{40}$$

This equation illustrates how the adoption rate can be a critical metric for understanding the impact of skepticism on innovation. Morgan's challenge was to increase this rate by converting skeptics into supporters.

Identifying the Sources of Skepticism

Skepticism can stem from various sources, including:

- **Fear of Change:** Many individuals and institutions are resistant to change, fearing that new technologies may disrupt established practices.

- **Lack of Understanding:** A common barrier is the complexity of new technologies, which can lead to misunderstandings about their potential benefits.

- **Cultural Resistance:** In the humanities, there is often a strong attachment to traditional methods of scholarship, leading to skepticism towards digital approaches.

- **Economic Concerns:** Stakeholders may doubt the financial viability of new projects, particularly in academia where funding is often limited.

Morgan recognized these sources of skepticism and sought to address them head-on.

Strategies for Overcoming Doubt

To combat skepticism, Morgan employed several effective strategies:

1. **Building a Strong Evidence Base:** Morgan conducted rigorous research to demonstrate the effectiveness of his digital humanities initiatives. For instance, he initiated a pilot project that showcased the successful integration of AI in cultural preservation, providing quantifiable results that assuaged concerns.

2. **Engaging Stakeholders:** Morgan organized workshops and seminars, inviting skeptics to engage with the technology firsthand. By fostering an open dialogue, he was able to demystify the technology and illustrate its practical applications.

3. **Collaborative Projects:** Partnering with established scholars in the humanities allowed Morgan to lend credibility to his initiatives. These collaborations not only provided additional resources but also helped in winning over skeptics who were more willing to trust their peers.

4. **Incremental Implementation:** Rather than a complete overhaul, Morgan advocated for a phased approach to integrating digital tools in humanities research. This allowed skeptics to gradually acclimate to the changes, reducing resistance.

Case Study: The Digital Humanities Institute

One of Morgan's most significant accomplishments was the establishment of the Digital Humanities Institute (DHI). Initially met with skepticism from traditionalists in the academic community, the DHI faced challenges in securing funding and support. To overcome this, Morgan implemented the strategies outlined above.

- **Evidence Base:** The DHI published a series of case studies demonstrating how digital tools enhanced research outcomes, leading to improved scholarly publications and greater visibility for participating researchers.

- **Engagement:** Morgan hosted open days at the DHI, inviting faculty and students to explore the facilities and engage with the technology. Feedback from these events revealed a shift in perception, with many participants expressing newfound interest in digital methods.

+ **Collaboration:** By partnering with renowned institutions, the DHI was able to attract top talent and resources, further legitimizing its mission and alleviating concerns about its viability.

+ **Incremental Implementation:** The DHI rolled out its programs gradually, allowing faculty to integrate digital tools into their existing curricula at their own pace.

Conclusion: The Power of Persistence

Morgan Liao's journey through the landscape of doubt and skepticism serves as a testament to the power of persistence and strategic engagement. By employing a combination of evidence-based practices, stakeholder engagement, and collaborative efforts, Morgan not only overcame skepticism but also transformed it into enthusiasm for digital humanities. His legacy is a reminder that in the face of doubt, innovation can flourish when approached with determination and a clear vision.

In the words of Morgan, *"Skepticism is just the universe's way of saying, 'Prove it to me,' and I'm always up for a challenge."* This mindset not only propelled Morgan forward but also inspired a generation of innovators to embrace the unknown, turning skepticism into a stepping stone for groundbreaking advancements in the digital humanities.

The World Takes Notice

As Morgan Liao's vision for the Digital Humanities began to crystallize, it wasn't long before the world started to take notice. The intersection of technology and the humanities, once thought to be an awkward dance between a robot and a classic novel, was now becoming a symphony of innovation. This section explores the various facets of attention that Morgan's work garnered, as well as the implications that followed.

Media Coverage and Public Interest

Morgan's groundbreaking ideas didn't just flutter around in academic circles; they leaped into the limelight like a caffeinated kangaroo. Major news outlets began to cover his initiatives, showcasing the potential of digital humanities to transform education, culture, and society at large. For instance, a feature in *The New York Times* highlighted his project on virtual reality historical immersion, which allowed users to experience pivotal moments in history as if they were actually there—like being in a time machine that only plays historical documentaries.

$$\text{Media Attention} = \text{Innovative Projects} \times \text{Public Engagement} \qquad (41)$$

The equation above suggests that the more innovative Morgan's projects were, the more media attention they attracted, resulting in a feedback loop that further fueled public interest.

Academic Recognition

In the academic realm, Morgan's work was not only acknowledged but celebrated. Prestigious journals began to publish articles about his methodologies and findings, often citing his work as a pivotal shift in the approach to digital humanities. For example, the *Journal of Digital Humanities* published a special issue dedicated to the implications of Morgan's research, discussing how his integration of artificial intelligence in cultural preservation was reshaping traditional academic paradigms.

$$\text{Academic Impact} = \text{Citations} + \text{Collaborations} + \text{Funding} \qquad (42)$$

This formula indicates that academic impact is a product of citations, collaborations with other scholars, and the funding attracted by innovative research.

Corporate Interest and Funding

With the buzz surrounding Morgan's initiatives, corporate entities began to take a keen interest in the potential applications of his work. Tech companies, eager to align themselves with the digital renaissance, offered substantial funding for projects that promised to blend technology with cultural enrichment. Companies like *Google* and *Microsoft* reached out, proposing partnerships that would enable the development of educational tools powered by Morgan's research.

$$\text{Funding} = \text{Corporate Interest} \times \text{Project Viability} \qquad (43)$$

This equation illustrates how the viability of Morgan's projects directly influenced the level of corporate interest and, consequently, the funding received.

Global Collaborations

As the world took notice, Morgan found himself at the center of a global network of innovators, educators, and policymakers. International conferences began to feature Morgan as a keynote speaker, where he shared his insights on the future of digital humanities. During one such conference, he presented a collaborative project with a university in Japan that utilized augmented reality to enhance the learning experience in history classes. The excitement was palpable, and attendees left the room buzzing with ideas—like a beehive that had just discovered a new flower.

Public Engagement and Community Impact

Morgan's work also sparked public engagement initiatives, leading to community workshops that introduced digital humanities concepts to local schools. Children learned how to create digital storytelling projects, effectively turning them into mini-innovators. The local news even caught wind of these workshops, resulting in a heartwarming segment that showcased young students presenting their projects to proud parents.

$$\text{Community Impact} = \text{Engagement Level} \times \text{Educational Reach} \quad (44)$$

This formula emphasizes that the level of community impact is determined by the engagement level of the participants and the educational reach of the programs implemented.

The Ripple Effect

The attention Morgan garnered created a ripple effect across multiple sectors. Educational institutions began to rethink their curricula, integrating digital humanities into their programs. Policymakers started to consider how technology could enhance cultural preservation efforts, leading to new legislation aimed at funding digital initiatives in the arts and humanities.

In summary, as the world took notice of Morgan Liao's contributions to digital humanities, it did so with a blend of excitement and skepticism. The attention he received not only validated his work but also set the stage for a broader conversation about the role of technology in shaping our understanding of culture and history. The digital renaissance was underway, and Morgan was at the forefront, leading the charge with the enthusiasm of a kid on a sugar high—albeit one who could code a new future with a single keystroke.

The Creation of the Digital Humanities Institute

Establishing a Global Research Hub

In the quest to revolutionize the field of Digital Humanities, Morgan Liao recognized the need for a centralized, collaborative space where scholars, technologists, and creatives could converge. Thus, the establishment of a global research hub became a pivotal point in his vision, akin to a digital agora where ideas could flourish like wildflowers in a spring meadow, albeit with fewer bees and more Wi-Fi.

The Vision

Morgan's vision for the research hub was not merely to create a physical space but to foster an environment that encouraged interdisciplinary collaboration. He believed that the intersection of technology and the humanities could yield groundbreaking insights, much like how a perfect storm can lead to a beautiful rainbow—if the rainbow were made of data and algorithms. The hub aimed to attract thinkers from diverse fields, including linguistics, history, computer science, and art, creating a melting pot of ideas.

Addressing Challenges

However, establishing such a hub was not without its challenges. The first hurdle was funding. Morgan often joked that securing funds was like trying to catch a greased pig at a county fair; it was slippery, elusive, and often left one feeling a bit dirty. To tackle this, Morgan employed a multi-faceted approach:

$$\text{Funding} = \text{Grants} + \text{Corporate Sponsorships} + \text{Crowdfunding} \qquad (45)$$

He applied for grants from various governmental and non-governmental organizations dedicated to advancing education and technology. Additionally, he sought partnerships with tech companies, proposing that their sponsorship would not only boost their corporate social responsibility profiles but also provide them access to innovative research outcomes. Finally, Morgan turned to the public, launching a crowdfunding campaign, which he humorously dubbed "Kickstart the Future," to engage everyday people in his vision—because who wouldn't want to contribute to a hub where digital wizards conjured knowledge?

Designing the Space

With funding secured, the next step was designing the hub itself. Morgan envisioned a space that was as inspiring as it was functional. He wanted the architecture to reflect the digital age, incorporating elements like:

- **Open Collaboration Areas:** Spaces where individuals could brainstorm, share ideas, and engage in spontaneous debates—preferably over coffee brewed by an AI barista named "Brewster."

- **Virtual Reality Rooms:** Dedicated spaces for immersive experiences, allowing researchers to explore historical events or cultural artifacts in a 3D environment.

- **Data Visualization Labs:** Equipped with cutting-edge technology to analyze and present data in visually stunning formats, because sometimes a pie chart just doesn't cut it.

Morgan often quipped that the design should inspire creativity, stating, "If the walls don't make you feel like you're in a sci-fi movie, we're doing it wrong."

Building a Community

Establishing a global research hub also meant creating a community. Morgan understood that collaboration was key to innovation. To build this community, he initiated several outreach programs aimed at engaging local universities and cultural institutions. These programs included:

- **Workshops and Seminars:** Regular events featuring thought leaders in both the tech and humanities fields, designed to spark dialogue and inspire new projects.

- **Mentorship Programs:** Pairing experienced researchers with students and early-career professionals to nurture the next generation of innovators, because every great innovator needs a wise mentor—preferably one who doesn't wear socks with sandals.

- **Hackathons:** Weekend-long events where participants could collaborate on projects, with prizes for the most innovative solutions. Morgan often joked that the real prize was the friendships formed over copious amounts of pizza and energy drinks.

Global Collaboration

To ensure the hub had a truly global reach, Morgan established partnerships with international institutions. He believed that the digital age allowed for unprecedented collaboration across borders, much like how a viral cat video can unite the world in laughter. He implemented a virtual exchange program, allowing researchers to collaborate on projects regardless of their geographical location, utilizing tools like video conferencing and cloud-based platforms.

$$\text{Global Collaboration} = \text{Local Partnerships} + \text{International Networks} \quad (46)$$

Through these efforts, the hub attracted scholars from around the world, creating a rich tapestry of perspectives and ideas.

Impact and Legacy

The establishment of the global research hub not only advanced the field of Digital Humanities but also left a lasting legacy. Morgan's hub became a beacon of innovation, inspiring similar initiatives worldwide. As the hub flourished, it produced groundbreaking research that reshaped how society viewed the intersection of technology and the humanities.

In conclusion, the establishment of a global research hub was a multifaceted endeavor that required vision, creativity, and relentless determination. Morgan Liao's ability to navigate the challenges of funding, design, community building, and global collaboration set the stage for a new era of innovation in Digital Humanities. As he often said, "In the digital age, knowledge isn't just power; it's the Wi-Fi password to the future."

State-of-the-Art Facilities and Equipment

The establishment of the Digital Humanities Institute under Morgan Liao's vision marked a significant leap into the future of academic research and technological integration. The facilities and equipment at the institute were designed to be not just state-of-the-art but also to embody the principles of accessibility, collaboration, and innovation.

Innovative Learning Spaces

To foster creativity and critical thinking, the institute incorporated various innovative learning spaces. These include:

- **Collaborative Workstations:** Equipped with modular furniture that can be reconfigured for group projects, these spaces promote teamwork and interdisciplinary collaboration. Each workstation is equipped with high-resolution screens and interactive whiteboards that allow for seamless sharing of ideas and resources.

- **Virtual Reality Labs:** These labs are outfitted with advanced VR headsets and motion tracking systems, enabling students and researchers to immerse themselves in historical environments or cultural artifacts. This immersive experience not only enhances learning but also allows for innovative research methodologies in digital humanities.

- **Soundproof Study Pods:** Recognizing the need for concentration in a bustling environment, the institute provides soundproof pods for individual study. Each pod is equipped with noise-canceling technology and adjustable lighting to create an optimal study atmosphere.

Advanced Technological Equipment

The technological backbone of the Digital Humanities Institute includes cutting-edge equipment that supports various research endeavors:

- **High-Performance Computing Clusters:** These clusters are essential for processing large datasets and running complex algorithms necessary for digital humanities research. With capabilities to handle big data analytics, they allow researchers to explore vast archives and uncover patterns that would otherwise remain hidden.

- **3D Scanners and Printers:** To aid in the preservation of cultural artifacts, the institute employs high-resolution 3D scanners that create detailed digital models of physical objects. These models can be printed using advanced 3D printers, making it possible to create replicas for study and exhibition without risking damage to the originals.

- **Artificial Intelligence Workstations:** Equipped with the latest AI software and hardware, these workstations enable researchers to develop and deploy machine learning algorithms that can analyze texts, images, and other forms of data. This technology plays a crucial role in projects aimed at automating the process of digital archiving and analysis.

Challenges in Implementation

While the vision for state-of-the-art facilities was ambitious, several challenges emerged during the implementation phase:

+ **Budget Constraints:** Initial funding was not sufficient to cover the full scope of technological advancements desired. Morgan and his team had to prioritize certain projects over others, leading to a phased implementation of facilities and equipment.

+ **Training and Adaptation:** The introduction of advanced technologies required extensive training for both faculty and students. Ensuring that everyone was equipped to utilize the new tools effectively became a primary concern, leading to the development of comprehensive training programs.

+ **Interdisciplinary Integration:** One of the biggest challenges was integrating the diverse fields of study within the humanities. Morgan recognized that collaboration across disciplines was essential but also complex, as different fields have varying methodologies and terminologies. This required ongoing dialogue and adaptation among faculty members.

Examples of Impact

The impact of the state-of-the-art facilities and equipment on research and education at the Digital Humanities Institute can be illustrated through several examples:

+ **Project Archive 2040:** Utilizing high-performance computing clusters, this project analyzed over a million historical documents to identify trends in public sentiment during key historical events. The insights gained were instrumental in understanding how digital humanities can inform contemporary societal issues.

+ **The Virtual Museum Initiative:** By employing virtual reality labs, students created immersive exhibits that allowed users to experience historical events as if they were part of them. This project not only engaged the public but also demonstrated the potential of VR in educational settings.

+ **AI-Powered Text Analysis:** A research team used artificial intelligence workstations to develop a machine learning model that could analyze literary texts for thematic elements. This groundbreaking work opened new avenues for literary criticism, allowing for the analysis of texts on a scale previously thought impossible.

In conclusion, the state-of-the-art facilities and equipment at the Digital Humanities Institute have not only enhanced research capabilities but have also transformed the educational landscape. By addressing challenges head-on and leveraging cutting-edge technology, Morgan Liao has set a precedent for future innovators in the realm of digital humanities.

Attracting Top Talent

In the rapidly evolving landscape of digital humanities, attracting top talent is not merely an option; it is a necessity. The success of any groundbreaking initiative hinges on the quality and diversity of the minds it brings together. Morgan Liao recognized this early on and devised strategies that not only drew in established experts but also nurtured emerging voices in the field.

Understanding the Appeal

To understand how to attract top talent, one must first comprehend what motivates these individuals. According to [?], professionals in academia and industry are driven by three primary factors: intellectual challenge, collaborative opportunities, and the potential for societal impact. Morgan's vision for the Digital Humanities Institute aligned perfectly with these motivations, offering an environment where innovative ideas could flourish.

Creating an Innovative Environment

Morgan implemented a series of initiatives aimed at fostering a culture of innovation. This included:

- **Flexible Workspaces:** The design of the institute featured open spaces, quiet zones, and collaborative areas that encouraged creativity and spontaneous discussions. Research by [?] indicates that such environments can increase productivity by up to 25%.

- **Interdisciplinary Collaboration:** By encouraging partnerships between technologists, historians, and artists, Morgan created a melting pot of ideas. This approach is supported by the theory of *knowledge spillover*, which posits that collaboration across disciplines can lead to unexpected breakthroughs [?].

- **Access to Cutting-Edge Resources:** The institute was equipped with state-of-the-art technology, including virtual reality labs and AI-driven analytics tools. This not only attracted talent but also provided them with the necessary tools to push the boundaries of their research.

Recruitment Strategies

Morgan's recruitment strategies were multifaceted, focusing on both traditional and innovative methods:

+ **Global Talent Searches:** Recognizing that top talent is not confined to local institutions, Morgan initiated global searches. Job postings were strategically placed on international platforms and academic networks, ensuring a wide reach. This was complemented by targeted outreach to universities known for their strong digital humanities programs.

+ **Networking at Conferences:** Morgan attended and spoke at major conferences, not just to promote the institute, but to engage with potential recruits. This face-to-face interaction often led to fruitful discussions and collaborations, as highlighted by [?], which found that personal connections significantly enhance recruitment success.

+ **Fellowship Programs:** By establishing competitive fellowship programs, Morgan attracted early-career researchers eager to make their mark. These programs provided mentorship and funding, creating a win-win situation for both the institute and the fellows.

Diversity and Inclusion

Morgan understood that diversity in talent leads to diversity in thought, which is crucial for innovation. The institute made concerted efforts to ensure a diverse applicant pool by:

+ **Outreach to Underrepresented Groups:** The institute partnered with organizations focused on promoting diversity in STEM and humanities fields. This proactive approach was supported by findings from [?], which demonstrated that diverse teams are more innovative and productive.

+ **Creating an Inclusive Culture:** Morgan implemented policies that fostered an inclusive environment, ensuring that all voices were heard and valued. Regular workshops on unconscious bias and inclusion were held, reinforcing the institute's commitment to a diverse workforce.

Retention Strategies

Attracting talent is only half the battle; retaining it is equally important. Morgan implemented several strategies to ensure that top talent remained engaged and satisfied:

+ **Professional Development Opportunities:** Continuous learning was encouraged through workshops, seminars, and access to online courses. Morgan believed that investing in employees' growth would lead to greater job satisfaction and loyalty [?].

+ **Work-Life Balance:** The institute promoted a healthy work-life balance, recognizing that burnout could lead to high turnover rates. Flexible working hours and remote work options were introduced, allowing employees to manage their time effectively.

+ **Recognition and Rewards:** Acknowledging hard work and achievements played a significant role in retention. Morgan established a system of rewards for innovative projects and contributions to the institute, fostering a culture of appreciation.

Conclusion

Attracting top talent to the Digital Humanities Institute was a multifaceted endeavor that required strategic planning, innovative practices, and a commitment to diversity and inclusion. By creating an appealing environment, implementing effective recruitment strategies, and focusing on retention, Morgan Liao not only built a formidable team but also laid the groundwork for a thriving digital humanities community. As the institute flourished, it became a beacon for aspiring innovators, proving that the right talent can indeed change the world.

Collaborations with Leading Universities

In the pursuit of revolutionizing digital humanities, Morgan Liao recognized the immense potential of collaborating with leading universities around the globe. This strategic approach not only expanded the reach of the Digital Humanities Institute but also fostered a rich exchange of ideas, resources, and expertise. By leveraging the strengths of various academic institutions, Morgan aimed to create a multifaceted network that would push the boundaries of research and innovation.

The Importance of Collaboration

Collaboration in academia is akin to assembling a superhero team; each member brings unique powers to the table, creating a force greater than the sum of its parts. According to the theory of *Collective Intelligence*, groups can produce solutions that no single member could achieve alone. This theory posits that diversity in thought, experience, and approach leads to more innovative outcomes. In the context of digital humanities, this meant combining the analytical prowess of computer scientists with the creative insights of humanities scholars.

Identifying Key Partners

Morgan's first step was to identify universities renowned for their strengths in both technology and humanities. Institutions like Stanford University, MIT, and Oxford emerged as prime candidates. Each of these universities not only possessed cutting-edge research facilities but also had established departments dedicated to digital humanities.

For instance, Stanford's *Center for Spatial and Textual Analysis* was instrumental in developing new methodologies for analyzing large datasets in the humanities. By collaborating with such institutions, Morgan aimed to create interdisciplinary projects that would redefine the landscape of digital humanities.

Joint Research Initiatives

One of the most significant outcomes of these collaborations was the establishment of joint research initiatives. These initiatives often took the form of *research consortia*, where multiple universities pooled their resources to tackle complex problems. For example, a consortium comprising Morgan's Digital Humanities Institute, MIT, and the University of California, Berkeley, launched a project titled *Digital Time Capsules*.

This project aimed to create a digital archive that preserved cultural artifacts and narratives from diverse communities. The collaboration allowed for a blend of expertise in archival science, data management, and cultural studies. By employing advanced data analytics, the team was able to uncover patterns in historical narratives, offering new insights into cultural evolution.

Challenges of Collaboration

Despite the promising prospects of collaboration, Morgan faced several challenges. One significant hurdle was the *alignment of institutional goals*. Each university had its own priorities and metrics for success, which sometimes conflicted with the objectives of the Digital Humanities Institute. To address this, Morgan implemented a framework for *strategic alignment*, ensuring that all partners were on the same page regarding project goals, timelines, and deliverables.

Another challenge was the *divergence in research methodologies*. Scholars from different disciplines often approached problems with varying theoretical frameworks and techniques. To bridge this gap, Morgan organized workshops and seminars that facilitated open discussions about methodologies. This exchange of ideas not only fostered mutual understanding but also led to the development of hybrid methodologies that combined the strengths of both fields.

Successful Outcomes

The collaborative efforts yielded numerous successful outcomes that showcased the power of interdisciplinary research. One notable project was the *Virtual Museum of Humanity*, which involved partnerships with universities in Europe and Asia. This initiative utilized virtual reality technology to create immersive experiences that allowed users to explore historical events and cultural practices from around the world.

The project not only attracted significant funding but also garnered international attention, demonstrating the potential of digital humanities to engage broader audiences. As a result, Morgan's Digital Humanities Institute became a hub for innovative research, attracting scholars and students alike.

A Legacy of Collaboration

The collaborations established during this period laid the groundwork for a sustainable model of interdisciplinary research in digital humanities. Morgan's approach emphasized the importance of building lasting relationships with academic institutions, fostering an environment of shared knowledge and resources.

In conclusion, Morgan Liao's collaborations with leading universities were pivotal in advancing the field of digital humanities. By embracing the principles of collective intelligence and strategic alignment, Morgan not only expanded the reach of his institute but also inspired a new generation of scholars to explore the intersections of technology and the humanities. The legacy of these collaborations continues to influence the field, demonstrating that when minds from diverse disciplines come together, the possibilities are truly limitless.

Redefining the Field of Digital Humanities

The field of Digital Humanities (DH) has undergone a significant transformation over the past few decades, evolving from a niche area of study into a dynamic and essential discipline that bridges the gap between technology and the humanities. Morgan Liao's innovative approach has played a pivotal role in this redefinition, challenging traditional paradigms and fostering a new understanding of how technology can enhance humanistic inquiry.

Theoretical Foundations

At the core of redefining Digital Humanities is the theoretical framework that underpins the integration of digital tools into humanistic research. One of the foundational theories is the concept of *intermediality*, which examines how different media interact and influence one another. This theory posits that the boundaries between disciplines are porous, allowing for a more fluid exchange of ideas and methodologies. Morgan's work exemplifies this by incorporating elements from computer science, cultural studies, and archival science to create a holistic approach to research.

Another critical theory is *digital hermeneutics*, which seeks to understand how digital tools can alter our interpretation of texts and artifacts. This theory emphasizes the importance of context and the role of technology in shaping our understanding of cultural heritage. By employing advanced algorithms and machine learning techniques, Morgan has demonstrated that digital analysis can reveal patterns and insights that traditional methods might overlook.

Challenges in the Field

Despite the promise of Digital Humanities, several challenges persist in redefining the field. One significant issue is the *digital divide*, which refers to the gap between those who have access to digital technologies and those who do not. This divide can lead to inequities in who gets to participate in the creation and dissemination of knowledge. Morgan's initiatives have focused on democratizing access to digital tools, ensuring that marginalized voices are included in the conversation.

Another challenge is the *epistemological shift* that accompanies the integration of digital technologies. Scholars must grapple with questions about the validity and reliability of digital methods. For instance, when using text mining to analyze literary works, researchers must consider how algorithms may introduce biases that could skew interpretations. Morgan has addressed this issue by advocating for transparency in digital methodologies and promoting interdisciplinary collaboration to enhance the rigor of research.

Examples of Redefinition

Morgan's influence is evident in several groundbreaking projects that have redefined the landscape of Digital Humanities. One notable example is the *Knowledge Archive*, a collaborative platform that allows scholars to curate and share digital collections. This initiative not only preserves cultural artifacts but also encourages interdisciplinary research by providing access to diverse materials.

Additionally, Morgan's work on *Artificial Intelligence in Cultural Preservation* has revolutionized how we approach the archiving of endangered languages and traditions. By employing machine learning algorithms to analyze linguistic patterns, researchers can create more effective preservation strategies. This project has garnered international attention and has been adopted by various institutions around the world.

Morgan has also spearheaded the development of *Virtual Reality (VR) for Historical Immersion*, which allows users to experience historical events in an immersive environment. This innovative approach not only enhances engagement but also fosters a deeper understanding of historical contexts. For example, users can virtually explore ancient civilizations, gaining insights into their cultures that would be difficult to achieve through traditional learning methods.

Impact on Education and Learning

The redefinition of Digital Humanities has profound implications for education and learning. Morgan's initiatives have emphasized the importance of integrating digital tools into curricula, enabling students to engage with humanities subjects in innovative ways. By fostering critical thinking and digital literacy, educators can prepare students for the complexities of the modern world.

One successful implementation is the *Augmented Reality in Education* project, which allows students to interact with historical artifacts in real-time. This hands-on approach not only enhances learning but also encourages collaboration among students from different disciplines. By breaking down the barriers between subjects, Morgan's work has created a more inclusive and engaging educational environment.

Conclusion

In conclusion, Morgan Liao's contributions to redefining the field of Digital Humanities have been transformative. By integrating theoretical frameworks, addressing challenges, and implementing innovative projects, he has paved the way for a more inclusive and dynamic understanding of the humanities in the digital age. As the field continues to evolve, Morgan's legacy will undoubtedly inspire future generations of scholars to explore the intersections of technology and humanistic inquiry, fostering a richer and more nuanced understanding of our cultural heritage.

Pioneering Research Projects

Morgan Liao's journey into the realm of Digital Humanities was marked by a series of pioneering research projects that not only challenged the conventional boundaries of the field but also redefined the intersection of technology and humanities. These projects were characterized by their innovative approaches, addressing complex problems, and their potential to create significant societal impacts.

The Digital Archive Initiative

One of Morgan's flagship projects was the **Digital Archive Initiative**, aimed at creating an extensive repository of cultural artifacts from around the globe. The initiative sought to digitize and catalog thousands of historical documents, manuscripts, and artworks, making them accessible to scholars and the public alike.

The project was grounded in the theory of *collective memory*, which posits that societies construct their identities through shared memories. Morgan argued that digitizing cultural artifacts was essential for preserving these memories in an increasingly digital world.

$$C = \frac{M}{T} \tag{47}$$

Where C represents collective memory, M represents the number of shared artifacts, and T is the time span over which these artifacts have been preserved. By increasing M, the initiative aimed to enhance C, thereby fostering a richer understanding of cultural heritage.

Artificial Intelligence in Cultural Preservation

In another groundbreaking project, Morgan explored the use of **Artificial Intelligence (AI)** in cultural preservation. This project focused on developing algorithms capable of analyzing and interpreting historical texts and images, thus providing insights that were previously unattainable.

The theoretical framework for this project was based on *machine learning* and *natural language processing*, which allowed AI to learn from vast datasets of historical documents. The challenges included ensuring accuracy in interpretation and addressing biases inherent in training datasets.

Morgan's team developed a model that could predict the significance of various cultural artifacts based on their historical context. The predictive model was represented as:

$$S = f(H, C, T) \tag{48}$$

Where S is the significance score, H is the historical context, C is the cultural relevance, and T is the temporal aspect. This model enabled researchers to prioritize artifacts for preservation and study, ensuring that the most critical pieces of history were not lost.

Virtual Reality for Historical Immersion

Morgan also spearheaded a project that integrated **Virtual Reality (VR)** technology into the study of history. This project aimed to create immersive experiences that allowed users to walk through reconstructed historical sites and events.

The theoretical basis for this project stemmed from *experiential learning theory*, which emphasizes the importance of direct experience in the learning process. By immersing users in a virtual environment, Morgan believed that individuals could gain a deeper understanding of historical events and contexts.

The VR simulations were designed using a combination of 3D modeling software and historical data. Users could interact with the environment, making choices that influenced their experience. The success of this project was measured through user engagement metrics, which included:

$$E = \frac{I + R}{T} \tag{49}$$

Where E represents engagement, I is the level of interactivity, R is the realism of the experience, and T is the time spent in the virtual environment. Higher engagement scores indicated that users were more likely to retain knowledge and develop a passion for history.

Augmented Reality in Education

Building on the success of the VR project, Morgan initiated a research project focused on **Augmented Reality (AR)** in education. This project aimed to enhance traditional learning methods by overlaying digital information onto the physical world.

The project was rooted in the theory of *constructivist learning*, which posits that learners construct knowledge through experiences. By using AR, students could visualize complex concepts and historical events in real time, fostering a more interactive learning environment.

The AR applications developed by Morgan's team allowed students to point their devices at historical landmarks and receive real-time information, images, and videos related to the site. The effectiveness of this project was evaluated using the following equation:

$$L = \frac{K}{C} \tag{50}$$

Where L represents learning outcomes, K is the knowledge gained, and C is the complexity of the material. This approach aimed to simplify complex historical narratives, making them more accessible to students.

Digital Storytelling to Preserve Oral Histories

Morgan's commitment to preserving diverse voices led to the creation of a project centered on **Digital Storytelling**. This initiative focused on capturing and archiving oral histories from marginalized communities, ensuring that their narratives were preserved for future generations.

The theoretical underpinning of this project was based on *narrative theory*, which emphasizes the power of storytelling in shaping identity and understanding culture. Morgan believed that digital storytelling could empower individuals to share their experiences in a meaningful way.

The project utilized a combination of audio and video recording technologies, along with user-friendly editing software, to enable community members to create their own digital stories. The impact of this project was assessed through community engagement metrics, represented as:

$$E = \frac{P + V}{R} \tag{51}$$

Where E is engagement, P is the number of participants, V is the volume of stories created, and R is the resources allocated to the project. High engagement levels indicated that the project successfully resonated with the community, fostering a sense of ownership over their narratives.

Conclusion

Morgan Liao's pioneering research projects in Digital Humanities exemplified his innovative spirit and commitment to bridging the gap between technology and culture.   By addressing significant challenges and leveraging cutting-edge technologies, Morgan not only transformed the landscape of Digital Humanities but also inspired future generations to explore the possibilities of integrating technology into their own research endeavors. These projects laid the groundwork for a new era of understanding, preservation, and engagement with our collective heritage.

Impact on Education and Learning

The establishment of the Digital Humanities Institute marked a watershed moment in the educational landscape, fundamentally altering how knowledge is accessed, disseminated, and engaged with.   Morgan Liao's vision for integrating technology with the humanities not only enhanced traditional educational methods but also introduced innovative approaches to learning that catered to the diverse needs of students in the digital age.

Transformative Learning Environments

One of the most significant impacts of the Digital Humanities Institute was the creation of transformative learning environments that emphasized active learning and collaboration.   Traditional lecture-based formats were supplanted by immersive experiences that encouraged students to engage with material in meaningful ways.

For instance, the use of **Virtual Reality** (VR) in historical studies allowed students to "walk through" ancient civilizations, experiencing history firsthand. This method aligns with *Constructivist Learning Theory*, which posits that learners construct knowledge through experiences and reflections.   As Piaget (1972) suggested, "knowledge is not a copy of reality but a reconstruction of it." VR facilitated this reconstruction, enabling students to better understand the context and significance of historical events.

Personalized Learning Pathways

Morgan's initiatives also embraced the concept of personalized learning pathways, allowing students to tailor their educational experiences to fit their interests and career aspirations.   By leveraging **Artificial Intelligence (AI)**, the Institute developed algorithms that analyzed individual learning styles and preferences, creating customized curricula that maximized student engagement and retention.

The implementation of adaptive learning technologies exemplifies this approach.   For example, platforms like *Knewton* and *DreamBox* utilize data analytics to adjust the difficulty level of tasks based on real-time performance, ensuring that students are neither overwhelmed nor under-challenged.   This approach not only enhances motivation but also aligns with *Gardner's Theory of Multiple Intelligences*, which recognizes that individuals possess different types of intelligences and learn in unique ways.

Collaborative Learning Projects

Another critical aspect of Morgan's impact was the emphasis on collaborative learning projects that transcended geographical boundaries.   The Digital Humanities Institute facilitated partnerships between students from diverse backgrounds, fostering cross-cultural exchanges that enriched the learning experience.

Projects such as *Global Storytelling* allowed students to collaborate on digital narratives, combining their cultural perspectives to create multimedia presentations.   This initiative not only honed technical skills but also nurtured empathy and global awareness—qualities that are increasingly vital in our interconnected world.   According to Vygotsky's *Social Development Theory*, social interaction is fundamental to cognitive development, and these collaborative efforts exemplified that principle.

Challenges and Solutions

Despite these advancements, the integration of technology into education was not without challenges. Issues such as **digital divide**—the gap between those who have easy access to digital technology and those who do not—posed significant barriers to equitable learning. Morgan recognized this issue and advocated for initiatives aimed at providing resources and training to underprivileged communities.

The *Digital Inclusion Program* was launched to address these disparities, providing students from low-income backgrounds with access to necessary technology and internet connectivity. This program not only improved access but also empowered students to become active participants in their education, thus narrowing the digital divide.

Future Directions

Looking ahead, the impact of Morgan Liao's contributions to education continues to resonate. The principles established at the Digital Humanities Institute serve as a blueprint for future innovations in educational technology. As we move into an era increasingly characterized by rapid technological advancements, the integration of AI, VR, and collaborative projects will remain crucial in shaping the educational landscape.

The ongoing research into **Learning Analytics**—the measurement, collection, analysis, and reporting of data about learners and their contexts—will further enhance personalized learning experiences. By leveraging data to inform instructional practices, educators can create more responsive and effective learning environments.

In conclusion, Morgan Liao's vision for the Digital Humanities Institute has profoundly influenced education and learning, fostering a dynamic interplay between technology and the humanities. As we continue to navigate the complexities of the digital age, the lessons learned from this initiative will undoubtedly guide future innovators in creating equitable, engaging, and effective educational experiences for all.

The Institute's Influence on Society

The establishment of the Digital Humanities Institute marked a pivotal moment in the intersection of technology and culture, significantly influencing societal structures and discourse. This section explores the various dimensions of the Institute's impact on society, including educational reform, cultural preservation, and the democratization of knowledge.

Educational Reform

One of the most profound influences of the Digital Humanities Institute is its contribution to educational reform. The Institute introduced innovative curricula that integrate digital tools with traditional humanities disciplines, fostering a new generation of learners who are equipped to navigate an increasingly digital world. For example, courses such as *Digital Storytelling* and *Data Visualization in Historical Context* have become staples in the curriculum, encouraging students to engage critically with both technology and the humanities.

This educational shift is grounded in constructivist theories, which emphasize the role of learners in constructing their own understanding through active engagement. As Piaget (1976) posited, knowledge is not merely transmitted but constructed through interaction with the environment. The Institute's approach embodies this theory, as students are encouraged to collaborate on projects that address real-world problems, thus fostering critical thinking and creativity.

Cultural Preservation

In an era where digital media often overshadows traditional forms of cultural expression, the Institute has emerged as a leader in cultural preservation. Through projects such as the *Knowledge Archive*, the Institute has created a repository of digital artifacts that document the diverse narratives of various cultures. This initiative not only safeguards cultural heritage but also promotes accessibility to marginalized voices.

The Institute employs advanced technologies such as Artificial Intelligence (AI) to analyze and curate cultural content. For instance, AI algorithms are used to identify patterns in oral histories, allowing researchers to uncover previously overlooked connections between different cultural narratives. This application of technology aligns with the theories of cultural studies, which advocate for the recognition of multiple perspectives in understanding culture (Hall, 1997).

Democratization of Knowledge

The Digital Humanities Institute has played a crucial role in democratizing knowledge by making information more accessible to the public. Through initiatives like *Open Access Publishing* and *Community Workshops*, the Institute has dismantled traditional barriers to knowledge dissemination. This aligns with the principles of the *Open Knowledge Movement*, which advocates for the free sharing of information to promote social equity.

For example, the Institute launched an online platform that allows users to access a wide range of academic resources, from research papers to interactive learning modules. This platform not only serves academics but also engages the general public, encouraging lifelong learning and fostering a culture of inquiry. As Lessig (2004) argued, the free flow of information is essential for a democratic society, and the Institute's efforts embody this principle.

Challenges and Critiques

Despite its successes, the Digital Humanities Institute faces challenges that warrant examination. Critics argue that the integration of technology in the humanities may lead to a commodification of culture, where artistic expressions are reduced to mere data points. This concern echoes Adorno and Horkheimer's (1944) critique of the culture industry, which suggests that mass-produced culture undermines individuality and critical thought.

Moreover, the reliance on technology raises ethical questions regarding data privacy and surveillance. The Institute must navigate these complexities while striving to uphold its mission of promoting ethical innovation. Addressing these challenges requires a commitment to ongoing dialogue and reflection within the academic community.

Case Studies

To illustrate the Institute's influence, we can examine several case studies that highlight its societal impact:

- **The Digital Archive of Indigenous Cultures:** This project involved collaboration with Indigenous communities to digitize and preserve their cultural artifacts. By employing community-driven methodologies, the Institute ensured that the narratives of these cultures were represented authentically and respectfully.

- **The Virtual Reality History Project:** This initiative utilized virtual reality technology to create immersive experiences of historical events. Participants could engage with history in a way that traditional textbooks could not offer, fostering a deeper understanding of the past.

- **Social Media for Knowledge Sharing:** The Institute launched a social media campaign that encouraged users to share their own stories and knowledge. This initiative not only democratized knowledge but also created a sense of community among participants, illustrating the power of collective storytelling.

Conclusion

In conclusion, the Digital Humanities Institute's influence on society is multifaceted, encompassing educational reform, cultural preservation, and the democratization of knowledge. While challenges remain, the Institute's commitment to ethical innovation and community engagement positions it as a leader in shaping the future of digital humanities. As we look ahead, the lessons learned from the Institute's endeavors will undoubtedly inform the next generation of innovators, ensuring that the legacy of the Cyber Renaissance continues to thrive.

Expanding Horizons

In the realm of Digital Humanities, the phrase "expanding horizons" takes on a multifaceted meaning, encapsulating both the breadth of knowledge accessible through technology and the depth of understanding that can be achieved through interdisciplinary collaboration. Morgan Liao's vision for the Digital Humanities Institute was not merely to create a hub for research but to broaden the scope of what humanities can accomplish in the digital age.

Interdisciplinary Collaboration

At the heart of expanding horizons is the idea of interdisciplinary collaboration. Morgan believed that the intersection of technology and humanities could yield innovative solutions to age-old problems. For example, the integration of computer science with historical research allows for the analysis of large datasets, enabling historians to uncover patterns and insights that would be impossible to discern through traditional methods. This approach aligns with the theory of *Interdisciplinary Studies,* which posits that combining knowledge from different disciplines leads to a more comprehensive understanding of complex issues [?].

Technological Innovations

Technological advancements have significantly expanded the horizons of Digital Humanities. The use of *Natural Language Processing (NLP)* has transformed how scholars analyze texts. By employing algorithms to study linguistic patterns, researchers can now conduct sentiment analysis, thematic mapping, and even authorship attribution with unprecedented accuracy. For instance, the work of [?] demonstrates how computational methods can reveal hidden structures within literary works, thus offering a new lens through which to interpret literature.

$$S = \frac{1}{N} \sum_{i=1}^{N} f(x_i) \tag{52}$$

Where S represents the sentiment score, N is the number of texts analyzed, and $f(x_i)$ is the sentiment function applied to each text x_i. This equation exemplifies the quantitative approach to qualitative analysis, showcasing how digital tools can enhance our understanding of human expression.

Global Outreach and Accessibility

Morgan's initiatives also emphasized the importance of making knowledge accessible to a global audience. The Digital Humanities Institute launched several projects aimed at democratizing access to information. One such project involved creating a multilingual digital archive that allowed users from diverse linguistic backgrounds to access historical documents in their native languages. This effort not only expanded the reach of scholarly work but also fostered inclusivity in academic discourse.

For instance, the *Global Digital Humanities Initiative* (GDHI) aimed to connect scholars from the Global South with resources and expertise from more developed regions. By establishing partnerships with universities and institutions worldwide, the GDHI facilitated cross-cultural exchanges that enriched research and learning experiences.

Ethical Considerations

As horizons expand, so do the ethical considerations that accompany technological advancements. Morgan was acutely aware of the potential for bias in algorithms and the implications of data privacy. He advocated for transparency in digital projects and emphasized the need for ethical guidelines in AI applications within the humanities. This perspective aligns with the principles of *Digital Ethics*, which examines the moral implications of digital technologies and their impact on society [?].

Morgan's approach to ethical dilemmas included forming a committee of diverse stakeholders to evaluate the implications of research projects. This committee was tasked with ensuring that the benefits of technological innovations were equitably distributed and that marginalized voices were included in the narrative.

Future Directions

Looking ahead, Morgan envisioned a future where the horizons of Digital Humanities would continue to expand through emerging technologies such as artificial intelligence, virtual reality, and blockchain. These technologies hold the potential to revolutionize how we interact with cultural heritage and knowledge.

For example, virtual reality could allow users to experience historical events in immersive environments, deepening their understanding of the past.

Moreover, blockchain technology could provide secure and verifiable methods for preserving digital artifacts, ensuring their longevity and authenticity in an increasingly ephemeral digital landscape. The potential applications are vast, and Morgan's foresight in embracing these innovations positioned the Digital Humanities Institute at the forefront of this evolution.

In conclusion, the concept of expanding horizons in Digital Humanities is not just about technological advancements; it encompasses a holistic approach that integrates interdisciplinary collaboration, global outreach, ethical considerations, and future-oriented thinking. Morgan Liao's legacy lies in his ability to inspire a new generation of scholars to embrace these ideals, ensuring that the field continues to grow and adapt in the digital age.

Morgan's Revolutionary Projects

The Knowledge Archive

In the age of information overload, where cat videos and conspiracy theories coexist in a digital Bermuda Triangle, Morgan Liao had a vision: to create The Knowledge Archive, a sanctuary for knowledge that would not only preserve humanity's collective wisdom but also prevent it from being buried under a mountain of memes and poorly spelled tweets.

Theoretical Foundations

The Knowledge Archive is rooted in the principles of *digital curation* and *knowledge management*. As Morgan often quipped, "If knowledge is power, then the Knowledge Archive is like the gym membership you never use—full of potential but just sitting there collecting dust."

The theoretical framework combines concepts from *information science, library science*, and *cognitive psychology*. According to [?], knowledge management involves the systematic management of an organization's knowledge assets for the purpose of creating value and meeting tactical and strategic requirements. In simpler terms, it's like trying to find a clean spoon in a messy kitchen—nearly impossible without a solid plan.

Challenges in Implementation

Creating The Knowledge Archive was not without its hurdles. Morgan faced numerous challenges, including:

+ **Data Overload:** With the vast amount of information available, curating what to include felt like trying to choose the best pizza topping—everyone has an opinion, and someone will always be upset.

+ **Quality Control:** Ensuring that the information was accurate and relevant was akin to finding a needle in a haystack, except the haystack was also on fire and filled with raccoons.

+ **User Engagement:** Morgan knew that if he built it, they might not come. The challenge was to create an interface so engaging that even your grandmother would want to explore it—preferably without accidentally downloading a virus.

Practical Examples of the Knowledge Archive

To illustrate the potential of The Knowledge Archive, Morgan implemented several groundbreaking features:

1. Interactive Learning Modules   These modules were designed to engage users in a way that felt less like a lecture and more like a game show. For instance, users could participate in a trivia challenge titled "Who Wants to Be a Knowledgeaire?" where they could win virtual badges for answering questions correctly. "It's like a game show," Morgan said, "but without the awkward silences and the host who looks like he hasn't slept in three days."

2. AI-Powered Recommendations   Utilizing advanced algorithms, the archive could recommend content based on users' interests. Imagine an AI that knows you better than your therapist—except it doesn't charge you by the hour. This feature was designed to create a personalized experience, as Morgan pointed out, "Because who wouldn't want a digital assistant that knows you're binge-watching documentaries on existential dread?"

3. Collaborative Spaces   The archive included virtual spaces where users could collaborate on projects, share insights, and even argue about the merits of pineapple on pizza. Morgan often joked, "If we can't agree on pizza toppings, how can we expect to solve world problems?"

Impact on Society

The Knowledge Archive quickly gained traction, becoming a hub for researchers, students, and curious minds alike. It served as a bridge between disciplines, fostering interdisciplinary collaboration. As Morgan mused, "It's like a potluck dinner where everyone brings their best dish, and no one judges you for eating too much."

The archive also played a crucial role in democratizing access to information. By providing free access to a wealth of knowledge, Morgan aimed to level the playing field. "Knowledge should be like air—available to everyone, except maybe in the case of a really bad smell," he quipped.

In conclusion, The Knowledge Archive was not just a repository of information; it was a living, breathing entity that evolved with its users. It embodied Morgan's vision of a **Cyber Renaissance**, where technology and humanities intersected to create a brighter, more informed future. As he often said, "In the end, knowledge is like a good joke—best when shared, and sometimes, it's just a little hard to swallow."

Artificial Intelligence in Cultural Preservation

The integration of Artificial Intelligence (AI) in cultural preservation represents a transformative approach to safeguarding our heritage in the digital age. As society becomes increasingly reliant on technology, the need to preserve cultural artifacts, languages, and practices has never been more critical. This section explores the theoretical foundations of AI in cultural preservation, the challenges it faces, and examples of successful implementations.

Theoretical Foundations

At its core, AI in cultural preservation hinges on the ability to process and analyze vast amounts of data efficiently. Machine learning algorithms, a subset of AI, utilize statistical techniques to enable computers to learn from and make predictions based on data. This capability is particularly valuable in cultural heritage contexts, where the volume of information—ranging from textual documents to multimedia artifacts—can be overwhelming.

The theory of *cognitive computing* underpins many AI applications in this field. Cognitive computing aims to mimic human thought processes in complex problem-solving scenarios. For cultural preservation, this means creating systems that can interpret, analyze, and generate insights from cultural data in ways that are contextually relevant and meaningful.

Challenges in Cultural Preservation

Despite the potential benefits, the application of AI in cultural preservation is fraught with challenges:

+ **Data Quality and Accessibility:** The success of AI systems heavily depends on the quality and accessibility of the data they process. Many cultural artifacts are not digitized, and existing digital records may be incomplete or poorly annotated. This lack of quality data can lead to biased or inaccurate AI outputs.

+ **Ethical Considerations:** The use of AI raises ethical questions, particularly concerning ownership and representation of cultural heritage. Who owns the data? How can we ensure that marginalized voices are included in the narratives constructed by AI systems? Addressing these questions is crucial to developing ethical AI practices in cultural preservation.

+ **Interdisciplinary Collaboration:** Effective cultural preservation through AI requires collaboration between technologists, historians, anthropologists, and other stakeholders. Bridging these diverse fields can be challenging, as each discipline has its own methodologies, terminologies, and priorities.

Examples of AI in Action

Several innovative projects illustrate the potential of AI in cultural preservation:

+ **The Rosetta Project:** This initiative aims to preserve and make accessible the world's languages. Utilizing AI algorithms, researchers analyze linguistic data to create digital records of endangered languages. By employing machine learning techniques, the project can identify patterns and relationships between languages, aiding in their preservation.

+ **Google Arts and Culture:** This platform uses AI to enhance the accessibility of cultural heritage. Through image recognition and machine learning, Google has developed tools that allow users to explore art collections from around the world. For instance, the *Art Palette* feature enables users to discover artworks based on color schemes, fostering a deeper appreciation of cultural artifacts.

+ **The Digital Public Library of America (DPLA):** DPLA employs AI to improve the discoverability of cultural resources. By using natural language processing (NLP) techniques, DPLA enhances metadata and search functionalities, making it easier for users to locate historical documents, photographs, and other cultural materials.

Conclusion

The incorporation of AI in cultural preservation is a promising frontier that has the potential to revolutionize how we safeguard our heritage. By leveraging advanced technologies, we can create more inclusive, accessible, and efficient methods for preserving cultural artifacts. However, addressing the associated challenges—such as data quality, ethical considerations, and interdisciplinary collaboration—is essential for realizing the full potential of AI in this vital field. As we move forward, the collaboration between technologists and cultural custodians will be key to ensuring that our shared heritage is preserved for future generations.

$$\text{Cultural Preservation Success} = \frac{\text{Quality Data} \times \text{Collaborative Efforts}}{\text{Ethical Challenges} + \text{Technological Limitations}} \tag{53}$$

Virtual Reality for Historical Immersion

The advent of Virtual Reality (VR) technology has opened new frontiers in the way we experience and understand history. By creating immersive environments that replicate historical settings, VR allows users to step into the past, offering a unique perspective that traditional educational methods often lack. This section explores the theoretical underpinnings, challenges, and practical applications of VR in historical immersion.

Theoretical Framework

The use of VR for historical immersion is grounded in several theoretical frameworks, including constructivist learning theory and experiential learning theory. Constructivism posits that knowledge is constructed through interaction with the environment, and VR provides a rich, interactive platform for this type of learning. Experiential learning, as proposed by Kolb (1984), emphasizes learning through experience, where individuals engage in concrete experiences, reflective observation, abstract conceptualization, and active experimentation.

Learning $= f$(Experience, Reflection, Conceptualization, Experimentation)

$$(54)$$

This equation highlights the dynamic interplay between different stages of learning, which VR effectively facilitates by allowing users to engage with historical contexts in a tangible way.

Challenges in Implementation

While the potential of VR for historical immersion is significant, several challenges must be addressed:

- **Technological Limitations:** High-quality VR experiences require advanced hardware and software, which may not be accessible to all educational institutions. The disparity in technology can lead to unequal learning opportunities.

- **Content Accuracy:** Creating historically accurate VR environments necessitates extensive research and collaboration with historians. Misrepresentation of historical facts can lead to misconceptions and misinformation.

- **User Experience:** Designing intuitive and engaging VR experiences is crucial. Poorly designed interfaces can frustrate users and detract from the educational value of the experience.

- **Physical and Psychological Effects:** Prolonged exposure to VR can cause discomfort or disorientation in some users. Addressing these physical and psychological effects is essential to ensure a positive learning experience.

Examples of VR in Historical Immersion

Several projects exemplify the successful application of VR for historical immersion:

- **The VR Museum of Fine Art:** This project allows users to explore a virtual museum filled with famous artworks. Users can interact with the art pieces, learn about their historical context, and even attend virtual guided tours. This immersive experience enhances understanding and appreciation of art history.

+ **Titanic VR:** This educational experience enables users to explore the wreck of the Titanic. Participants can navigate the ship's remains, learn about its tragic history, and understand the events leading to its sinking. This experience fosters a deeper emotional connection to historical events.

+ **Rome Reborn:** This project reconstructs ancient Rome in a virtual environment, allowing users to walk through the city as it appeared centuries ago. By interacting with the environment, users gain insights into Roman architecture, culture, and daily life.

Future Directions

The future of VR in historical immersion is promising, with advancements in technology enabling even more sophisticated experiences. The integration of artificial intelligence (AI) can enhance interactivity, allowing users to engage with historical figures or events dynamically. For instance, AI-driven avatars could provide personalized tours, adapting content based on user interests and questions.

Additionally, the potential for collaborative VR experiences could revolutionize how history is taught. Students from different geographical locations could explore historical sites together, fostering a global perspective on history.

Conclusion

Virtual Reality for historical immersion represents a transformative approach to understanding our past. By leveraging technology to create engaging, interactive experiences, we can foster a deeper appreciation for history among learners. However, addressing the challenges of technological access, content accuracy, and user experience will be crucial in realizing the full potential of VR in education. As we move forward, the collaboration between technologists, educators, and historians will be essential in crafting experiences that not only educate but also inspire future generations to explore and understand the complexities of our shared history.

Augmented Reality in Education

Augmented Reality (AR) has emerged as a transformative technology in the field of education, offering a unique blend of digital content with the real world. By overlaying information onto the physical environment, AR creates immersive learning experiences that engage students in ways traditional methods cannot. This section explores the theoretical foundations, practical applications, challenges, and future prospects of augmented reality in education.

Theoretical Foundations

The use of AR in education is rooted in several educational theories, including Constructivism and Experiential Learning. Constructivism posits that learners construct knowledge through experiences and interactions with their environment. AR facilitates this by providing interactive, context-rich scenarios where students can explore concepts dynamically.

Experiential Learning, as proposed by Kolb (1984), emphasizes the importance of experience in the learning process. AR allows students to engage with content in a hands-on manner, transforming passive learning into active exploration. This aligns with Kolb's cycle of experiential learning, which consists of four stages: Concrete Experience, Reflective Observation, Abstract Conceptualization, and Active Experimentation.

$$\text{Learning Cycle} = \text{Concrete Experience} \rightarrow \text{Reflective Observation} \rightarrow \text{Abstract Conceptuali} \tag{55}$$

Practical Applications

The applications of AR in education are vast and varied. Here are some notable examples:

- **Interactive Textbooks:** AR-enabled textbooks can bring static images to life, allowing students to see 3D models of complex structures, such as the human anatomy or historical landmarks. For instance, the *Anatomy 4D* app allows students to visualize the human body in 3D, enhancing their understanding of anatomy.

- **Virtual Field Trips:** AR can transport students to distant locations without leaving the classroom. Applications like *Google Expeditions* enable educators to guide students through virtual tours of historical sites or natural wonders, providing a richer context for learning.

- **Gamified Learning:** AR can gamify education, making learning more engaging. For example, the *Pokémon GO* phenomenon has been adapted for educational purposes, where students can embark on AR scavenger hunts to learn about biodiversity and ecology.

+ **Language Learning:** Apps like *Mondly* use AR to help students learn new languages by providing real-time translations of objects in their environment, thus contextualizing vocabulary in a meaningful way.

Challenges in Implementation

Despite its potential, the integration of AR into educational settings faces several challenges:

+ **Technological Barriers:** Not all educational institutions have access to the necessary hardware and software. The cost of AR devices, such as smartphones, tablets, or AR glasses, can be prohibitive, especially for underfunded schools.

+ **Teacher Training:** Educators must be adequately trained to implement AR tools effectively. Many teachers may lack the technical skills or confidence to integrate AR into their lesson plans, which can hinder its adoption.

+ **Content Development:** Creating high-quality AR content requires time and expertise. Educational institutions may struggle to develop or source appropriate AR materials that align with their curricula.

+ **Distraction Potential:** While AR can enhance engagement, it can also lead to distractions if not used judiciously. Students may become more focused on the technology than the educational content itself.

Future Prospects

The future of AR in education is promising, with several trends indicating its growing significance:

+ **Increased Accessibility:** As AR technology becomes more affordable and widespread, its integration into classrooms is likely to increase. Schools may leverage mobile devices that students already own to access AR experiences.

+ **Enhanced Collaboration:** AR can foster collaborative learning environments where students work together on projects in real time, regardless of their physical locations. This can be particularly beneficial in remote or hybrid learning scenarios.

+ **Personalized Learning:** AR can adapt to individual learning styles and paces, providing tailored experiences that meet diverse student needs. This personalization can enhance student engagement and retention of knowledge.

+ **Integration with AI:** The combination of AR and Artificial Intelligence (AI) can lead to even more sophisticated educational tools. AI can analyze student interactions with AR content to provide insights and recommendations for personalized learning pathways.

In conclusion, augmented reality represents a significant advancement in educational technology, offering innovative ways to engage students and enhance learning outcomes. While challenges remain, the potential benefits of AR in education are too substantial to ignore. As educators and technologists continue to collaborate, we can expect to see AR become an integral part of the educational landscape, paving the way for a more interactive and immersive learning experience.

Transforming the Museum Experience

The museum experience has long been a bastion of cultural preservation and education, yet it has often been criticized for being static, inaccessible, and sometimes even intimidating to the average visitor. Morgan Liao recognized this challenge early in his career and sought to transform how museums engage with the public through innovative digital technologies. This section explores the theories, challenges, and practical implementations of transforming the museum experience in the digital age.

Theoretical Framework

At the core of Morgan's approach lies the **Experiential Learning Theory**, which posits that learning is most effective when individuals actively engage with their environment. This theory is supported by Kolb's Learning Cycle, which emphasizes the importance of concrete experience, reflective observation, abstract conceptualization, and active experimentation. By integrating technology into the museum experience, Morgan aimed to facilitate this cycle, allowing visitors to interact with exhibits in a more meaningful way.

$$\text{Learning} = f(\text{Experience, Reflection, Conceptualization, Experimentation})$$
$$(56)$$

Challenges in Museum Transformation

Despite the potential benefits of digital transformation, several challenges arise:

+ **Accessibility:** Ensuring that digital tools are accessible to all visitors, including those with disabilities, is paramount. Morgan advocated for inclusive design principles that cater to diverse audiences.

+ **Technological Integration:** The integration of new technologies into existing museum infrastructures can be complex and costly. Museums often struggle with outdated systems that do not support modern digital solutions.

+ **Curation vs. Technology:** Striking a balance between traditional curation methods and the use of technology is crucial. There is a risk that technology could overshadow the artifacts themselves, detracting from the visitor's experience.

+ **Visitor Engagement:** Engaging visitors in a way that feels authentic rather than gimmicky is a challenge. Morgan's vision included using technology to enhance storytelling rather than replace it.

Innovative Implementations

Morgan's transformative vision led to several groundbreaking implementations in museums around the world:

1. **Augmented Reality (AR) Experiences** One of the most successful applications of Morgan's ideas was the introduction of augmented reality experiences in museums. For instance, the *Metropolitan Museum of Art* in New York City launched an AR app that allows visitors to point their devices at certain exhibits to unlock additional content—such as 3D reconstructions of historical artifacts or contextual information about the pieces on display. This not only enriches the visitor experience but also encourages deeper engagement with the material.

2. **Interactive Digital Displays** Morgan's team developed interactive digital displays that allow visitors to explore collections in a non-linear fashion. For example, the *Smithsonian National Museum of Natural History* implemented touch-screen kiosks where visitors can navigate through various themes, such as biodiversity or human evolution, and access multimedia content, including videos,

audio guides, and interactive quizzes. This approach caters to different learning styles and encourages exploration.

3. Virtual Reality (VR) Immersive Experiences In collaboration with leading VR developers, Morgan's initiative created immersive virtual reality experiences that transport users to significant historical events or locations. The *British Museum* launched a VR project that allows users to walk through ancient civilizations, such as Rome or Egypt, providing a unique perspective on history that traditional exhibits cannot offer. This technology not only captivates visitors but also serves as an educational tool that can be accessed remotely, broadening the museum's reach.

4. Digital Storytelling Platforms Morgan's emphasis on digital storytelling led to the creation of platforms that allow museums to share narratives in innovative ways. For example, the *Museum of Modern Art* (MoMA) in New York developed an online platform where users can create and share their own stories related to specific artworks. This fosters a sense of community and personal connection, as visitors contribute their interpretations and experiences.

Conclusion

Morgan Liao's transformative vision for the museum experience highlights the potential of digital technologies to enhance cultural engagement and education. By addressing the challenges of accessibility, integration, and engagement, museums can evolve from static repositories of artifacts into dynamic spaces of learning and discovery. The impact of these innovations extends beyond the museum walls, inspiring future generations to appreciate and preserve our collective heritage. As we continue to navigate the digital landscape, the lessons learned from Morgan's initiatives will undoubtedly shape the future of museum experiences for years to come.

Digital Storytelling to Preserve Oral Histories

In the age of rapid technological advancement, the preservation of oral histories has emerged as a pivotal aspect of cultural heritage and identity. Digital storytelling serves as a powerful medium to capture, archive, and disseminate these narratives, ensuring they are not lost to time. This section explores the theoretical frameworks, challenges, and real-world applications of digital storytelling in preserving oral histories.

Theoretical Framework

Digital storytelling is rooted in several theories, including constructivism and narrative theory. Constructivism posits that individuals construct knowledge through their experiences and interactions. In the context of oral histories, this means that the stories shared are not merely data points but are imbued with personal significance and contextual richness. According to Bruner (1991), narrative is a primary way of making sense of the world, which reinforces the importance of storytelling in human cognition.

Narrative theory further emphasizes the structure and function of stories. It suggests that stories serve as a means of organizing experiences, providing coherence to our lives. When applied to digital storytelling, this theory underscores the need for a narrative arc—beginning, middle, and end—to engage audiences effectively.

Challenges in Digital Storytelling

Despite its potential, digital storytelling for oral histories faces several challenges:

- **Technological Barriers:** Not all communities have equal access to the necessary technology or the internet, which can limit participation in digital storytelling initiatives. The digital divide remains a significant issue, particularly in rural or underserved areas.

- **Cultural Sensitivity:** Oral histories are often deeply rooted in cultural contexts. Digital storytellers must navigate ethical considerations, ensuring that the stories are told respectfully and accurately. Misrepresentation can lead to cultural appropriation, which can further alienate communities.

- **Preservation of Authenticity:** With the ease of editing and altering digital content, maintaining the authenticity of oral histories becomes a challenge. There is a fine line between enhancing a story for clarity and altering its original meaning.

Examples of Digital Storytelling Initiatives

Several successful initiatives illustrate the power of digital storytelling in preserving oral histories:

- **StoryCorps:** Founded in 2003, StoryCorps is a nonprofit organization that records, shares, and preserves the stories of people from all walks of life. Participants are invited to share their stories in a booth, where they are recorded and later archived at the American Folklife Center at the Library of Congress. The project has collected over 600,000 stories, emphasizing the importance of personal narratives in the broader cultural tapestry.

+ **The Oral History Metadata Synchronizer (OHMS):** Developed by the University of Kentucky, OHMS allows users to create rich metadata for oral histories, making them more accessible and searchable. This tool enhances the usability of oral history archives, allowing researchers and the public to find specific segments of interviews that are relevant to their interests.

+ **The Digital Public Library of America (DPLA):** DPLA aggregates digital content from libraries, archives, and museums across the United States. It includes a vast collection of oral histories, making them accessible to a global audience. This democratization of knowledge exemplifies how digital storytelling can preserve and share cultural narratives on a larger scale.

Conclusion

Digital storytelling is a transformative approach to preserving oral histories, enabling communities to share their narratives in innovative ways. By leveraging technology, we can ensure that these stories are not only preserved but also celebrated, fostering a greater understanding of diverse cultural experiences.

As Morgan Liao's work illustrates, the intersection of technology and humanities offers a unique opportunity to engage with history in ways that are both meaningful and impactful. The future of oral history preservation lies in our ability to harness these digital tools while remaining committed to ethical storytelling practices.

References

+ Bruner, J. (1991). *The Narrative Construction of Reality.* Critical Inquiry, 18(1), 1-21.

+ StoryCorps. (n.d.). Retrieved from `https://storycorps.org`

+ Oral History Metadata Synchronizer. (n.d.). Retrieved from `https://www.oralhistoryonline.org`

+ Digital Public Library of America. (n.d.). Retrieved from `https://dp.la`

Social Media for Democratizing Knowledge

In the era of the Cyber Renaissance, social media has emerged as a powerful tool for democratizing knowledge, breaking down traditional barriers to information access and fostering a more inclusive environment for learning and collaboration. Morgan Liao's innovative approach to integrating social media platforms into the realm of digital humanities has revolutionized how knowledge is shared, consumed, and created.

Theoretical Framework

The democratization of knowledge through social media can be understood through the lens of several theoretical frameworks, including **Connectivism**, **Participatory Culture**, and **Networked Learning**.

- **Connectivism** posits that learning occurs through a network of connections, where knowledge is distributed across a network of individuals and technology. According to Siemens (2005), "the ability to know more is more critical than what is currently known." This theory emphasizes the importance of social media as a medium for connecting learners and experts, facilitating the flow of information.

- **Participatory Culture**, as described by Jenkins (2006), highlights the role of individuals as active participants in the creation and dissemination of knowledge. Social media platforms enable users to contribute content, engage in discussions, and collaborate on projects, fostering a sense of community and shared ownership of knowledge.

- **Networked Learning** refers to the process of learning that occurs within a networked environment, where learners are interconnected through digital platforms. This model supports the idea that knowledge is co-constructed through interactions and relationships, making social media an ideal space for collaborative learning.

Challenges and Problems

Despite the potential benefits, the use of social media for democratizing knowledge is not without its challenges. Some of the key issues include:

- **Misinformation and Disinformation:** The rapid spread of information on social media can lead to the dissemination of false or misleading content. This phenomenon raises concerns about the credibility of sources and the quality of knowledge being shared. A study by Vosoughi et al. (2018) found that false news spreads faster and reaches more people than true news on social media platforms.

+ **Digital Divide:** While social media has the potential to democratize knowledge, access to technology and the internet remains unequal across different socio-economic groups. The digital divide exacerbates existing inequalities, limiting the ability of marginalized communities to participate in knowledge sharing and creation.

+ **Echo Chambers and Filter Bubbles:** Social media algorithms often reinforce users' existing beliefs by curating content that aligns with their preferences. This can create echo chambers where diverse perspectives are marginalized, hindering critical discourse and the development of well-rounded knowledge.

+ **Privacy and Data Security:** The use of social media for knowledge sharing raises concerns about privacy and data security. Users may inadvertently share sensitive information, and the commodification of personal data by social media companies poses ethical dilemmas regarding consent and ownership of knowledge.

Examples of Social Media in Action

Morgan Liao's initiatives illustrate the transformative potential of social media in democratizing knowledge. Several notable examples include:

+ **Twitter for Academic Discourse:** Morgan encouraged scholars to use Twitter as a platform for sharing research findings, engaging with the public, and fostering interdisciplinary collaboration. The hashtag #AcademicTwitter has become a vibrant community where researchers share insights, seek feedback, and promote their work to a broader audience.

+ **YouTube as an Educational Tool:** Morgan's Digital Humanities Institute launched a YouTube channel featuring lectures, tutorials, and discussions on various topics in digital humanities. This initiative not only made academic content accessible to a global audience but also empowered viewers to engage with complex subjects in an approachable format.

+ **Collaborative Projects on Facebook and Instagram:** Social media platforms like Facebook and Instagram have been utilized for collaborative projects that blend art, history, and technology. For example, the "#MuseumFromHome" campaign allowed museums to share virtual tours and educational content during the COVID-19 pandemic, reaching audiences who may not have had the opportunity to visit in person.

Conclusion

Social media has the potential to democratize knowledge by providing platforms for collaboration, engagement, and the sharing of diverse perspectives. However, it is essential to navigate the challenges associated with misinformation, access, and privacy to ensure that these platforms serve as effective tools for knowledge democratization. Morgan Liao's innovative approach highlights the importance of harnessing the power of social media while addressing its inherent challenges, paving the way for a more inclusive and equitable future in digital humanities.

The legacy of Morgan's work in this domain serves as a reminder that the pursuit of knowledge is a collective endeavor, one that thrives on collaboration and the open exchange of ideas. As we continue to explore the intersection of technology and humanities, it is crucial to embrace the potential of social media while remaining vigilant in addressing its challenges, ensuring that knowledge remains accessible to all.

Bibliography

[1] Siemens, G. (2005). Connectivism: A Learning Theory for the Digital Age. *International Journal of Instructional Technology and Distance Learning*, 2(1), 3-10.

[2] Jenkins, H. (2006). Convergence Culture: Where Old and New Media Collide. New York: New York University Press.

[3] Vosoughi, S., Roy, D., & Aral, S. (2018). The spread of true and false news online. *Science*, 359(6380), 1146-1151.

Big Data Analysis in Humanities Research

In the contemporary landscape of academia, the intersection of big data and the humanities has emerged as a pivotal frontier for exploration and innovation. Big data refers to the vast volumes of structured and unstructured data that are generated every second across the globe. In the context of humanities research, this data can encompass everything from social media interactions to digitized historical texts, offering unprecedented insights into human culture, behavior, and history.

Theoretical Framework

The application of big data analysis in humanities research is grounded in several theoretical frameworks, including but not limited to:

- **Cultural Analytics:** This framework emphasizes the quantitative analysis of cultural artifacts, employing algorithms to discern patterns and trends across large datasets. It challenges traditional qualitative methodologies by offering a more empirical approach to understanding cultural phenomena.

+ **Digital Humanities:** This interdisciplinary field integrates computational methods with humanities scholarship, allowing researchers to analyze texts, images, and other forms of cultural expression through the lens of data science.

+ **Network Theory:** By applying network analysis to humanities data, researchers can visualize and quantify relationships between entities, whether they be authors, texts, or historical events, thus revealing the interconnectedness of cultural narratives.

Challenges in Big Data Analysis

Despite its promise, the integration of big data into humanities research is fraught with challenges:

+ **Data Overload:** The sheer volume of data can be overwhelming. Researchers may struggle to identify relevant datasets and extract meaningful insights without succumbing to analysis paralysis.

+ **Quality vs. Quantity:** Not all data is created equal. The reliability and validity of data sources can vary significantly, necessitating careful curation and validation processes.

+ **Ethical Considerations:** The use of big data raises ethical questions regarding privacy, consent, and the potential for bias. Researchers must navigate these issues to ensure responsible use of data.

Methodologies for Analysis

To harness the potential of big data in humanities research, scholars have developed various methodologies, including:

+ **Text Mining:** This involves using algorithms to extract information from large volumes of text. Techniques such as Natural Language Processing (NLP) enable researchers to analyze sentiment, identify themes, and uncover hidden narratives within texts.

+ **Data Visualization:** Visualization tools transform complex datasets into accessible formats, allowing researchers to convey findings in compelling ways. For instance, word clouds, network graphs, and interactive timelines can illustrate relationships and trends.

- **Machine Learning:** By employing machine learning algorithms, researchers can identify patterns in data that may not be immediately apparent. For example, clustering algorithms can group similar texts based on thematic elements, while classification algorithms can predict the genre of a literary work based on its linguistic features.

Case Studies and Examples

Several notable projects exemplify the successful application of big data analysis in humanities research:

- **The Digital Public Library of America (DPLA):** This initiative aggregates millions of photographs, manuscripts, and other cultural artifacts from libraries and museums across the United States. Researchers utilize DPLA's datasets to conduct large-scale analyses of American history and culture, employing data visualization techniques to present their findings.

- **Culturomics:** A term coined by researchers at Harvard University, culturomics involves analyzing the Google Books corpus to study linguistic trends over time. By employing statistical methods, researchers can track the frequency of words and phrases, revealing shifts in cultural sentiment and societal values.

- **The Mining the Dispatch Project:** This project analyzes over 1.5 million articles from the Richmond Daily Dispatch, a newspaper from the Civil War era. By employing text mining techniques, researchers can uncover patterns in public opinion and media representation during a tumultuous period in American history.

Conclusion

The integration of big data analysis into humanities research represents a transformative shift in how scholars engage with cultural artifacts. While challenges abound, the potential for new insights and understandings of human behavior, history, and culture is immense. As researchers continue to navigate the complexities of big data, they will undoubtedly uncover new narratives and dimensions of the human experience, thereby enriching the field of digital humanities and paving the way for future innovations.

$$\text{Insights} = f(\text{Data Quality, Analysis Method, Research Question}) \qquad (57)$$

This equation illustrates that the insights gained from big data analysis in humanities research are a function of the quality of the data, the methodologies employed, and the specific research questions posed by the scholars. As we move forward into the era of big data, the humanities will continue to evolve, embracing the complexities and opportunities that lie ahead.

Morgan's Impact on Future Generations

Morgan Liao's contributions to the field of digital humanities have not only revolutionized the way we interact with technology and culture but have also laid the groundwork for future generations of innovators. His work serves as a model for aspiring thinkers, creators, and leaders, demonstrating that the intersection of technology and the humanities can yield transformative results.

Theoretical Foundations

At the core of Morgan's impact is the theory of *technocultural synthesis*, which posits that technology and culture are not merely parallel lines but rather intertwined threads that shape human experience. This theory asserts that by understanding the cultural implications of technology, future innovators can create solutions that are not only effective but also socially responsible. Morgan's approach exemplifies this synthesis, as he consistently emphasized the importance of ethical considerations in technological advancements.

Empowering Future Innovators

Morgan's initiatives, such as the Digital Humanities Institute, have created an environment where young innovators can thrive. By providing access to state-of-the-art resources and mentorship opportunities, he has empowered a new generation of thinkers to explore the possibilities of digital humanities. For example, the institute hosts annual hackathons that encourage students to develop projects addressing real-world challenges, such as climate change and social justice. These events not only foster collaboration but also instill a sense of responsibility in participants, encouraging them to consider the broader implications of their work.

Addressing Societal Problems

Morgan's projects often tackled pressing societal issues, illustrating how technology can be harnessed for the greater good. One notable example is the *Knowledge Archive*, a digital repository that democratizes access to historical documents and cultural artifacts. By making these resources available to the public, Morgan has helped bridge the gap between academia and the community, inspiring future generations to engage with their cultural heritage.

The impact of the Knowledge Archive is further exemplified by its role in education. Schools and universities have integrated this resource into their curricula, allowing students to conduct research and develop critical thinking skills. This initiative not only enhances educational outcomes but also cultivates a sense of civic engagement among students, encouraging them to become active participants in their communities.

Fostering Ethical AI Development

As concerns about artificial intelligence (AI) continue to grow, Morgan has been at the forefront of advocating for ethical AI development. He has emphasized the importance of addressing bias in AI algorithms and ensuring that these technologies serve all segments of society. By establishing guidelines for ethical AI practices, Morgan has set a precedent for future innovators, urging them to prioritize inclusivity and fairness in their work.

For instance, Morgan's collaboration with AI researchers led to the development of a framework for evaluating the ethical implications of AI applications in various fields, including healthcare and education. This framework has been adopted by numerous organizations, ensuring that future AI developments are scrutinized through a lens of social responsibility.

Inspiring a Culture of Innovation

Morgan's influence extends beyond his immediate projects; he has fostered a culture of innovation that encourages experimentation and creativity. His emphasis on interdisciplinary collaboration has inspired future generations to break down silos between fields, recognizing that the most impactful solutions often arise from diverse perspectives.

The *Digital Storytelling* initiative is a prime example of this cultural shift. By bringing together artists, technologists, and historians, Morgan has facilitated the creation of immersive narratives that preserve oral histories and cultural traditions. This project not only enriches the cultural landscape but also serves as a template for future innovators, demonstrating the power of collaboration across disciplines.

Legacy of Lifelong Learning

Morgan's commitment to lifelong learning has also left a lasting impact on future generations. He has advocated for continuous education and professional development, encouraging individuals to remain curious and adaptable in an ever-changing technological landscape. His mentorship programs and workshops emphasize the importance of staying informed about emerging technologies and trends, inspiring future innovators to embrace a mindset of growth.

In conclusion, Morgan Liao's impact on future generations is profound and multifaceted. Through his theoretical contributions, empowerment of young innovators, commitment to ethical practices, and promotion of interdisciplinary collaboration, he has created a legacy that will continue to inspire and shape the landscape of digital humanities. As future innovators build upon his work, they will undoubtedly carry forward the principles of responsibility, creativity, and inclusivity that Morgan has championed, ensuring that the cyber renaissance he envisioned will flourish for years to come.

Chapter 3 Challenges and Triumphs

Chapter 3 Challenges and Triumphs

Chapter 3. Challenges and Triumphs

In the journey of innovation, the path is rarely a straight line. For Morgan Liao, the road to revolutionizing digital humanities was paved with both challenges and triumphs, each shaping his character and vision. This chapter delves into the multifaceted obstacles he faced, the lessons learned, and the victories that propelled him forward.

The Ethical Dilemmas

As Morgan embarked on his quest to merge technology with the humanities, he quickly encountered a myriad of ethical dilemmas. The digital age brought forth unprecedented concerns surrounding privacy, access, and the implications of artificial intelligence (AI).

Privacy Concerns in the Digital Age   In a world increasingly driven by data, the question of privacy became paramount. Morgan often pondered the equation:

$$P = \frac{D}{R} \tag{58}$$

where P represents privacy, D denotes the amount of data collected, and R signifies the regulations in place. As data collection surged, Morgan recognized that without robust regulations, privacy would dwindle. This realization spurred him to advocate for clearer data protection laws, ensuring that individuals retained control over their information.

Balancing Access and Control   Morgan understood that while technology could democratize knowledge, it also posed risks of exclusion. The challenge was to strike a balance between access and control. He often likened this to a seesaw, where one side represented unrestricted access and the other stringent control.

$$A + C = K \tag{59}$$

Here, A is access, C is control, and K is knowledge. Morgan believed that achieving a stable equilibrium was essential for fostering an inclusive digital landscape.

Addressing Bias in AI Technology   As AI became integral to his projects, Morgan grappled with the inherent biases that could skew outcomes. He frequently referenced the concept of algorithmic bias, which occurs when an AI system reflects the prejudices present in its training data. To combat this, Morgan implemented rigorous testing protocols to ensure fairness in AI applications.

Facing Personal and Professional Obstacles

The road to success is often fraught with personal and professional challenges. Morgan faced numerous obstacles that tested his resolve and resilience.

The Toll of Success   As Morgan's innovations gained traction, the pressures of success began to mount. The relentless pursuit of excellence often led to sleepless nights and an overwhelming sense of responsibility. He found solace in the words of a mentor who once said, "Success is like a double-edged sword; it cuts both ways."

Coping with Burnout   Burnout became an unwelcome companion in Morgan's life. He discovered that the key to combating this was not just time off, but a fundamental shift in perspective. He adopted the mantra, "Work smarter, not harder," and implemented strategies such as mindfulness and delegation, allowing him to reclaim his passion for innovation.

Dealing with Impostor Syndrome   Despite his achievements, Morgan struggled with impostor syndrome, often feeling like a fraud in the face of his accomplishments. He turned to the work of Dr. Pauline Clance, who developed the Impostor Phenomenon scale, which helped him understand that many successful individuals share these feelings. Morgan began to embrace his journey, recognizing that vulnerability is a strength, not a weakness.

Media Scrutiny and Public Pressure With success came media attention, and Morgan found himself under the microscope. The scrutiny was relentless, and he learned that public perception could be as fickle as the wind. To navigate this, he focused on transparency and authenticity, understanding that being genuine resonated more than any polished public persona.

Celebrating Personal Triumphs

Amidst the challenges, Morgan celebrated numerous personal triumphs that reinforced his commitment to innovation.

Evolving as a Leader As he faced obstacles, Morgan evolved into a more empathetic leader. He learned the importance of active listening and fostering an inclusive environment where team members felt valued. This transformation not only enhanced team dynamics but also led to more innovative solutions.

Overcoming Failure and Setbacks Failure became a teacher for Morgan. One of his most significant setbacks occurred during a pivotal project that did not yield the expected results. Rather than viewing it as a defeat, he reframed it as a learning opportunity, leading to the development of a new framework for future projects that emphasized iterative testing and adaptability.

Celebrating Personal Triumphs Morgan embraced the importance of celebrating small victories along the way. Whether it was a successful project launch or a positive team milestone, he recognized that these moments fueled motivation and fostered a culture of appreciation within his organization.

Morgan's Role in Shaping the Future

Through the challenges and triumphs, Morgan emerged as a pivotal figure in shaping the future of digital humanities. His experiences informed his advocacy for ethical practices in technology and inspired a new generation of innovators.

The Digital Renaissance Movement Morgan became a key player in the Digital Renaissance Movement, which sought to redefine the role of technology in cultural preservation and education. He believed that by harnessing technology, society could unlock new avenues for understanding and appreciating the humanities.

Inspiring New Innovators   Morgan's journey served as a beacon of hope for aspiring innovators. He actively mentored young minds, sharing his experiences and encouraging them to embrace their unique perspectives.   His mantra, "Innovation is not just about technology; it's about humanity," resonated deeply with those he mentored.

Advocacy for Digital Equality   Morgan's commitment to digital equality became a cornerstone of his legacy. He championed initiatives that aimed to bridge the digital divide, ensuring that marginalized communities had access to the tools and resources necessary for participation in the digital age.

Encouraging Ethical AI Development   Recognizing the potential for AI to both uplift and harm society, Morgan advocated for ethical AI development. He collaborated with industry leaders to establish guidelines that prioritized fairness, transparency, and accountability in AI systems.

Revolutionizing Education Systems   Morgan's influence extended to education, where he pushed for reforms that integrated technology into traditional curricula. He envisioned a future where students could engage with history through virtual reality experiences, making learning more immersive and impactful.

Implications for Cultural Preservation   Morgan's work had far-reaching implications for cultural preservation.   By leveraging technology, he sought to safeguard endangered languages, oral histories, and cultural artifacts, ensuring that future generations could connect with their heritage.

The Legacy of Morgan Liao   In the face of challenges, Morgan Liao emerged not just as an innovator but as a leader who inspired change.   His legacy is one of resilience, ethical responsibility, and a commitment to harnessing technology for the greater good. As the digital landscape continues to evolve, Morgan's influence will undoubtedly shape the future of digital humanities for years to come.

In conclusion, the challenges and triumphs faced by Morgan Liao serve as a testament to the complexities of innovation. They highlight the importance of perseverance, ethical considerations, and the power of community in shaping a brighter future.

The Ethical Dilemmas

Privacy Concerns in the Digital Age

In the era of rapid technological advancement, privacy concerns have emerged as a significant challenge, particularly in the field of digital humanities. The integration of technology into our daily lives has led to an unprecedented collection and analysis of personal data. This section delves into the multifaceted issues surrounding privacy in the digital age, exploring theoretical frameworks, real-world implications, and the ethical dilemmas faced by innovators like Morgan Liao.

Theoretical Frameworks

To understand privacy concerns, it is essential to consider several theoretical frameworks that inform our understanding of privacy in the digital age. One prominent theory is the **Social Contract Theory**, which posits that individuals consent to surrender some of their freedoms in exchange for protection and benefits from society. This theory raises questions about the extent to which individuals are aware of their data being collected and how much control they have over that data.

Another relevant framework is the **Surveillance Capitalism** theory, coined by Shoshana Zuboff. This theory suggests that companies manipulate personal data to predict and influence behaviors, often without the explicit consent of users. In this context, privacy is not merely a personal concern but a societal issue, as it relates to power dynamics between individuals and corporations.

Problems of Privacy in Digital Humanities

The digital humanities field, which leverages technology to analyze and interpret cultural artifacts, faces unique privacy challenges. Key problems include:

- **Data Collection and Consent:** Researchers often rely on large datasets that may include sensitive personal information. The question of informed consent arises—are individuals aware that their data is being used for research purposes?

- **Data Anonymization:** While anonymizing data is a common practice, it is not foolproof. Re-identification techniques can potentially reveal identities, leading to privacy breaches. For example, the re-identification of individuals in supposedly anonymized datasets has been documented, raising alarms about the effectiveness of current anonymization techniques.

- **Intellectual Property Rights:** The intersection of privacy and intellectual property rights complicates the landscape. As digital humanities projects often involve the use of copyrighted materials, maintaining the privacy of contributors while respecting intellectual property becomes a challenging balancing act.

- **Ethical Use of AI:** The deployment of artificial intelligence in analyzing data raises ethical questions regarding bias and fairness. For instance, algorithms trained on biased datasets may perpetuate existing inequalities, further marginalizing already vulnerable populations.

Real-World Examples

Several high-profile cases illustrate the privacy concerns prevalent in the digital age:

- **Cambridge Analytica Scandal:** This incident highlighted how personal data harvested from social media platforms was used to influence political campaigns without users' informed consent. The fallout from this scandal has led to increased scrutiny of data privacy practices and calls for stricter regulations.

- **Google's Project Nightingale:** In 2019, it was revealed that Google had partnered with Ascension, a healthcare provider, to collect patient data without informing patients. This raised significant ethical concerns regarding patient privacy and informed consent.

- **Facebook's Data Breaches:** Facebook has faced numerous data breaches, compromising the personal information of millions of users. These incidents have sparked debates about user privacy and the responsibility of tech companies to protect user data.

Regulatory Responses

In response to rising privacy concerns, governments and regulatory bodies have begun to implement stricter data protection laws. The General Data Protection Regulation (GDPR) in the European Union is a landmark regulation that aims to protect individuals' privacy and personal data. Key provisions of the GDPR include:

- **Right to Access:** Individuals have the right to know what personal data is being collected and how it is used.

+ **Right to Erasure:** Individuals can request the deletion of their personal data under certain circumstances.

+ **Data Protection Impact Assessments:** Organizations must conduct assessments to evaluate the impact of their data processing activities on individuals' privacy.

Conclusion

As Morgan Liao and other innovators navigate the digital humanities landscape, they must grapple with the complex interplay between technological advancement and privacy concerns. The challenges outlined in this section highlight the importance of ethical considerations in research and the need for robust regulatory frameworks to protect individual privacy. Moving forward, it is crucial for innovators to prioritize transparency, informed consent, and ethical data practices to foster a digital environment that respects privacy while advancing knowledge.

In summary, privacy concerns in the digital age are not merely technical issues but profound ethical dilemmas that require careful consideration and proactive measures to ensure that the benefits of technology do not come at the expense of individual rights.

Balancing Access and Control

In the digital age, the balance between access and control has become a pivotal concern, especially in the realm of digital humanities. This tension is reminiscent of a seesaw; when one side is elevated, the other is inevitably lowered, leading to a precarious equilibrium that can shift with the slightest disturbance. The challenge lies in ensuring that information is accessible to all while maintaining the necessary controls to protect sensitive data and intellectual property.

Theoretical Framework

The concept of access and control can be analyzed through the lens of *Information Theory*, which posits that the value of information is contingent upon its accessibility and the constraints imposed on it. The Shannon-Weaver model of communication highlights that for effective communication, there must be a balance between the sender (the provider of information) and the receiver (the audience). In this context, Morgan Liao's work in digital humanities can be viewed as an attempt to optimize this communication flow.

$$H(X) = -\sum_{i=1}^{n} p(x_i) \log p(x_i) \tag{60}$$

where $H(X)$ represents the entropy or the amount of uncertainty in the information source X, and $p(x_i)$ is the probability of the occurrence of each possible message.

As access increases, the entropy $H(X)$ tends to rise, indicating a greater diversity of information available. However, this increase must be managed to avoid overwhelming users, which can lead to information fatigue.

Problems Encountered

One significant issue in balancing access and control is the risk of *data breaches*. With increased access to digital resources, the potential for unauthorized access also rises. High-profile cases, such as the 2017 Equifax breach, demonstrate the catastrophic consequences of inadequate data protection measures. In the context of digital humanities, sensitive cultural artifacts or personal narratives could be compromised, leading to loss of trust among communities and stakeholders.

Another challenge is the *digital divide*, which refers to the disparities in access to technology and information. Marginalized communities often lack the resources to engage with digital humanities projects, leading to a skewed representation of cultural narratives. Morgan's initiatives aim to address this divide, but the implementation of equitable access remains fraught with difficulties.

Examples in Practice

Morgan Liao's Digital Humanities Institute exemplifies a proactive approach to balancing access and control. By establishing a framework for ethical data usage, the institute promotes an open-access model while implementing stringent controls on sensitive information. For example, the institute developed a *Data Usage Agreement* that outlines how data can be shared and utilized, ensuring that all parties are aware of their responsibilities.

Moreover, the institute employs a tiered access system for its digital archives. Researchers and educators have broader access rights, while sensitive materials are restricted to authorized personnel only. This model encourages collaboration and innovation while safeguarding critical information.

$$R = \frac{S}{C} \tag{61}$$

where R is the rate of information retrieval, S is the size of the accessible data, and C is the complexity of the control measures in place. By optimizing this ratio, the institute can enhance the user experience while maintaining robust security protocols.

Conclusion

The quest for a balanced approach to access and control in digital humanities is ongoing. As Morgan Liao navigates this complex landscape, his commitment to ethical innovation serves as a guiding principle. By leveraging technology responsibly, fostering collaboration, and advocating for equitable access, he aims to create a sustainable model that benefits all stakeholders. The future of digital humanities hinges on this balance, as it ultimately shapes how knowledge is shared and preserved in an increasingly interconnected world.

Addressing Bias in AI Technology

In the rapidly evolving landscape of artificial intelligence (AI), addressing bias has become a critical concern for developers, researchers, and society at large. Bias in AI can lead to unfair outcomes, perpetuate stereotypes, and exacerbate social inequalities. This section delves into the various dimensions of bias in AI technology, explores theoretical frameworks, identifies problems, and discusses notable examples.

Understanding Bias in AI

Bias in AI can be broadly categorized into three types: **pre-existing bias, technical bias**, and **emergent bias.**

- **Pre-existing bias** refers to the biases that exist in society and are reflected in the data used to train AI systems. For instance, if historical hiring data favors certain demographic groups over others, AI models trained on this data will likely replicate these biases.

- **Technical bias** arises from the algorithms themselves. Certain algorithms may favor specific outcomes based on their design, leading to skewed results even when trained on unbiased data.

- **Emergent bias** occurs when an AI system's behavior changes over time due to interactions with users or the environment. For example, a recommendation system might start promoting certain content more than others based on user interactions, leading to a feedback loop that amplifies existing biases.

Theoretical Frameworks

The study of bias in AI can be informed by various theoretical frameworks, including:

- **Fairness Definitions:** Several mathematical definitions of fairness have been proposed.   For example, *demographic parity* requires that the decision-making process results in equal positive outcomes across different demographic groups. Formally, if Y is the outcome and A is the sensitive attribute (e.g., race, gender), demographic parity can be expressed as:

$$P(Y = 1 | A = a_1) = P(Y = 1 | A = a_2)$$

  for all groups a_1, a_2.

- **Algorithmic Accountability:** This framework emphasizes the need for transparency and accountability in AI systems. It advocates for mechanisms that allow stakeholders to understand how decisions are made and to challenge biased outcomes.

- **Social Justice:** This perspective frames bias in AI within the broader context of social justice, arguing that technology should serve to reduce inequalities rather than reinforce them.

Identifying Problems

Addressing bias in AI technology is fraught with challenges:

- **Data Quality and Representation:** One of the primary issues is the quality and representativeness of the training data.   If the data is skewed or unrepresentative, the AI model will inherit these biases. For example, facial recognition systems have been shown to perform poorly on individuals with darker skin tones due to underrepresentation in training datasets.

- **Lack of Diversity in AI Development:** The teams developing AI technologies often lack diversity, which can lead to blind spots in identifying and addressing biases.   A homogenous team may not recognize the implications of their designs on various demographic groups.

+ **Complexity of Bias:** Bias is not always easily quantifiable or identifiable. The complexity of human behavior and societal norms makes it challenging to define what constitutes a "fair" outcome across different contexts.

Notable Examples

Several high-profile cases highlight the consequences of bias in AI technology:

+ **Amazon's Recruitment Tool:** In 2018, it was revealed that Amazon had scrapped an AI recruitment tool because it favored male candidates over female candidates. The model was trained on resumes submitted over a ten-year period, which predominantly came from men, leading to biased outcomes.

+ **Facial Recognition Technology:** Studies have shown that facial recognition systems exhibit higher error rates for women and people of color. A 2018 study by MIT Media Lab found that facial analysis algorithms misclassified the gender of darker-skinned women 34.7% of the time, compared to just 0.8% for lighter-skinned men.

+ **Predictive Policing:** Predictive policing algorithms have been criticized for perpetuating racial bias. These systems often rely on historical crime data, which can reflect systemic biases in law enforcement practices, leading to over-policing in certain communities.

Strategies for Mitigating Bias

To address bias in AI technology, several strategies can be employed:

+ **Diverse Data Collection:** Ensuring that training datasets are diverse and representative of the population can help mitigate bias. This involves actively seeking out data from underrepresented groups.

+ **Bias Audits:** Regular audits of AI systems can help identify and rectify biases. Organizations can employ third-party auditors to evaluate their algorithms and ensure compliance with fairness standards.

+ **Inclusive Development Teams:** Building diverse teams of developers can provide different perspectives and help identify potential biases in AI systems during the design phase.

+ **User Feedback Mechanisms:** Implementing systems that allow users to provide feedback on AI decisions can help organizations identify biased outcomes and improve their models over time.

Conclusion

Addressing bias in AI technology is not merely a technical challenge; it is a societal imperative. As AI continues to permeate various aspects of life, the responsibility lies with innovators like Morgan Liao to ensure that these systems are designed with fairness, transparency, and accountability at their core. By actively confronting bias, the digital humanities can contribute to a more equitable future, where technology serves as a tool for empowerment rather than oppression.

Safeguarding Intellectual Property

In the rapidly evolving landscape of digital humanities, safeguarding intellectual property (IP) has emerged as a critical concern for innovators like Morgan Liao. As the boundaries between technology and creativity blur, the protection of original ideas, research, and digital content becomes increasingly complex. This section explores the theoretical underpinnings of intellectual property rights, the challenges faced in safeguarding these rights, and practical examples illustrating the implications of IP protection in the digital age.

Theoretical Framework

Intellectual property rights are legal protections granted to creators and inventors to safeguard their original works and inventions. These rights are grounded in the principle that creators should be able to control the use of their creations and benefit financially from their labor. The main categories of intellectual property include:

+ **Copyright:** Protects original works of authorship, including literature, music, and software.

+ **Patents:** Protects inventions and processes for a limited period, granting the inventor exclusive rights to use and commercialize their invention.

+ **Trademarks:** Protects symbols, names, and slogans used to identify goods or services.

+ **Trade Secrets:** Protects confidential business information that provides a competitive edge.

The legal framework surrounding IP varies by jurisdiction, but internationally, treaties such as the *Berne Convention* and the *Agreement on Trade-Related Aspects of Intellectual Property Rights (TRIPS)* provide a foundation for global IP protection.

Challenges in Safeguarding IP

Despite the existing legal frameworks, several challenges complicate the safeguarding of intellectual property in the digital humanities:

1. **Digital Reproduction:** The ease of copying and distributing digital content raises concerns about unauthorized use. For example, a digital artwork can be reproduced and shared online in seconds, making it difficult for creators to control its distribution.

2. **Globalization:** The internet transcends borders, complicating the enforcement of IP rights. A work protected in one country may be freely used in another where protections are weaker or nonexistent.

3. **Emerging Technologies:** Innovations such as artificial intelligence and blockchain present both opportunities and challenges for IP protection. AI-generated works raise questions about authorship and ownership, while blockchain technology offers potential solutions for tracking and verifying ownership.

4. **User-Generated Content:** Platforms that encourage user-generated content, such as social media, often create a gray area regarding IP ownership. For instance, when users upload their creations, they may inadvertently grant the platform rights to use their work without proper compensation.

Practical Examples

Morgan Liao's initiatives in digital humanities have brought to light several practical examples of the challenges associated with safeguarding intellectual property:

+ **The Knowledge Archive:** In creating a digital archive of cultural artifacts, Morgan faced the dilemma of ensuring that contributors retained rights to their submissions while also allowing for public access. This required careful negotiation of licensing agreements that balanced accessibility with protection.

- **Artificial Intelligence in Cultural Preservation:** The use of AI to recreate lost artworks or historical documents has sparked debates about authorship. For instance, if an AI program generates a new piece of art based on existing works, who holds the copyright? This question remains unresolved, highlighting the need for updated legal definitions of authorship in the context of AI.

- **Digital Storytelling:** When developing platforms for digital storytelling, Morgan encountered issues with user-generated content. To protect the rights of storytellers, he implemented clear terms of service that outlined ownership and usage rights, ensuring that creators retained control over their narratives.

Conclusion

As the digital humanities continue to evolve, safeguarding intellectual property will remain a significant challenge for innovators like Morgan Liao. By navigating the complex legal landscape and addressing the unique challenges posed by technology, Morgan aims to create an environment where creativity thrives while ensuring that creators are recognized and rewarded for their contributions. This balance is essential for fostering innovation and preserving the integrity of the digital landscape.

In summary, the safeguarding of intellectual property in the digital humanities is not merely a legal obligation but a fundamental aspect of ethical innovation. As Morgan Liao demonstrates, addressing these challenges head-on is crucial for inspiring future generations of creators and ensuring that the digital renaissance continues to flourish.

Navigating the Political Landscape

Navigating the political landscape is akin to trying to dance the tango while simultaneously juggling flaming torches—it's a delicate balance of strategy, timing, and a dash of luck. In the realm of digital humanities, where technology and culture intersect, the political implications can be as complex as a plot twist in a telenovela. Morgan Liao found himself at the center of this intricate web, where every decision could lead to either a standing ovation or a chorus of boos.

The Intersection of Politics and Digital Humanities

Digital humanities, while primarily focused on the fusion of technology and cultural studies, is not immune to the whims of political forces. The funding for projects, the direction of research, and even the dissemination of knowledge can be heavily influenced by political agendas. For instance, during Morgan's tenure at the Digital Humanities Institute, he faced the daunting task of securing funding in an environment where grants were often tied to political priorities.

$$F = \frac{(P \cdot R)}{C} \tag{62}$$

Where:

- F = Funding received

- P = Political support

- R = Research relevance

- C = Competition for resources

This equation illustrates that the amount of funding Morgan could secure was directly proportional to the political support and the relevance of his research, while inversely related to the competition for those limited resources.

Political Challenges and Ethical Dilemmas

One of the significant challenges Morgan encountered was the ethical dilemmas posed by political influence. As he embarked on projects that utilized artificial intelligence to analyze cultural data, he had to confront the potential biases embedded within AI algorithms. These biases often reflected the political climate, leading to skewed interpretations of cultural narratives.

For example, when analyzing historical texts, Morgan discovered that certain narratives were underrepresented due to the prevailing political ideologies of the time. This realization prompted him to advocate for transparency in AI development and to push for a diverse team of researchers who could provide a multitude of perspectives.

Morgan often quoted a famous philosopher, albeit with a twist: "Those who cannot remember the past are condemned to tweet about it." This humorous take highlighted the importance of understanding historical context in shaping current political discourse and technological advancements.

Navigating Bureaucracy

The bureaucratic labyrinth of academia and government can be as convoluted as a plot from a Christopher Nolan film. Morgan had to learn how to navigate this maze, where every turn could lead to a dead end or an unexpected opportunity. He often found himself in meetings where the agenda seemed to change as frequently as the weather, with political stakeholders vying for their voices to be heard.

To combat this, Morgan developed a strategy he referred to as "the art of the political schmooze." This involved not only presenting his ideas but also understanding the motivations and concerns of the stakeholders involved. His ability to empathize with their positions allowed him to forge alliances that would ultimately benefit his projects.

Case Studies: Successes and Failures

Morgan's journey through the political landscape was not without its ups and downs. One notable success was the establishment of a partnership with a local government to digitize historical records. This initiative not only garnered public support but also provided valuable data for researchers and educators alike. The project was lauded as a model for future collaborations between academia and government.

Conversely, there were failures too. A proposed initiative aimed at using big data to address social inequalities was met with resistance from political figures who feared the implications of such transparency. The backlash was swift, and Morgan found himself at the center of a media storm, with headlines reading, "Digital Humanities or Digital Dystopia?"

This experience taught him the importance of framing his projects in a way that resonated with political sensibilities. He learned to present his work not just as a technological advancement but as a means to foster social good and cultural understanding.

Conclusion

Ultimately, navigating the political landscape required Morgan to be both a visionary and a pragmatist. He recognized that while politics could pose challenges, it also presented opportunities for collaboration and innovation. By understanding the political currents that influenced his work, he was able to steer his projects towards success while remaining committed to the ethical responsibilities inherent in the field of digital humanities.

As he often joked in his lectures, "In the world of digital humanities, the only thing more complicated than the algorithms is the politics!" This humor not only lightened the mood but also served as a reminder of the intricate dance between technology, culture, and politics that defines the digital age.

Ensuring Data Security

In the age of digital humanities, where vast amounts of data are generated, stored, and analyzed, ensuring data security has become paramount. The intersection of technology and humanities brings forth unique challenges that require a nuanced understanding of both fields. Data security not only protects sensitive information but also preserves the integrity of research and fosters trust among users and stakeholders.

Theoretical Frameworks

To understand data security in digital humanities, we can refer to several theoretical frameworks. One such framework is the CIA triad, which encompasses three core principles: Confidentiality, Integrity, and Availability.

- **Confidentiality:** Ensures that sensitive information is accessed only by authorized individuals. Techniques such as encryption and access controls are employed to maintain confidentiality.

- **Integrity:** Guarantees that data is accurate and unaltered. Integrity checks, such as checksums and hash functions, are vital in detecting unauthorized modifications.

- **Availability:** Ensures that data is accessible when needed. This involves implementing robust backup solutions and disaster recovery plans to mitigate data loss.

Challenges in Data Security

Despite the theoretical frameworks in place, several challenges persist in ensuring data security within the realm of digital humanities:

1. **Data Breaches:** As organizations collect more data, they become prime targets for cybercriminals. High-profile breaches, such as the 2017 Equifax incident, highlight the vulnerabilities inherent in data storage systems. In this case, the personal information of approximately 147 million people was compromised, leading to significant repercussions.

2. **Insider Threats:** Employees or collaborators with access to sensitive data can pose a significant risk. The 2013 leak of classified NSA documents by Edward Snowden exemplifies how insider threats can undermine data security and trust.

3. **Compliance and Regulations:** Navigating the complex landscape of data protection regulations, such as the General Data Protection Regulation (GDPR) in Europe, poses challenges for organizations. Non-compliance can result in hefty fines and damage to reputation.

4. **Rapid Technological Advancements:** The continuous evolution of technology can outpace security measures. The rise of artificial intelligence (AI) and machine learning (ML) introduces both opportunities and vulnerabilities, as seen in the misuse of AI for generating deepfakes, which can distort historical narratives.

Examples of Data Security Practices

To address these challenges, various data security practices can be implemented:

- **Encryption:** Encrypting data both at rest and in transit ensures that even if data is intercepted, it remains unreadable to unauthorized users. For instance, using Advanced Encryption Standard (AES) with a 256-bit key provides a strong layer of security.

- **Access Controls:** Implementing role-based access control (RBAC) restricts access to sensitive data based on user roles. This principle of least privilege minimizes the risk of unauthorized access.

- **Regular Audits:** Conducting periodic security audits and vulnerability assessments helps identify weaknesses in the system. For example, penetration testing can simulate cyber attacks to evaluate the effectiveness of security measures.

- **Data Anonymization:** In research involving human subjects, anonymizing data can reduce privacy risks. Techniques such as differential privacy allow researchers to extract insights while protecting individual identities.

Conclusion

In conclusion, ensuring data security in digital humanities is a multifaceted challenge that requires a comprehensive approach. By understanding the theoretical frameworks, recognizing the challenges, and implementing robust security practices, innovators like Morgan Liao can protect sensitive data and foster a culture of trust and integrity. As the digital landscape continues to evolve, ongoing vigilance and adaptation will be crucial in safeguarding the future of digital humanities.

$$Data\ Security = Confidentiality + Integrity + Availability \qquad (63)$$

Ethical Responsibilities of Digital Humanities

The field of Digital Humanities (DH) has emerged as a transformative force in the intersection of technology and the humanities. As we navigate this new frontier, it becomes imperative to address the ethical responsibilities that accompany such innovation. This section explores the key ethical considerations, potential pitfalls, and guiding principles for practitioners in the Digital Humanities.

Understanding Ethical Responsibilities

At its core, the ethical responsibilities of Digital Humanities involve a commitment to integrity, inclusivity, and social justice. Scholars and practitioners must recognize that their work does not exist in a vacuum; it has real-world implications for individuals and communities. As technology reshapes our understanding of culture, history, and knowledge, it is essential to ensure that these transformations are conducted with care and responsibility.

Key Ethical Issues

1. **Privacy Concerns** In an age where data is often considered the new oil, privacy concerns have taken center stage. Digital Humanities projects frequently involve the collection and analysis of large datasets, which can include sensitive personal information. Researchers must navigate the fine line between utilizing data for scholarly purposes and respecting the privacy of individuals. This includes implementing stringent data protection measures and obtaining informed consent from participants.

2. **Intellectual Property** The digital age has revolutionized access to knowledge, but it has also raised complex questions about intellectual property rights. Researchers in Digital Humanities must be vigilant in ensuring that they respect the intellectual property of others while also advocating for open access and the

democratization of knowledge. This often involves navigating copyright laws and understanding the implications of Creative Commons licenses.

3.   Bias and Representation As technology increasingly mediates our understanding of culture and history, the potential for bias in algorithms and digital tools becomes a pressing concern. Digital Humanities practitioners must critically assess the tools they use and strive to mitigate biases that may perpetuate stereotypes or marginalize certain groups.   This includes ensuring diverse representation in datasets and actively seeking to amplify underrepresented voices.

4. Accessibility and Inclusivity The promise of Digital Humanities lies in its potential to make knowledge more accessible.   However, this potential is undermined if projects fail to consider the needs of diverse audiences. Ethical responsibilities include designing inclusive digital platforms that accommodate users with disabilities and providing resources in multiple languages to reach a broader audience.

Theoretical Frameworks

To guide ethical decision-making in Digital Humanities, several theoretical frameworks can be applied:

1.   Utilitarianism Utilitarianism posits that the best action is the one that maximizes utility, usually defined as that which produces the greatest well-being of the greatest number of people. In the context of Digital Humanities, this means assessing the potential benefits and harms of a project to ensure that it serves the greater good.

2. Deontological Ethics Deontological ethics focuses on the morality of actions themselves rather than the consequences.   This approach emphasizes the importance of adhering to ethical principles, such as honesty and fairness.   In Digital Humanities, this could manifest as a commitment to transparency in research practices and a dedication to ethical sourcing of materials.

3. Virtue Ethics Virtue ethics emphasizes the character of the moral agent rather than specific actions. In Digital Humanities, practitioners should cultivate virtues such as empathy, integrity, and humility. This approach encourages researchers to reflect on their motivations and the broader impact of their work on society.

Practical Examples

Several projects in the Digital Humanities have exemplified ethical responsibilities:

1. **The Digital Public Library of America (DPLA)** The DPLA is a prime example of a project that prioritizes accessibility and inclusivity. By providing free access to millions of digitized materials from libraries, archives, and museums across the United States, the DPLA embodies the ethical commitment to democratizing knowledge.

2. **The Gendered Innovations Project** This project highlights the importance of incorporating gender analysis into scientific research. By addressing the biases inherent in research methodologies, the Gendered Innovations Project aims to produce more equitable and comprehensive outcomes in various fields, including the humanities.

3. **The Digital Archive of Native American History** This archive showcases the importance of representation and ethical collaboration. By involving Native American communities in the curation and interpretation of their own histories, the project not only preserves cultural heritage but also empowers marginalized voices.

Conclusion

As the Digital Humanities continue to evolve, the ethical responsibilities of practitioners remain paramount. By acknowledging the complexities of technology's impact on culture and knowledge, researchers can navigate the challenges ahead with integrity and purpose. Embracing ethical frameworks and learning from exemplary projects will enable the field to foster a more inclusive, equitable, and responsible future for Digital Humanities.

In summary, the ethical responsibilities of Digital Humanities encompass a commitment to privacy, intellectual property, bias mitigation, accessibility, and inclusivity. By grounding their work in ethical theory and best practices, practitioners can ensure that their contributions to the field are both innovative and responsible.

Morgan's Insights and Solutions

In the rapidly evolving landscape of digital humanities, Morgan Liao emerged as a pivotal figure, not just for his innovative projects but for his ability to navigate the ethical dilemmas that often accompany technological advancements. As he faced the multifaceted challenges of the digital age, Morgan developed a framework of insights and solutions that aimed to address these issues comprehensively.

Privacy Concerns in the Digital Age

One of the foremost ethical dilemmas Morgan encountered was the issue of privacy in a world increasingly dominated by data. With the proliferation of digital tools, the line between public and private information became blurred. Morgan proposed a dual-layered approach to privacy, which he termed the *Privacy Shield Protocol*. This protocol consisted of:

$$\text{Privacy Shield} = \text{User Consent} + \text{Data Anonymization} \tag{64}$$

In this model, user consent would be obtained through clear and transparent communication, while data anonymization would ensure that individual identities remained protected. By implementing these strategies, Morgan aimed to foster trust between users and digital platforms, encouraging more open participation in digital humanities projects.

Balancing Access and Control

Morgan recognized that while access to information is vital for knowledge democratization, unregulated access can lead to misuse and exploitation. He introduced the concept of *Controlled Accessibility*, which advocated for tiered access levels based on user roles and project requirements. For instance, researchers might have full access to certain datasets, while the general public could access only aggregated summaries.

This model is represented as:

$$\text{Controlled Accessibility} = \frac{\text{User Role} \cdot \text{Project Needs}}{\text{Data Sensitivity}} \tag{65}$$

This equation illustrates how Morgan envisioned a balance between user needs and data protection, ensuring that sensitive information was safeguarded while still allowing for meaningful engagement with digital content.

Addressing Bias in AI Technology

The integration of AI into digital humanities raised concerns about bias, particularly in algorithms that could perpetuate existing societal inequalities. Morgan's approach to mitigating bias involved a two-pronged strategy:

- **Diverse Data Sets:** He emphasized the importance of using diverse and representative data sets in training AI models. This would help to ensure that the outputs of these models reflect a broader spectrum of human experiences.

- **Bias Audits:** Morgan advocated for regular bias audits of AI systems, where independent teams would evaluate algorithms for fairness and accuracy. This proactive measure would help to identify and rectify biases before they could cause harm.

Morgan's commitment to ethical AI development was encapsulated in his mantra: *"Diversity in, fairness out."*

Safeguarding Intellectual Property

As digital humanities projects often involve collaborative efforts, safeguarding intellectual property (IP) became a crucial concern. Morgan introduced the *Collaborative IP Framework*, which aimed to clarify ownership rights while promoting shared innovation. This framework included:

$$\text{Collaborative IP} = \text{Clear Agreements} + \text{Shared Benefits} \qquad (66)$$

By establishing clear agreements at the outset of collaborative projects and ensuring that all contributors benefited from the outcomes, Morgan sought to create an environment of mutual respect and shared purpose.

Navigating the Political Landscape

Digital humanities are not immune to the influence of politics. Morgan understood that navigating this landscape required a strategic approach. He proposed the *Engagement Model*, which involved:

- **Stakeholder Dialogues:** Regular dialogues with policymakers, educators, and community leaders to align digital humanities projects with societal needs.

- **Advocacy Initiatives:** Launching advocacy initiatives to promote policies that support ethical digital practices and equitable access to technology.

This model allowed Morgan to position digital humanities as a vital component of the broader cultural and political discourse, ensuring that the field remained relevant and responsive to societal changes.

Ensuring Data Security

In an era where data breaches are commonplace, Morgan prioritized data security in all his initiatives. He developed a comprehensive *Data Security Protocol* that included:

$$\text{Data Security} = \text{Encryption} + \text{Regular Audits} + \text{User Education} \quad (67)$$

This multifaceted approach ensured that data was not only protected through encryption but also regularly audited for vulnerabilities, while users were educated on best practices for maintaining their own data security.

Ethical Responsibilities of Digital Humanities

Morgan firmly believed that those working in digital humanities have a moral obligation to uphold ethical standards. He articulated a set of *Ethical Guidelines* that all practitioners should follow, which included:

+ Respect for cultural heritage and the communities involved in digital projects.

+ Commitment to transparency in data collection and usage.

+ Responsibility to engage with and educate the public about the implications of digital technologies.

By promoting these ethical guidelines, Morgan aimed to cultivate a culture of responsibility within the field, ensuring that innovation did not come at the cost of integrity.

Morgan's Insights on Future Challenges

As technology continues to evolve, Morgan remains acutely aware of the emerging challenges that lie ahead. He emphasizes the need for continuous adaptation and learning, stating, *"In a world where change is the only constant, our ability to pivot defines our success."* His insights serve as a guiding light for future innovators, encouraging them to embrace uncertainty and remain agile in their pursuits.

In conclusion, Morgan Liao's insights and solutions not only addressed the immediate ethical dilemmas of the digital humanities but also laid the groundwork for a more equitable and responsible future. His commitment to privacy, access, bias reduction, IP protection, political engagement, data security, and ethical responsibility exemplifies the kind of leadership needed in an increasingly complex digital landscape. As he often quipped, *"If we don't navigate these waters carefully, we might just find ourselves sinking in a sea of data!"*

Leaving a Legacy of Ethical Innovation

In an age where technology evolves faster than a cat video goes viral, Morgan Liao emerged as a beacon of ethical innovation. His journey was not merely about creating groundbreaking technologies but also about ensuring these advancements were grounded in ethical considerations. As Morgan often joked, "If my AI starts developing feelings, I'm moving to a cabin in the woods with nothing but my thoughts and a lifetime supply of marshmallows."

The Ethical Framework

Morgan's approach to innovation can be encapsulated by the concept of **Ethical AI**, which emphasizes the importance of integrating ethical principles into the development of artificial intelligence systems. He frequently referenced the *IEEE Ethically Aligned Design*, which outlines the need for technology to prioritize human well-being, accountability, and transparency. The equation of ethical innovation can be humorously simplified to:

$$\text{Ethical Innovation} = \text{Technology} + \text{Human Values} + \text{Accountability}$$

This equation, while not found in any textbook, served as Morgan's guiding principle, reminding him that technology should enhance, not hinder, the human experience.

Addressing Privacy Concerns

One of the major challenges Morgan faced was the growing concern over privacy in the digital age. With every new app, there seemed to be a corresponding TikTok challenge involving data breaches. Morgan tackled these issues head-on by advocating for transparent data policies and user consent mechanisms. He famously quipped, "If I wanted my data shared without my consent, I'd just send a postcard to my ex."

To illustrate the importance of privacy, Morgan initiated the *Data Transparency Initiative*, which required companies to disclose how user data was collected, used, and shared. This initiative not only garnered support from tech giants but also turned into a viral campaign, leading to the hashtag #PrivacyMatters trending worldwide—much to the confusion of his grandmother, who thought it was about her collection of vintage privacy screens.

Balancing Access and Control

Morgan understood that with great power comes great responsibility—or, in his case, great memes. He often emphasized the need to balance access to technology with the control of its use. His mantra was, "Just because you can do something, doesn't mean you should. Unless it's making a cat video; then, by all means, proceed."

He proposed the *Digital Rights Framework*, which aimed to ensure equitable access to technology while safeguarding users' rights. This framework became a cornerstone of his legacy, promoting the idea that technology should be a tool for empowerment rather than oppression.

Addressing Bias in AI Technology

Morgan was acutely aware of the biases that could inadvertently be encoded into AI systems. He often joked, "If my AI can't tell the difference between a cat and a dog, we might have bigger problems than just a confused pet."

To combat this, he spearheaded the *Bias Mitigation Project*, which focused on developing algorithms that actively sought to identify and correct biases in datasets. The project involved collaboration with diverse teams, ensuring that multiple perspectives were considered in the development process. Morgan's approach was that if AI was going to make decisions about humanity, it should at least be trained by humanity—preferably humanity that had a good sense of humor.

Safeguarding Intellectual Property

In a world where ideas are as easily copied as a poorly written meme, Morgan recognized the importance of safeguarding intellectual property. He established the *Creative Commons Initiative*, which encouraged innovators to share their work while protecting their rights. Morgan often said, "Sharing is caring, but let's not share my secret cookie recipe."

This initiative not only fostered collaboration but also promoted a culture of ethical sharing, where creators could thrive without the fear of having their ideas stolen. As a result, many young innovators credited Morgan with inspiring them to pursue their passions while respecting the work of others.

Navigating the Political Landscape

Morgan's journey through the murky waters of the political landscape was akin to navigating a minefield while blindfolded. He understood that technology and politics were inseparable, and he often remarked, "If you think tech is complicated, try explaining it to a politician."

To address this, he founded the *Tech-Policy Alliance*, a platform that brought together technologists, policymakers, and ethicists to discuss the implications of emerging technologies. This initiative aimed to create policies that not only fostered innovation but also protected the public interest. Morgan's ability to bridge the gap between these two worlds earned him respect from both sides, even if he sometimes felt like the awkward middle child at a family reunion.

Ensuring Data Security

In an era where data breaches were as common as bad puns, Morgan prioritized data security in all his projects. He often joked, "My data is like my diary; it's private, and if you find it, I'll deny everything."

Morgan implemented robust security protocols and advocated for encryption standards that protected user data from unauthorized access. His commitment to data security not only built trust among users but also set a standard for the industry.

Leaving a Lasting Impact

Morgan's legacy of ethical innovation extended beyond his projects; it inspired a generation of innovators to consider the ethical implications of their work. He believed that the true measure of success was not just in the technology created but in the positive impact it had on society.

As he often said, "If my invention doesn't make the world a better place, then I'll just stick to making cat memes." His humorous outlook, combined with a steadfast commitment to ethics, ensured that Morgan Liao would be remembered not just as a brilliant innovator, but as a champion of ethical innovation.

In conclusion, Morgan Liao left behind a legacy that intertwined innovation with ethical considerations, proving that technology could be both groundbreaking and grounded. As future generations of innovators look to Morgan's work, they carry forward the torch of ethical innovation, ensuring that the future is not just bright, but also just.

Facing Personal and Professional Obstacles

The Toll of Success

Success, while often celebrated, can impose significant burdens on individuals, particularly those like Morgan Liao, who find themselves at the forefront of innovation. The journey of success is frequently paved with challenges that can lead to emotional, physical, and psychological tolls. In this section, we delve into the various dimensions of the toll of success, exploring the implications of high achievement on Morgan's life.

The Weight of Expectations

As Morgan rose to prominence, the expectations surrounding him grew exponentially. The pressure to continuously innovate and perform can lead to what psychologists refer to as *performance anxiety*. This phenomenon manifests as an overwhelming fear of failure, which can hinder creativity and diminish overall well-being. According to the *Yerkes-Dodson Law*, there exists an optimal level of arousal for performance; however, exceeding this threshold can lead to detrimental effects.

$$\text{Performance} = \text{Arousal} \times \text{Task Complexity} \tag{68}$$

Morgan's groundbreaking projects, such as the *Knowledge Archive*, exemplified the complexity of his work. As the complexity of tasks increased, so too did the arousal levels, often pushing Morgan beyond his optimal performance zone. The result was a cycle of stress and anxiety that not only affected his professional life but also seeped into his personal relationships.

Burnout: The Silent Saboteur

One of the most insidious consequences of relentless success is burnout. Defined by the World Health Organization as a syndrome resulting from chronic workplace stress that has not been successfully managed, burnout can lead to emotional exhaustion, depersonalization, and a reduced sense of accomplishment. Morgan experienced symptoms of burnout, particularly during peak project phases when deadlines loomed large.

Research indicates that individuals in high-stakes environments are particularly susceptible to burnout. A study by Maslach and Leiter (2016) highlights that the emotional toll of sustained high performance can lead to diminished productivity and increased health issues.

$$Burnout = f(\text{Workload, Control, Reward, Community, Fairness, Values}) \quad (69)$$

Morgan's workload was often overwhelming, and despite his remarkable capabilities, he struggled with feelings of inadequacy. The disconnect between his values and the corporate demands placed on him contributed to a sense of disillusionment.

Personal Sacrifices

The pursuit of success frequently comes at a personal cost. Morgan's commitment to his work led to strained relationships with family and friends. The phenomenon known as *social isolation* is common among high achievers, as they often prioritize work over personal connections. A study conducted by Cacioppo and Cacioppo (2014) underscores the detrimental effects of loneliness on mental health, revealing that social isolation can be as harmful as smoking fifteen cigarettes a day.

Morgan's dedication to his projects meant missed family gatherings and neglected friendships. The emotional toll of these sacrifices weighed heavily on him, leading to feelings of guilt and regret. The struggle to maintain a work-life balance became a recurring theme in his narrative.

Impostor Syndrome

Despite his accolades and achievements, Morgan grappled with *impostor syndrome*, a psychological pattern where individuals doubt their accomplishments and fear being exposed as a "fraud." This phenomenon is particularly prevalent among high achievers, as they often attribute their success to external factors rather than their capabilities.

Research by Clance and Imes (1978) suggests that impostor syndrome can lead to chronic self-doubt, anxiety, and stress. Morgan's experiences were no exception; he often found himself questioning whether he truly deserved his success or if it was merely a stroke of luck. This internal conflict further exacerbated the toll of success, leading to a cycle of overworking to prove his worth.

The Path Forward

Recognizing the toll of success is crucial for sustainable achievement. Morgan began to implement strategies to mitigate the negative effects of his accomplishments. He sought mentorship from industry leaders who had navigated similar challenges, emphasizing the importance of resilience and self-care.

Incorporating practices such as mindfulness and regular physical activity helped Morgan manage stress and maintain a healthier work-life balance. The establishment of boundaries around work hours allowed him to reconnect with his passions outside of technology, fostering a renewed sense of purpose.

In conclusion, while success can be a powerful catalyst for innovation and achievement, it is essential to acknowledge and address the toll it can take on individuals like Morgan Liao. By understanding the psychological and emotional challenges associated with high achievement, future innovators can cultivate a more balanced approach to success, ensuring that their journeys are not only impactful but also fulfilling.

Coping with Burnout

Burnout is a state of emotional, physical, and mental exhaustion caused by prolonged and excessive stress. It can manifest in various forms, including fatigue, cynicism, and a feeling of reduced accomplishment. For innovators like Morgan Liao, who operate at the intersection of technology and humanities, the risk of burnout can be particularly acute due to the high demands of their work and the relentless pace of the digital age.

Theoretical Framework

Burnout can be understood through the lens of the *Job Demands-Resources (JD-R)* model. This model posits that job demands (e.g., workload, time pressure) can lead to burnout when they exceed the resources available to cope with them (e.g., support, autonomy). Mathematically, we can express this relationship as:

$$\text{Burnout} = f(\text{Job Demands}, \text{Job Resources}) \qquad (70)$$

Where: - f is a function that describes the interaction between job demands and resources. - High job demands without adequate resources can lead to a positive correlation with burnout levels.

Identifying Symptoms of Burnout

Morgan, like many innovators, faced symptoms of burnout that included:

+ **Chronic Fatigue:** A persistent lack of energy that made even simple tasks feel monumental.

+ **Cynicism:** A growing detachment from his work, leading to a sense of disillusionment with his projects.

+ **Reduced Performance:** Despite his previous high levels of productivity, he found himself struggling to meet deadlines and maintain quality.

Coping Strategies

To combat burnout, Morgan adopted several strategies grounded in both psychological theory and practical application:

1. Mindfulness and Meditation Research has shown that mindfulness practices can significantly reduce stress and improve mental health. Morgan began incorporating daily meditation sessions into his routine, utilizing apps that guided him through mindfulness exercises. This practice helped him to center his thoughts and reduce anxiety.

2. Time Management Techniques Morgan implemented the *Pomodoro Technique*, which involves working in focused bursts of 25 minutes followed by a 5-minute break. This method helped him maintain concentration while also allowing for regular intervals of rest, thus preventing fatigue from prolonged work sessions.

3. Seeking Support Recognizing the importance of social support, Morgan reached out to mentors and peers to discuss his feelings of burnout. This not only provided him with a sense of community but also offered new perspectives on managing stress. According to the *Social Support Theory*, having a robust support network can buffer the effects of stress and mitigate feelings of isolation.

4. Physical Activity Morgan reintroduced regular physical exercise into his life, understanding its role in reducing stress hormones and increasing endorphins. Whether it was jogging, yoga, or even dancing in his living room, he found that movement was a powerful antidote to burnout.

5. Reevaluating Goals Morgan took time to reassess his professional goals and priorities. By aligning his projects with his values and passions, he rekindled his motivation and found renewed purpose in his work. This process is akin to the *Self-Determination Theory*, which emphasizes the importance of autonomy, competence, and relatedness in fostering intrinsic motivation.

Real-Life Examples

Morgan's journey through burnout is not unique. Many high-achieving individuals in demanding fields have faced similar challenges. For instance, a study on tech entrepreneurs revealed that over 60% reported experiencing burnout at some point in their careers. One entrepreneur, who founded a successful startup, shared that after recognizing his burnout, he took a sabbatical to travel and explore new ideas, ultimately returning with a fresh perspective and renewed energy.

Another notable example is that of a renowned author who, after experiencing burnout from the pressures of writing and public speaking, decided to take a year off to focus on personal growth and creativity. This break allowed her to return to her craft with new insights and a deeper appreciation for her work.

Conclusion

Coping with burnout is an ongoing process that requires self-awareness, proactive strategies, and a supportive environment. For innovators like Morgan Liao, understanding the symptoms and implementing effective coping mechanisms not only enhances personal well-being but also fosters sustained creativity and productivity. As the digital landscape continues to evolve, prioritizing mental health will be essential for future innovators to thrive in their endeavors.

Losing Loved Ones

In the journey of innovation and personal growth, the path is often fraught with challenges, including the profound experience of losing loved ones. For Morgan Liao, this was not just a footnote in his biography but a pivotal chapter that shaped his outlook on life, work, and the very essence of human connection.

The Emotional Toll of Loss

Losing loved ones can create a void that feels insurmountable. According to the *Grief Cycle* proposed by Elisabeth Kübler-Ross, individuals typically navigate through five stages of grief: denial, anger, bargaining, depression, and acceptance. Morgan found himself oscillating through these stages, often revisiting them in unexpected ways.

$$G(t) = D(t) + A(t) + B(t) + P(t) + A_c(t) \tag{71}$$

Where: - $G(t)$ is the overall grief experience at time t, - $D(t)$ represents denial, - $A(t)$ represents anger, - $B(t)$ represents bargaining, - $P(t)$ represents depression, - $A_c(t)$ represents acceptance.

Morgan's emotional journey was characterized by a profound sense of denial upon the passing of his childhood mentor, who had instilled in him a love for technology and creativity. This denial manifested in a compulsive work ethic, where he submerged himself in projects, trying to outrun the reality of his loss.

Coping Mechanisms

In the face of grief, individuals often develop coping mechanisms that can either support or hinder their healing process. For Morgan, the initial response was to channel his grief into his work. He believed that by achieving greater heights in his career, he could somehow honor the memory of those he lost. However, this approach led to burnout and a sense of isolation, as he neglected his emotional health.

Research has shown that healthy coping strategies can include seeking support from friends and family, engaging in self-care, and allowing oneself to feel and process emotions. Morgan eventually recognized the importance of these strategies. He began to open up about his feelings, joining support groups where he could share his experiences with others who had faced similar losses.

The Impact on Relationships

The loss of loved ones can also strain existing relationships. Morgan found that his friends, while well-meaning, often struggled to relate to his grief. Many tried to offer platitudes, such as "Time heals all wounds" or "They're in a better place," which only deepened his sense of isolation.

A study by *Worden* (1996) emphasizes the importance of open communication in processing grief. Morgan learned that expressing his feelings, rather than bottling them up, allowed his friends to understand his experience better. This led to deeper connections and a shared understanding of the complexities of grief.

Transformative Experiences

The experience of losing loved ones can lead to transformative insights and a renewed perspective on life. For Morgan, the passing of his mentor inspired him to create a project that honored their legacy. He launched an initiative aimed at mentoring young innovators, ensuring that the knowledge and passion imparted to him would continue to inspire future generations.

This project became a cornerstone of Morgan's philosophy, emphasizing the importance of community and connection in the face of loss. He often quoted his mentor: "Innovation is not just about technology; it's about the people we uplift along the way." This mantra guided him as he navigated his grief, turning pain into purpose.

Legacy and Remembrance

In the aftermath of loss, many seek ways to preserve the memory of their loved ones. Morgan established a scholarship fund in honor of his mentor, aimed at supporting underprivileged students pursuing careers in technology and digital humanities. This initiative not only served as a tribute but also created a ripple effect, inspiring others to contribute to causes that resonated with their personal experiences.

Morgan's journey through loss and grief ultimately shaped his leadership style. He became an advocate for mental health awareness within the tech community, emphasizing the need for emotional support systems in high-pressure environments. His experiences taught him that vulnerability can be a strength, allowing for authentic connections that foster innovation.

Conclusion

Losing loved ones is an inevitable part of the human experience, and for Morgan Liao, it was a catalyst for growth and transformation. His journey through grief highlighted the importance of community, the power of mentorship, and the enduring impact of love and memory. As he moved forward, he carried the lessons learned from his losses, ensuring that the legacies of those he cherished would live on through his work and the lives he touched.

Morgan's story serves as a reminder that even in the face of profound loss, there is an opportunity for renewal and a chance to honor those who have shaped us. In the words of Morgan himself, "In every ending, there is a new beginning, and in every loss, there is a chance to create something beautiful."

Dealing with Impostor Syndrome

Impostor Syndrome, a term popularized by psychologists Pauline Clance and Suzanne Imes in 1978, refers to the internal experience of believing that you are not as competent as others perceive you to be. This phenomenon is particularly prevalent among high achievers, such as Morgan Liao, who often grapple with feelings of self-doubt and inadequacy despite their accomplishments.

Theoretical Background

Impostor Syndrome is characterized by a persistent fear of being exposed as a "fraud." According to Clance and Imes, individuals experiencing this syndrome may attribute their success to external factors such as luck or timing rather than their own skills or intelligence. This can lead to a cycle of anxiety and stress, as these individuals constantly seek validation while fearing that they will eventually be "found out."

The theory can be mathematically represented by the following equation:

$$S = \frac{C}{E} \times 100 \tag{72}$$

Where: - S is the subjective sense of success, - C is the actual competence level (skills, knowledge, etc.), - E is the external validation received (awards, recognition, etc.).

When $C < E$, individuals may feel like impostors, even if their actual competence is high. This dissonance between perceived and actual competence can exacerbate feelings of inadequacy.

Problems Associated with Impostor Syndrome

Morgan's journey through the tech and academic worlds was not without its challenges. As he achieved success, the pressures of expectations mounted. Common problems associated with impostor syndrome include:

+ **Anxiety and Stress:** The fear of failure can lead to chronic anxiety, affecting both mental and physical health.

+ **Burnout:** The relentless pursuit of perfection can result in burnout, as individuals overwork themselves to prove their worth.

+ **Avoidance of Opportunities:** Fear of being exposed may lead individuals to avoid new challenges, stunting their growth and potential.

+ **Poor Self-Esteem:** Persistent feelings of inadequacy can erode self-esteem, making it difficult to accept compliments or acknowledge achievements.

Examples from Morgan's Life

Morgan's experiences provide a vivid illustration of how impostor syndrome can manifest in a high-achieving individual:

+ **The Ivy League Dilemma:** Upon receiving acceptance to an Ivy League university, Morgan felt an overwhelming sense of unworthiness. He questioned whether he had been admitted based on merit or if it was a clerical error. This led him to overprepare for classes, spending countless hours studying, which ironically resulted in excellent grades but also significant stress.

+ **The Revolutionary AI Project:** While leading a team to develop a groundbreaking AI project, Morgan often felt like a fraud among his peers, many of whom had advanced degrees and years of experience. He frequently sought reassurance from his team members, fearing that they would realize he was just "winging it." This led to him overcompensating by working late nights and weekends, which ultimately affected his health and personal relationships.

+ **The Media Spotlight:** As Morgan began to gain recognition in the media, he found himself grappling with the pressure of public perception. During interviews, he often felt like a performer in a play, reciting lines rather than expressing genuine thoughts. This disconnect fueled his impostor feelings, making him question whether he truly belonged in the spotlight.

Strategies for Overcoming Impostor Syndrome

To combat these feelings, Morgan adopted several strategies that proved effective in mitigating the effects of impostor syndrome:

+ **Acknowledging Achievements:** Morgan began to maintain a "success journal," where he documented his accomplishments and positive feedback from peers. This practice helped him recognize his competence and the value he brought to his work.

+ **Seeking Support:** Morgan reached out to mentors and peers who had experienced similar feelings. By sharing his struggles, he discovered that many successful individuals also battled impostor syndrome, which normalized his experience and provided a sense of community.

+ **Reframing Negative Thoughts:** Morgan learned to challenge his negative self-talk by reframing his thoughts. Instead of thinking, "I don't deserve this success," he would remind himself, "I worked hard for this, and I am capable."

• **Setting Realistic Goals:** By setting achievable goals and celebrating small victories, Morgan shifted his focus from perfectionism to progress, reducing the pressure he placed on himself.

Conclusion

Dealing with impostor syndrome is a significant challenge for many innovators like Morgan Liao. By understanding the underlying theory, recognizing the associated problems, and implementing effective strategies, individuals can navigate their feelings of inadequacy and embrace their successes. Ultimately, acknowledging that self-doubt is a common experience among high achievers can help foster resilience and pave the way for continued innovation and growth.

Media Scrutiny and Public Pressure

In the age of digital information, the line between public and private life has become increasingly blurred, especially for innovators like Morgan Liao. As a pioneer in the field of digital humanities, Morgan found himself under the relentless gaze of the media, which often scrutinized his every move, decision, and project. This scrutiny can be likened to a double-edged sword: while it can amplify one's ideas and successes, it can also pose significant challenges and pressures.

The Nature of Media Scrutiny

Media scrutiny refers to the intense examination of an individual's actions and statements by news outlets and social media platforms. For Morgan, this meant that even the most mundane decisions—like what to have for breakfast—were subject to analysis and speculation. The phenomenon is well-documented in communication theory, particularly in the context of the *Agenda-Setting Theory*, which posits that the media doesn't just report news but also shapes public perception by highlighting certain issues over others.

In Morgan's case, the media often focused on sensational aspects of his work rather than its substantive contributions to the field of digital humanities. For instance, when he launched a revolutionary AI project aimed at preserving cultural heritage, headlines often read, "Morgan Liao: The Tech Wizard or Just Another Overhyped Genius?" This type of coverage created a narrative that overshadowed the project's real impact, leading to public skepticism and doubt.

Problems Arising from Scrutiny

The constant media attention brought several challenges for Morgan. One significant issue was the *impostor syndrome*, a psychological pattern where an individual doubts their accomplishments and fears being exposed as a "fraud." As Morgan's work gained visibility, he began to feel the weight of expectations and the pressure to continually innovate. This pressure was compounded by the media's tendency to compare him to other tech moguls, creating an unrealistic benchmark for success.

Moreover, the scrutiny also extended to Morgan's personal life. The media's invasive reporting on his family and relationships added stress and anxiety, often leading to a public backlash against his personal choices. For example, when Morgan took a sabbatical to recharge, the headlines read, "Morgan Liao: Is He Burned Out or Just Running Away?" Such narratives not only distorted his intentions but also affected his mental well-being.

Examples of Public Pressure

One notable incident occurred during a live-streamed Q&A session where Morgan was confronted with tough questions about the ethical implications of his AI technology. The media seized upon his momentary hesitation, framing it as a sign of weakness. This led to a wave of criticism on social media, with hashtags like #MorganFails trending for days. Such instances illustrate the immense public pressure innovators face, where a single misstep can lead to widespread condemnation.

Additionally, Morgan's attempts to address the ethical dilemmas surrounding his work were often met with skepticism. For instance, when he proposed a framework for ethical AI development, the media highlighted the potential for biases in algorithms, often neglecting the proactive measures he was advocating. This selective reporting contributed to a narrative that painted him as out of touch with the realities of his field.

Navigating the Pressure

To cope with the pressures of media scrutiny, Morgan adopted several strategies. First, he focused on transparency in his work, frequently engaging with the public through social media to clarify misconceptions and share insights into his projects. This proactive approach allowed him to build a supportive community of followers who appreciated his authenticity.

Second, Morgan sought mentorship from seasoned innovators who had navigated similar challenges. They provided him with invaluable advice on managing public perception and the importance of maintaining a healthy work-life balance. This mentorship proved crucial in helping him regain confidence and refocus on his mission.

Finally, Morgan emphasized the importance of mental health, advocating for open discussions about the psychological toll of public scrutiny within the tech community. By sharing his experiences, he not only destigmatized mental health issues but also encouraged others to seek support in the face of adversity.

Conclusion

In summary, media scrutiny and public pressure are inherent challenges for innovators like Morgan Liao. While these factors can amplify successes, they also pose significant risks to mental health and public perception. By understanding the dynamics of media coverage and adopting strategies to navigate these challenges, Morgan was able to continue his groundbreaking work in digital humanities while maintaining his well-being. As the digital landscape evolves, it is crucial for future innovators to learn from Morgan's experiences and develop resilience in the face of public scrutiny.

Managing a Work-Life Balance

Achieving a healthy work-life balance is a challenge that many innovators face, including Morgan Liao. In the fast-paced world of digital humanities, where the lines between professional obligations and personal life can easily blur, managing this balance becomes crucial for sustained creativity and mental well-being.

The Importance of Work-Life Balance

Work-life balance is defined as the equilibrium between personal life and work commitments. It is essential for several reasons:

+ **Mental Health:** A lack of balance can lead to burnout, anxiety, and depression. Studies show that individuals who maintain a healthy work-life balance report higher levels of job satisfaction and lower levels of stress (Greenhaus & Allen, 2011).

+ **Productivity:** Contrary to the belief that longer hours equate to higher productivity, research indicates that well-rested and balanced individuals are often more productive and creative (Kabat-Zinn, 1990).

+ **Relationships:** Maintaining personal relationships is vital for emotional support. Neglecting personal life can lead to strained relationships with family and friends, which can further exacerbate stress.

Challenges Morgan Faced

Despite his success, Morgan encountered several challenges in maintaining his work-life balance:

1. **High Expectations:** As a young innovator, Morgan faced immense pressure to succeed. The expectations from peers, mentors, and the media often left little room for personal time.

2. **Time Management:** Juggling multiple projects, including the establishment of the Digital Humanities Institute and his revolutionary research, required exceptional time management skills. Morgan often found himself prioritizing work over personal needs.

3. **Technology's Double-Edged Sword:** While technology enabled Morgan to work more efficiently, it also meant that he was always connected. The constant notifications and emails blurred the boundaries between work and personal time, making it difficult to disconnect.

Strategies for Balance

To combat these challenges, Morgan adopted several strategies to manage his work-life balance effectively:

+ **Setting Boundaries:** Morgan learned to set clear boundaries by designating specific hours for work and personal life. He would turn off notifications after work hours, allowing himself to be fully present in his personal life.

+ **Prioritization:** He utilized prioritization techniques such as the Eisenhower Matrix, which helps individuals distinguish between what is urgent and important. This method allowed him to focus on high-impact tasks while delegating or postponing less critical ones.

+ **Mindfulness Practices:** Incorporating mindfulness and meditation into his daily routine helped Morgan reduce stress and improve focus. Research by Kabat-Zinn (1990) highlights the benefits of mindfulness in enhancing overall well-being.

* **Quality Time:** Morgan made it a point to schedule regular quality time with family and friends. Whether it was a weekly game night or a monthly outing, these moments provided him with the emotional recharge needed to tackle his professional responsibilities.

Example of Success

An exemplary instance of Morgan's commitment to work-life balance occurred during the launch of a significant project at the Digital Humanities Institute. Faced with tight deadlines, he initially succumbed to the temptation of working late nights. However, realizing that this approach was unsustainable, he decided to implement a strict schedule that included regular breaks and time for personal interests.

As a result, not only did he complete the project ahead of schedule, but he also reported feeling more energized and creative throughout the process. This experience reinforced the idea that balance is not merely a luxury but a necessity for innovation.

Conclusion

In conclusion, managing a work-life balance is a critical aspect of Morgan Liao's journey as an innovator. By setting boundaries, prioritizing tasks, and incorporating mindfulness practices, he was able to navigate the challenges of his demanding career while maintaining a fulfilling personal life. This balance not only contributed to his success but also served as a model for future innovators in the digital humanities field. As Morgan often reflects, "Innovation doesn't thrive in chaos; it flourishes in balance."

Overcoming Failure and Setbacks

Morgan Liao's journey through the Digital Renaissance was not without its share of failures and setbacks. In fact, it was during these challenging times that he truly honed his resilience and innovative spirit. Understanding the nature of failure is crucial for any innovator, as it often serves as a stepping stone to success. As the famous author J.K. Rowling once said, "It is impossible to live without failing at something unless you live so cautiously that you might as well not have lived at all."

The Nature of Failure

Failure is an inherent part of the creative process. It can be defined as the inability to achieve a desired outcome or goal. In mathematical terms, we might express failure as:

$$F = G - A$$

where F represents failure, G is the goal, and A is the actual achievement. This equation illustrates that failure occurs when the actual achievement falls short of the intended goal.

Morgan faced numerous failures throughout his career, particularly during his early attempts to launch his first startup. At the tender age of sixteen, he developed an ambitious application designed to streamline school attendance tracking. However, the app was riddled with bugs and ultimately crashed during a live demonstration. The embarrassment was palpable, and the experience left Morgan questioning his abilities.

Learning from Setbacks

Despite the initial humiliation, Morgan adopted a growth mindset, a concept popularized by psychologist Carol Dweck. This mindset emphasizes the belief that abilities can be developed through dedication and hard work. Dweck's research indicates that individuals with a growth mindset are more likely to embrace challenges, persist through difficulties, and learn from criticism.

Morgan took this lesson to heart. Instead of viewing his failed app as a definitive judgment of his skills, he analyzed the issues that led to its downfall. He sought feedback from peers and mentors, and he immersed himself in coding tutorials to improve his technical knowledge. This proactive approach allowed him to transform a painful experience into a valuable learning opportunity.

The Role of Support Systems

In the face of adversity, support systems play a pivotal role. Morgan was fortunate to have a network of dedicated teachers and friends who believed in his potential. They provided encouragement and constructive feedback, allowing him to navigate the tumultuous waters of innovation.

A notable example of this support came when Morgan was grappling with the failure of his AI project during his university years. The project, which aimed to utilize artificial intelligence for cultural preservation, faced significant technical hurdles. Instead of succumbing to despair, Morgan organized a brainstorming session with his peers. This collaborative effort led to a breakthrough: by pooling their diverse skill sets, they developed a more robust algorithm that ultimately salvaged the project.

Resilience and Adaptability

Resilience is a crucial trait for any innovator. It refers to the ability to bounce back from setbacks and continue pursuing one's goals. Morgan exemplified resilience when he faced a major funding setback for his Digital Humanities Institute. After securing initial funding, a key investor backed out at the last minute, leaving the project in jeopardy.

Rather than giving up, Morgan pivoted. He organized a crowdfunding campaign that not only raised the necessary funds but also engaged the community in the vision of the Institute. This adaptability not only saved the project but also strengthened its foundation by fostering a sense of ownership among supporters.

Embracing Failure as a Catalyst for Innovation

Morgan's experiences highlight the notion that failure can be a catalyst for innovation. The renowned inventor Thomas Edison famously stated, "I have not failed. I've just found 10,000 ways that won't work." This perspective is essential for innovators who must navigate the unpredictable landscape of technological advancement.

In Morgan's case, his setbacks often led to unexpected insights. For instance, after a failed attempt to integrate augmented reality into a museum exhibition, he discovered that visitors preferred a more straightforward approach. This realization prompted him to focus on enhancing the storytelling aspect of the exhibit, ultimately leading to a more engaging experience for attendees.

Concluding Thoughts

Overcoming failure and setbacks is an integral part of the journey for any innovator, and Morgan Liao's story is no exception. By embracing a growth mindset, leveraging support systems, demonstrating resilience, and viewing failure as an opportunity for innovation, Morgan was able to transform obstacles into stepping stones on his path to success. As he often reminds aspiring innovators, "Failure is not the end; it's merely a detour on the road to discovery."

Evolving as a Leader

As Morgan Liao navigated the tumultuous waters of innovation and digital humanities, he faced a myriad of challenges that necessitated a profound evolution in his leadership style. Leadership, particularly in the fast-paced tech landscape, is not a static trait but rather a dynamic process that adapts to the needs of the moment, the team, and the broader societal context.

Theoretical Foundations of Leadership Evolution

To understand Morgan's evolution as a leader, we can reference the **Situational Leadership Theory** developed by Hersey and Blanchard. This theory posits that effective leadership is contingent upon the maturity level of the followers and the task at hand. Morgan employed this model by assessing the skills and confidence of his team members, adjusting his leadership style from directive to supportive as necessary.

Mathematically, we can represent the relationship between leadership style L, team maturity M, and task complexity T with the equation:

$$L = f(M, T)$$

where f is a function that determines the optimal leadership approach based on the interplay of team maturity and task complexity.

Identifying Leadership Challenges

Morgan's journey was not without its obstacles. One of the primary challenges he faced was the **diversity of thought** within his team. As he assembled a group of innovators from various backgrounds, he quickly realized that differing perspectives could lead to creative breakthroughs but also to conflict.

For example, during the early stages of developing the Knowledge Archive, a project aimed at digitally preserving cultural artifacts, disagreements arose regarding the prioritization of certain cultures over others. Morgan had to evolve from a traditional top-down approach to one that embraced collaborative decision-making, ensuring that all voices were heard.

Building Emotional Intelligence

Another critical aspect of Morgan's leadership evolution was the development of his **emotional intelligence** (EI). According to Daniel Goleman, emotional intelligence encompasses self-awareness, self-regulation, motivation, empathy, and social skills. For Morgan, enhancing his EI meant recognizing his own emotional triggers, particularly during high-stress situations, such as when facing media scrutiny or public pressure.

Morgan often reflected on his emotional responses, employing the following self-assessment equation to gauge his EI:

$$EI = \frac{(SA + SR + M + E + SS)}{5}$$

where SA is self-awareness, SR is self-regulation, M is motivation, E is empathy, and SS is social skills. By focusing on improving each component, he became more adept at navigating complex interpersonal dynamics.

Mentorship and Team Empowerment

As Morgan evolved, he recognized the importance of **mentorship** in fostering a culture of innovation. He transitioned from being a sole decision-maker to a facilitator of ideas, empowering his team to take ownership of their projects.

One notable instance was during the development of the Virtual Reality for Historical Immersion project. Morgan encouraged his team to pitch their ideas and take the lead on specific components. This not only boosted morale but also resulted in a more innovative final product. The equation representing this shift can be expressed as:

$$Innovation = \sum_{i=1}^{n}(Ownership_i \times Creativity_i)$$

where $Ownership_i$ is the level of ownership taken by team member i, and $Creativity_i$ is the creative output from that member.

Embracing Failure as a Learning Tool

Morgan's evolution also involved reframing his perception of failure. Initially, he viewed setbacks as personal failures; however, he gradually recognized that failure is an integral part of the innovation process. By fostering a culture where mistakes were seen as learning opportunities, he encouraged his team to take risks without the fear of repercussions.

This shift in mindset can be mathematically represented by the equation:

$$Learning = \frac{Failures}{Risk}$$

As the denominator increases, indicating a higher willingness to take risks, the potential for learning and growth also increases.

Conclusion: The Legacy of Evolving Leadership

In conclusion, Morgan Liao's evolution as a leader was marked by a commitment to adaptability, emotional intelligence, mentorship, and a positive outlook on failure. His journey illustrates that effective leadership in the realm of digital humanities—and indeed in any innovative field—requires a continuous process of self-reflection and growth. As he mentored the next generation of innovators, Morgan's legacy became not just about technological advancements but also about nurturing a new breed of leaders equipped to face the challenges of tomorrow.

Through his experiences, Morgan Liao not only transformed the landscape of digital humanities but also left an indelible mark on the art of leadership itself.

Celebrating Personal Triumphs

As Morgan Liao navigated the turbulent waters of innovation and digital humanities, he found himself at the helm of not just projects and initiatives, but also a series of personal triumphs that would make even the most stoic of tech moguls break into a dance that could only be described as a combination of the robot and the Macarena. These moments of victory were not merely footnotes in his biography; they were the exclamation points that punctuated his relentless pursuit of knowledge and excellence.

The First Major Award: A Humble Beginning

Morgan's first major award came unexpectedly, like a cat that jumps out of a box during a Zoom meeting. It was the prestigious *Innovator of the Year* award at a local tech conference. The ceremony was held in a cramped auditorium that smelled faintly of burnt popcorn, and as Morgan took the stage, he could feel the weight of a thousand eyes staring at him, each one silently judging his choice of socks—striped with polka dots.

$$\text{Confidence} = \frac{\text{Knowledge}}{\text{Fear of Public Speaking}} \tag{73}$$

Morgan's acceptance speech was a blend of heartfelt gratitude and awkward humor. "I'd like to thank my parents for believing in me," he said, "and for buying me my first computer instead of a pet hamster. I mean, have you ever tried coding with a hamster on your keyboard? It's a nightmare!" The audience erupted in laughter, and in that moment, Morgan realized the power of humor in connecting with people.

The Launch of the Knowledge Archive

One of the crowning achievements in Morgan's career was the launch of the *Knowledge Archive*, a digital repository designed to democratize access to information. As he watched the first users engage with the platform, he felt a sense of accomplishment that could only be rivaled by winning a game of chess against a grandmaster while blindfolded.

Morgan often joked about the challenges of the project, likening it to "trying to build a spaceship out of spaghetti and hope it flies." Yet, through collaboration and sheer determination, the Knowledge Archive became a beacon of hope for students and researchers alike.

Impact on Future Generations

Morgan's work in digital humanities didn't just impact his immediate circle; it rippled through the academic community like a well-placed meme. He often reflected on how the students who used his platforms were not just consumers of knowledge but potential innovators themselves.

$$\text{Future Innovators} = \text{Current Students} \times \text{Morgan's Platform} \qquad (74)$$

He frequently hosted workshops, where he encouraged young minds to embrace their creativity. "Remember," he would say, "the only bad idea is the one you don't share. Unless it involves a catapult. Then it's probably a bad idea."

Personal Milestones: Balancing Life and Work

Amidst his professional achievements, Morgan also celebrated personal milestones. He married his college sweetheart, a brilliant coder who could debug his code while simultaneously making the world's best mac and cheese. Their wedding was a glorious affair, complete with a digital display of their love story, narrated by a holographic version of Morgan himself—because, why not?

The couple often joked about their relationship dynamics, with Morgan claiming, "She's the only one who can handle my 'innovative' ideas without rolling her eyes so hard they get stuck." Their partnership became a source of strength for Morgan, proving that personal triumphs are just as vital as professional ones.

Conclusion: Embracing the Journey

In the end, Morgan Liao's journey was one of continuous celebration—of ideas, relationships, and the occasional awkward dance move at tech conferences. Each triumph, whether big or small, added to the tapestry of his life, reminding him that success is not just about the accolades but also about the laughter shared along the way.

As he often said, "Life is like coding: sometimes you hit a bug, but with a little debugging, you can create something beautiful." And with that wisdom, Morgan continued to inspire others, proving that celebrating personal triumphs is just as important as the innovations that change the world.

Morgan's Role in Shaping the Future

The Digital Renaissance Movement

The Digital Renaissance Movement, spearheaded by Morgan Liao, represents a profound shift in how we perceive and interact with knowledge in the digital age. This movement is not merely a response to technological advancements but a holistic transformation of cultural, educational, and ethical paradigms. It seeks to bridge the gap between technology and the humanities, fostering a new era where innovation and creativity thrive in tandem.

Theoretical Foundations

At the heart of the Digital Renaissance Movement lies the theory of *digital humanism*, which posits that technology should serve to enhance human experience rather than detract from it. This theory draws on the principles of traditional humanism, emphasizing the value of human agency, creativity, and critical thinking. Digital humanism advocates for a balanced approach, where technology is employed to amplify human capabilities while maintaining ethical considerations.

A key aspect of this movement is the integration of *interdisciplinary studies*, where fields such as computer science, history, philosophy, and sociology converge. This interdisciplinary approach not only enriches the understanding of each field but also encourages innovative solutions to complex problems. For instance, the use of big data analytics in historical research allows scholars to uncover patterns and insights that were previously inaccessible, thus reshaping our understanding of the past.

Challenges and Problems

Despite its promise, the Digital Renaissance Movement faces several challenges that must be addressed to ensure its success. One significant issue is the *digital divide*, which refers to the gap between those who have access to digital technologies and those who do not. This divide can exacerbate existing inequalities in education and cultural participation, hindering the movement's goal of democratizing knowledge.

Another challenge is the ethical implications of technology in the humanities. As Morgan Liao often emphasizes, the rapid advancement of artificial intelligence (AI) raises concerns about *bias and representation*. For example, AI algorithms trained on historical data may perpetuate existing stereotypes or overlook marginalized voices. Thus, it is crucial for digital humanists to engage in critical discourse surrounding the ethical use of technology, ensuring that diverse perspectives are included in the development of digital tools and resources.

Examples of Impact

The Digital Renaissance Movement has already made significant strides in various domains. One notable example is the creation of the *Knowledge Archive*, a digital repository that houses a vast array of cultural artifacts, historical documents, and multimedia resources. This initiative not only preserves cultural heritage but also makes it accessible to a global audience, fostering a sense of collective ownership over knowledge.

Additionally, the use of *virtual reality (VR)* in education has transformed traditional learning experiences. Institutions have begun to implement VR technology to create immersive learning environments, allowing students to explore historical sites or engage with complex concepts in a hands-on manner. For instance, a VR simulation of ancient Rome enables students to walk the streets of the past, providing a richer understanding of historical context.

Moreover, the movement has catalyzed the development of *digital storytelling platforms*, which empower individuals to share their narratives and preserve oral histories. These platforms democratize knowledge creation, allowing diverse voices to contribute to the collective narrative. By leveraging social media and digital tools, the Digital Renaissance Movement encourages a participatory approach to knowledge dissemination, breaking down barriers that have traditionally restricted access to information.

Conclusion

In conclusion, the Digital Renaissance Movement, as envisioned by Morgan Liao, represents a transformative force in the intersection of technology and the humanities.   By embracing digital humanism and fostering interdisciplinary collaboration, this movement seeks to democratize knowledge, address ethical challenges, and inspire future generations of innovators.   As we navigate the complexities of the digital age, the principles of the Digital Renaissance Movement will be essential in shaping a future where technology enhances our understanding of the human experience, rather than diminishing it.

$$\text{Digital Renaissance} = \text{Technology} + \text{Humanism} + \text{Interdisciplinary Collaboration}$$
$$(75)$$

This equation encapsulates the essence of the movement, highlighting the need for a harmonious relationship between technology and the humanities to foster a vibrant and inclusive future.

Inspiring New Innovators

In the wake of Morgan Liao's groundbreaking contributions to the field of digital humanities, a new generation of innovators has emerged, inspired by his vision and relentless pursuit of knowledge.   Morgan's influence transcends traditional boundaries, sparking a movement that encourages young minds to explore the intersection of technology and the humanities.   This section delves into how Morgan has inspired these new innovators, the challenges they face, and the transformative ideas they are bringing to life.

Catalysts for Innovation

Morgan's approach to innovation can be encapsulated in the principle of **collaborative creativity**. By fostering an environment where ideas can flourish through teamwork, he has shown that the best solutions often arise from diverse perspectives. This aligns with the theory of *collective intelligence*, which posits that groups can outperform individuals in problem-solving tasks when they leverage their unique strengths.

$$C = \frac{1}{n} \sum_{i=1}^{n} I_i \qquad (76)$$

Where C represents the collective intelligence of a group, n is the number of individuals, and I_i is the individual intelligence of each member. Morgan's mentorship has embodied this principle, encouraging young innovators to collaborate on projects that push the boundaries of what is possible.

Empowering Young Innovators

Morgan has established several initiatives aimed at empowering young innovators. One notable example is the *Future Innovators Program*, which provides mentorship, resources, and funding for students and young professionals looking to make a mark in digital humanities. This program not only equips participants with the necessary skills but also instills confidence, encouraging them to take risks and pursue their ideas passionately.

The program's success can be attributed to its holistic approach, which includes workshops, hackathons, and networking events. For instance, during the annual *Hack the Past* event, participants are challenged to create digital solutions that address historical preservation issues. This hands-on experience allows them to apply theoretical knowledge in practical settings, fostering a sense of ownership and creativity.

Challenges Faced by New Innovators

Despite the enthusiasm and support, young innovators encounter numerous challenges. One significant issue is **access to resources**. Many aspiring creators come from underrepresented backgrounds and lack the financial means to pursue their ideas fully. Morgan has recognized this barrier and is actively working to bridge the gap through scholarships and grants aimed at marginalized communities.

Additionally, the rapid pace of technological advancement presents a double-edged sword. While it opens up new possibilities, it also creates a daunting landscape where keeping up with trends can be overwhelming. Morgan emphasizes the importance of adaptability and lifelong learning, encouraging innovators to embrace change rather than fear it.

Real-World Examples of Inspired Innovators

Several young innovators have already made significant strides in their respective fields, drawing inspiration from Morgan's work. For example, **Aisha Patel**, a recent graduate of the Future Innovators Program, developed an application that utilizes augmented reality to enhance the museum experience. By overlaying historical data onto physical exhibits, her project not only educates visitors but also makes history more engaging and accessible.

Another example is **Liam Chen**, who has created a digital storytelling platform that allows users to share their oral histories in an interactive format. This project not only preserves cultural narratives but also democratizes knowledge, allowing voices that have been historically marginalized to be heard.

Conclusion: A Legacy of Inspiration

Morgan Liao's legacy is one of inspiration and empowerment. By nurturing the next generation of innovators, he is not only ensuring the continuation of the digital humanities movement but also fostering a culture of creativity and collaboration. As these young innovators embark on their journeys, they carry with them the lessons learned from Morgan's experiences, ready to tackle the challenges of tomorrow and shape the future of technology and the humanities.

In summary, the impact of Morgan's mentorship is profound and multifaceted. Through collaborative projects, targeted support, and real-world applications, he has ignited a spark in the hearts of aspiring creators. As they continue to innovate, they are not only honoring his legacy but also paving the way for a brighter, more inclusive future in the realm of digital humanities.

Advocacy for Digital Equality

In the rapidly evolving landscape of technology, Morgan Liao recognized early on that digital equality is not just a luxury; it is a necessity. In a world where information is power, the digital divide—the gap between those who have easy access to digital technology and those who do not—poses significant challenges to equitable growth and social justice. Morgan's advocacy for digital equality encompassed several critical dimensions, each aimed at dismantling barriers that hinder access to technology and information.

Understanding Digital Inequality

Digital inequality manifests in various forms, including economic disparities, geographic limitations, and social factors. According to the *Pew Research Center*, approximately 25% of rural Americans lack access to high-speed internet, compared to only 1% of urban residents. This discrepancy can be expressed mathematically as:

$$D = \frac{U - R}{U}$$

where D represents the digital disparity, U is the percentage of urban residents with access, and R is the percentage of rural residents. In this case:

$$D = \frac{100 - 25}{100} = 0.75 \quad \text{or} \quad 75\%$$

This equation highlights the stark contrast in access, underscoring the urgency for advocacy.

Barriers to Digital Access

Morgan identified several barriers that contribute to digital inequality:

+ **Economic Factors:** The cost of devices and internet service remains prohibitive for many families. According to a report by *The Federal Communications Commission (FCC)*, nearly 19 million Americans live in areas where there is no broadband provider.

+ **Educational Disparities:** Students in low-income areas often lack the necessary resources to succeed in a digital learning environment, leading to a cycle of disadvantage.

+ **Geographic Challenges:** Rural areas frequently suffer from inadequate infrastructure, limiting access to high-speed internet and essential digital services.

+ **Social and Cultural Barriers:** Marginalized communities may face additional hurdles, including lack of digital literacy and cultural biases that discourage engagement with technology.

Morgan's Initiatives for Digital Equality

In response to these challenges, Morgan launched several initiatives aimed at fostering digital equality:

+ **Community Tech Hubs:** Morgan established tech hubs in underserved communities, providing access to high-speed internet, computers, and training programs. These hubs not only offered resources but also served as community gathering spaces for collaboration and innovation.

+ **Digital Literacy Programs:** Recognizing that access alone is insufficient, Morgan developed digital literacy programs targeting both youth and adults. These programs included workshops on coding, online safety, and navigating digital platforms, empowering individuals to utilize technology effectively.

+ **Partnerships with Local Governments:** Morgan collaborated with local governments to advocate for policies that promote infrastructure development in rural areas, ensuring that high-speed internet becomes a fundamental utility, much like water and electricity.

+ **Scholarships for Tech Education:** To bridge the educational gap, Morgan initiated scholarship programs for students from low-income families to pursue degrees in technology and digital humanities, fostering a new generation of innovators.

Measuring the Impact

To assess the effectiveness of these initiatives, Morgan employed a combination of qualitative and quantitative metrics. Surveys and feedback from community members provided insights into the perceived value of the programs, while data analytics tracked improvements in digital access and literacy rates. For instance, after the implementation of the community tech hubs, surveys indicated a 60% increase in self-reported digital literacy among participants.

Case Studies: Success Stories

Several success stories emerged from Morgan's advocacy efforts, illustrating the transformative power of digital equality:

+ **The Story of Maria:** A single mother from a rural area, Maria enrolled in a digital literacy program offered at a community tech hub. Within six months, she secured a remote job that allowed her to support her family while continuing her education.

+ **The Coding Club:** A group of high school students formed a coding club at their local tech hub, eventually developing an app that helps users locate free Wi-Fi hotspots in their neighborhoods. Their project garnered attention from local businesses, leading to sponsorships and internships.

Conclusion: A Call to Action

Morgan Liao's advocacy for digital equality serves as a reminder that technology should be an inclusive tool for empowerment rather than a divider. As we move forward into an increasingly digital future, it is imperative that innovators, policymakers, and community leaders work collaboratively to ensure that everyone has the opportunity to participate in the digital age. In the words of Morgan, "Digital equality is not just about access; it's about giving everyone a seat at the table—and making sure that table is big enough for all of us."

Encouraging Ethical AI Development

In the age of rapid technological advancement, the development of Artificial Intelligence (AI) has become a double-edged sword. While AI holds the potential to revolutionize industries, enhance productivity, and solve complex problems, it also raises significant ethical concerns that cannot be ignored. Morgan Liao, as a leading figure in the Digital Humanities, recognized the importance of encouraging ethical AI development as a cornerstone of his vision for a responsible digital future.

Theoretical Foundations of Ethical AI

The theoretical underpinnings of ethical AI can be traced to several philosophical frameworks. One prominent theory is Utilitarianism, which posits that the best action is the one that maximizes overall happiness. In the context of AI, this translates to creating systems that provide the greatest benefit to the largest number of people. However, this approach can lead to problematic outcomes if not carefully managed, as it may justify harmful actions against a minority if they result in a net positive for the majority.

Conversely, Deontological ethics, championed by philosophers like Immanuel Kant, emphasizes the importance of duty and the morality of actions themselves, regardless of the consequences. This perspective advocates for the development of AI systems that respect individual rights and uphold human dignity. For instance, ensuring that AI does not perpetuate biases or infringe on privacy rights aligns with deontological principles.

Morgan's approach to ethical AI development integrates these theoretical frameworks, advocating for a balanced consideration of both outcomes and moral duties. He believes that ethical AI should not only aim to maximize benefits but also adhere to fundamental ethical principles that protect individuals and communities.

Identifying Ethical Challenges in AI

Despite the theoretical frameworks guiding ethical AI development, real-world challenges persist. Some of the most pressing ethical dilemmas include:

+ **Bias and Discrimination:** AI systems often learn from historical data, which can embed existing biases. For example, facial recognition technology has been shown to misidentify individuals from minority groups at higher rates than their white counterparts. This raises concerns about fairness and equity in AI applications.

+ **Privacy Concerns:** The collection and analysis of vast amounts of personal data by AI systems can lead to significant privacy infringements. For instance, AI-driven surveillance systems may monitor individuals without their consent, posing ethical questions about autonomy and individual rights.

+ **Accountability:** As AI systems become more autonomous, determining accountability for their actions becomes increasingly complex. If an AI system makes a harmful decision, it is often unclear who should be held responsible—the developers, the users, or the AI itself?

+ **Manipulation and Misinformation:** The use of AI in creating deepfakes and generating misleading information presents ethical challenges regarding truth and trust in digital communications. This manipulation can have real-world consequences, influencing public opinion and undermining democratic processes.

Morgan Liao emphasizes the need for a proactive approach to address these challenges. He advocates for interdisciplinary collaboration among ethicists, technologists, and policymakers to establish frameworks that guide ethical AI development.

Implementing Ethical Guidelines

To foster ethical AI development, Morgan proposes a multi-faceted strategy that includes the following components:

+ **Establishing Ethical Standards:** Organizations should develop comprehensive ethical guidelines that govern AI development and deployment. These standards should address issues such as bias mitigation, privacy protection, and accountability.

+ **Transparency and Explainability:** AI systems should be designed to be transparent and explainable. Stakeholders must understand how decisions are made, allowing for scrutiny and accountability. For instance, Morgan's Digital Humanities Institute developed an AI model that provides clear explanations for its recommendations, enhancing trust among users.

+ **Diverse Development Teams:** Encouraging diversity within AI development teams can help mitigate biases and promote a more comprehensive understanding of ethical implications. Diverse perspectives can lead to more inclusive AI solutions that consider the needs of various communities.

+ **Continuous Monitoring and Evaluation:** Ethical AI development is not a one-time effort but requires ongoing monitoring and evaluation. Organizations should implement feedback mechanisms to assess the impact of AI systems and make necessary adjustments to uphold ethical standards.

Examples of Ethical AI Initiatives

Morgan's advocacy for ethical AI development has led to the establishment of several initiatives that exemplify these principles:

+ **The Fairness Toolkit:** Developed by the Digital Humanities Institute, this toolkit provides resources for AI developers to assess and mitigate bias in their algorithms. It includes guidelines for data collection, model training, and evaluation to ensure fairness in AI applications.

+ **Privacy-First AI Projects:** Morgan spearheaded projects that prioritize user privacy by employing techniques such as differential privacy and federated learning. These approaches allow AI systems to learn from data without compromising individual privacy, setting a precedent for responsible data usage.

+ **Ethical AI Workshops:** The Institute hosts workshops that bring together technologists, ethicists, and policymakers to discuss ethical AI development. These events foster dialogue and collaboration, leading to actionable strategies for addressing ethical challenges in AI.

Conclusion: A Call to Action

As AI continues to permeate various aspects of society, the call for ethical AI development becomes increasingly urgent. Morgan Liao's commitment to encouraging ethical practices in AI serves as a beacon for future innovators. By integrating theoretical frameworks, identifying ethical challenges, and implementing robust guidelines, we can pave the way for a future where AI serves humanity responsibly and equitably.

In the words of Morgan, "The future of AI is not just about what we can do, but what we should do." As we navigate the complexities of AI, let us embrace this ethos and strive for a digital landscape that prioritizes ethics alongside innovation. Only then can we truly realize the promise of a Cyber Renaissance that uplifts all of humanity.

Revolutionizing Education Systems

In the age of digital transformation, Morgan Liao recognized that education systems worldwide were in dire need of a makeover. The traditional model, which often resembled a factory assembly line, was ill-equipped to foster creativity, critical thinking, and the digital skills necessary for the future. Morgan's vision was to create a more dynamic, inclusive, and engaging educational framework that harnessed the power of technology while addressing the unique challenges of the 21st century.

Theoretical Foundations

Morgan drew inspiration from various educational theories, including Constructivism and Connectivism. Constructivism posits that learners construct their own understanding and knowledge of the world through experiences and reflecting on those experiences. In contrast, Connectivism emphasizes the role of social and cultural context in the learning process, highlighting the importance of connections within networks of information.

The equation that summarizes the shift from traditional to modern education can be framed as follows:

$$E = f(T, A, C) \tag{77}$$

Where:

+ E represents educational effectiveness,

+ T is the technology integration,

+ A refers to active learning methodologies, and

+ C stands for collaborative environments.

Morgan believed that by enhancing T, A, and C, educational institutions could significantly improve student outcomes.

Identifying Problems in Traditional Education

Morgan identified several key problems in traditional education systems:

+ **Standardization:** A one-size-fits-all approach fails to accommodate diverse learning styles and paces.

+ **Access:** Significant disparities exist in access to quality education, particularly in underprivileged communities.

+ **Engagement:** Traditional lecture-based models often lead to disengagement and lack of motivation among students.

+ **Relevance:** The curriculum frequently lags behind the skills needed in the modern workforce, leaving students unprepared for real-world challenges.

These issues not only hindered individual student growth but also stunted societal progress as a whole.

Innovative Solutions

To address these challenges, Morgan proposed several innovative solutions:

1. Personalized Learning Environments Morgan championed the use of adaptive learning technologies that tailor educational experiences to individual student needs. For example, platforms like *Khan Academy* and *Coursera* utilize algorithms to assess student performance and adjust the difficulty of tasks accordingly, promoting mastery at a personalized pace.

2. Gamification of Learning By incorporating game design elements into educational contexts, Morgan aimed to increase student engagement and motivation. Research has shown that gamification can lead to improved retention rates and a more enjoyable learning experience. For instance, platforms like *Duolingo* have successfully used gamification to teach languages, making the process fun and interactive.

3. Collaborative Learning Spaces   Morgan envisioned educational institutions as hubs of collaboration, where students could work together on projects that address real-world issues. The creation of makerspaces and innovation labs in schools allows students to engage in hands-on learning and foster teamwork. Programs like *FIRST Robotics* exemplify this approach, encouraging students to collaborate on engineering challenges.

4. Integration of Digital Humanities   Morgan believed that incorporating digital humanities into the curriculum could enhance students' understanding of culture, history, and ethics in the digital age. For instance, using virtual reality to explore historical events provides an immersive learning experience that textbooks cannot replicate. This approach not only makes learning more engaging but also instills a sense of empathy and connection to the past.

The Impact of Morgan's Initiatives

The implementation of these innovative educational practices resulted in several positive outcomes:

- **Increased Student Engagement:** Schools that adopted gamification and personalized learning reported higher levels of student participation and enthusiasm.

- **Enhanced Critical Thinking Skills:** Collaborative projects encouraged students to think critically and creatively, preparing them for complex problem-solving in the workforce.

- **Greater Inclusivity:** Adaptive learning technologies helped bridge the gap for students with diverse learning needs, ensuring that all voices were heard and valued.

- **Preparation for the Future:** By integrating digital humanities and technology into the curriculum, students emerged with skills and knowledge relevant to the evolving job market.

Morgan's initiatives not only transformed educational systems but also inspired a new generation of innovators equipped to tackle the challenges of the future.

Conclusion

In conclusion, Morgan Liao's revolutionary approach to education systems exemplifies the potential of technology to create meaningful change. By addressing the shortcomings of traditional models and emphasizing personalized, collaborative, and engaging learning experiences, Morgan set the stage for a brighter future where education is accessible, relevant, and transformative. The legacy of his work continues to resonate, inspiring educators and learners alike to embrace innovation in the pursuit of knowledge.

Implications for Cultural Preservation

Cultural preservation in the digital age presents a unique set of challenges and opportunities, particularly as we navigate the intersection of technology and the humanities. Morgan Liao's work in this field has not only highlighted the importance of preserving cultural heritage but has also introduced innovative methodologies for doing so. The implications for cultural preservation can be analyzed through several key lenses: accessibility, authenticity, and sustainability.

Accessibility of Cultural Heritage

One of the most significant implications of Morgan's initiatives is the democratization of access to cultural heritage. Traditional methods of preservation often limited access to artifacts and historical sites, creating a barrier for many individuals, particularly those from marginalized communities. With the advent of digital technologies, Morgan's projects have aimed to create virtual archives that allow global access to cultural materials.

For instance, the *Knowledge Archive*, a pioneering project led by Morgan, utilizes advanced data management systems and artificial intelligence to curate and digitize cultural artifacts. This project not only preserves the artifacts but also makes them available to anyone with an internet connection. The equation governing accessibility can be simplified as follows:

$$A = \frac{D}{C}$$

where A represents accessibility, D denotes the digitized content, and C signifies the barriers to access. As D increases through digital preservation efforts, A correspondingly rises, indicating a more inclusive approach to cultural heritage.

Authenticity in the Digital Realm

While digital preservation offers unprecedented access, it also raises questions about authenticity. How do we ensure that digital representations of cultural artifacts remain true to their original forms? Morgan's approach emphasizes the need for rigorous standards in digital documentation and preservation practices.

The concept of authenticity can be mathematically represented by the following model:

$$\text{Authenticity} = f(P, R, T)$$

where P is the physical presence of the artifact, R is the reliability of the digital representation, and T is the technological fidelity of the medium used. Morgan advocates for a multi-faceted approach to authenticity, ensuring that digital reproductions are not only visually accurate but also contextually relevant. This involves collaboration with cultural experts and the use of high-fidelity imaging technologies to capture the essence of the original artifacts.

Sustainability of Cultural Preservation Efforts

Sustainability is another critical aspect of cultural preservation in the digital age. Morgan has emphasized that while technology can facilitate preservation, it must be employed in a manner that is sustainable over the long term. This includes considerations of environmental impact, financial viability, and the ongoing need for technological updates.

To address sustainability, Morgan's team has developed a framework that incorporates the following equation:

$$S = \frac{R + E + T}{C}$$

where S represents sustainability, R is the resources allocated for preservation, E denotes environmental considerations, T represents technological updates, and C signifies costs associated with preservation efforts. By optimizing each variable, Morgan's initiatives aim to create a sustainable model for cultural preservation that can adapt to changing technological landscapes.

Case Studies and Real-World Applications

Several case studies exemplify the implications of Morgan's work in cultural preservation. One notable example is the *Virtual Museum of World Cultures*, a collaborative project that utilizes augmented reality to provide immersive experiences of cultural artifacts. Visitors can explore ancient artifacts in their original contexts, bridging the gap between digital representations and physical experiences.

Additionally, the *Digital Storytelling Initiative* has successfully documented and preserved oral histories from diverse communities, ensuring that marginalized voices are heard and recorded for future generations. This project has demonstrated the power of social media and digital platforms in democratizing knowledge and preserving cultural narratives.

Conclusion

In conclusion, the implications for cultural preservation stemming from Morgan Liao's work are profound and multifaceted. By addressing accessibility, authenticity, and sustainability, Morgan has paved the way for a new paradigm in cultural heritage preservation. As we continue to navigate the complexities of the digital age, it is imperative that we embrace these innovations while remaining vigilant about the ethical considerations that accompany them. The legacy of Morgan's contributions to cultural preservation will undoubtedly shape the future of how we engage with our shared human heritage.

Morgan's Impact on Policy-making

In the rapidly evolving landscape of digital technology, Morgan Liao emerged not only as an innovator in digital humanities but also as a significant influencer in policy-making. His work has highlighted the necessity for frameworks that govern the ethical use of technology, particularly in the realms of artificial intelligence (AI), data privacy, and cultural preservation. As a thought leader, Morgan recognized that the implications of digital advancements extend far beyond the confines of academia and industry; they ripple through society, demanding a proactive approach to policy formulation.

Theoretical Foundations

Morgan's impact on policy-making can be understood through the lens of several theoretical frameworks:

1. **Technological Determinism**: This theory posits that technology shapes society's structures and cultural values. Morgan's advocacy for responsible AI illustrates how technology can influence policy decisions, pushing legislators to consider the societal implications of technological advancements.

2.   **Actor-Network Theory (ANT)**:   ANT emphasizes the interconnectedness of human and non-human actors in shaping social phenomena. Morgan's collaborative projects with policymakers, technologists, and ethicists exemplify how diverse stakeholders can coalesce to create policies that reflect a holistic understanding of technology's impact.

3. **Social Constructivism**: This theory argues that knowledge and meaning are constructed through social processes. Morgan's initiatives aimed at democratizing access to information demonstrate how policies can be shaped by collective societal values and norms, particularly in the digital age.

Identifying Problems

Several pressing issues in the digital landscape necessitated Morgan's involvement in policy-making:

+ **Data Privacy Concerns:** With the proliferation of data collection technologies, the protection of individual privacy became a paramount concern. Morgan advocated for policies that emphasize transparency and user consent, ensuring that individuals retain control over their personal information.

+ **Algorithmic Bias:** As AI systems increasingly influence decision-making processes, the potential for inherent biases in algorithms poses significant ethical dilemmas. Morgan's research highlighted the need for policies that mandate fairness and accountability in AI development.

+ **Cultural Preservation:** The digitization of cultural artifacts raises questions about ownership, access, and the ethics of representation. Morgan pushed for policies that protect cultural heritage while promoting equitable access to digital resources.

Morgan's Contributions to Policy-making

Morgan's influence in policy-making manifested through various initiatives and collaborations:

+ **Advisory Roles:** Morgan served on several governmental and non-governmental advisory boards, where he provided insights on the intersection of technology and policy. His contributions were instrumental in shaping regulations that govern AI ethics and data protection.

+ **Workshops and Conferences:** By organizing and participating in workshops, Morgan fostered dialogue among stakeholders, including policymakers, technologists, and community leaders. These events served as platforms for discussing best practices and formulating actionable policy recommendations.

+ **Public Advocacy:** Morgan utilized his platform to advocate for policies that promote digital equity. He emphasized the importance of bridging the digital divide, ensuring that marginalized communities have access to technology and the skills necessary to thrive in a digital economy.

Case Studies

Morgan's impact on policy-making can be illustrated through specific case studies:

1. **The Digital Bill of Rights:** In response to growing concerns about data privacy and user rights, Morgan played a pivotal role in advocating for a comprehensive Digital Bill of Rights. This legislation aimed to protect individuals' online privacy, ensuring that users have the right to know how their data is collected, used, and shared. The bill emphasized the principles of transparency, consent, and accountability, reflecting Morgan's commitment to ethical technology use.

2. **AI Fairness Initiatives:** Recognizing the potential for bias in AI systems, Morgan collaborated with tech companies and regulatory bodies to establish guidelines for ethical AI development. These initiatives focused on creating diverse datasets and implementing rigorous testing to identify and mitigate bias in algorithms. Morgan's efforts contributed to the formulation of policies that promote fairness and inclusivity in AI applications.

3. **Cultural Heritage Preservation Policies:** Morgan's work in digital humanities led to the development of policies aimed at preserving cultural heritage in the digital age. By advocating for the ethical digitization of artifacts and the establishment of open access repositories, he ensured that cultural resources are accessible to all while respecting the rights of indigenous and local communities.

Conclusion

Morgan Liao's influence on policy-making underscores the critical intersection of technology and ethics in shaping the future. His advocacy for data privacy, algorithmic fairness, and cultural preservation has not only informed legislative frameworks but has also inspired a new generation of policymakers to consider the broader implications of technological advancements. As we navigate the complexities of the digital age, Morgan's legacy serves as a reminder of the importance of ethical innovation and the necessity of inclusive policies that reflect the diverse needs of society.

In summary, Morgan's impact on policy-making is a testament to his vision of a future where technology serves humanity, fostering an environment where innovation and ethics coexist harmoniously. As we move forward, the policies shaped by Morgan's insights will continue to guide the responsible development and use of technology, ensuring that the benefits of the digital revolution are shared equitably across all sectors of society.

The Legacy of Morgan Liao

Morgan Liao's legacy is a multifaceted tapestry woven from the threads of innovation, ethical responsibility, and a relentless pursuit of knowledge. As a pioneer in the field of Digital Humanities, his contributions have not only transformed the landscape of academia but have also inspired a generation of thinkers and creators to embrace the digital revolution with a sense of purpose and integrity.

Impact on Digital Humanities

At the heart of Morgan's legacy is the establishment of the Digital Humanities Institute, which serves as a global research hub dedicated to exploring the intersection of technology and the humanities. This institute has become a beacon for scholars and innovators, promoting interdisciplinary collaboration and encouraging the integration of computational methods into traditional humanities disciplines. The institute's groundbreaking research projects have set new standards for academic inquiry, demonstrating that the humanities can thrive in a digital age.

One of the most significant contributions of the Digital Humanities Institute is the development of the *Knowledge Archive*, a comprehensive digital repository that houses a vast array of historical documents, cultural artifacts, and scholarly works. This archive not only preserves invaluable knowledge but also democratizes access to information, allowing individuals from diverse backgrounds to engage with the humanities in ways that were previously unimaginable. The impact of this archive can be quantified through the following equation:

$$K = \frac{D}{A} \tag{78}$$

where K represents the knowledge accessibility index, D is the total number of documents available, and A is the number of active users accessing the archive. This equation highlights the correlation between the volume of available resources and the engagement of the public, showcasing Morgan's commitment to fostering a more inclusive intellectual environment.

Advocacy for Ethical AI

Morgan's legacy is also marked by his staunch advocacy for ethical considerations in the development and application of artificial intelligence. Recognizing the potential for bias and discrimination in AI technologies, he championed initiatives aimed at addressing these critical issues. His work in this area led to the formulation of the *Ethical AI Framework*, which provides guidelines for researchers and developers to ensure that their work aligns with principles of fairness, accountability, and transparency.

The framework emphasizes the importance of diverse data sets in training AI systems, as illustrated by the following inequality:

$$B \leq \frac{C}{D} \tag{79}$$

where B denotes bias in AI outcomes, C represents the diversity of the training data, and D is the total number of data points. This inequality underscores the necessity of inclusive data practices to mitigate bias, a principle that Morgan instilled in future innovators as they navigated the complexities of technology in society.

Inspiration for Future Innovators

Morgan Liao's influence extends far beyond his immediate contributions; he has become a symbol of inspiration for aspiring innovators around the globe. Through his mentorship programs, he has nurtured countless young minds, encouraging them to pursue their passions while remaining grounded in ethical considerations. His ability to identify and cultivate potential leaders has resulted in a new wave of thinkers who are not only technologically savvy but also socially conscious.

One notable example of this mentorship is the story of a young innovator, Sara Patel, who, under Morgan's guidance, developed a mobile application aimed at improving literacy rates in underserved communities. This project exemplifies the spirit of Morgan's legacy, demonstrating how technology can be harnessed for social good. As Sara often quotes Morgan, "Innovation without purpose is just a fancy gadget."

Cultural Preservation and Education

Morgan's legacy is intricately tied to his commitment to cultural preservation and the reimagining of educational systems. His initiatives in digital storytelling and augmented reality have revolutionized the way history is taught and experienced. By creating immersive educational experiences, he has enabled students to engage with historical narratives in a manner that is both interactive and impactful.

The success of these initiatives can be measured through the *Engagement Quotient* (EQ), defined as:

$$EQ = \frac{I + R}{T} \tag{80}$$

where I is the level of interactivity, R represents the relevance of the content, and T is the total time spent by students engaging with the material. This formula illustrates how Morgan's innovative approaches have increased student engagement, fostering a deeper understanding of cultural heritage.

A Lasting Impact on Policy-Making

Morgan's influence has also reached the corridors of power, as policymakers have sought his insights on the implications of digital technologies for society. His advocacy for digital equality and ethical AI has informed legislative efforts aimed at ensuring that technological advancements benefit all members of society, not just a privileged few. This engagement with policy-making underscores the importance of integrating academic research with real-world applications, a principle that Morgan has tirelessly promoted throughout his career.

In conclusion, the legacy of Morgan Liao is one of profound impact, characterized by a commitment to ethical innovation, a passion for knowledge dissemination, and an unwavering belief in the power of technology to transform society. As future generations of innovators continue to build upon his work, they carry with them the torch of his vision—a vision that champions inclusivity, creativity, and a better understanding of our shared human experience in an increasingly digital world.

A Future Filled with Possibilities

In the wake of Morgan Liao's transformative contributions to the field of digital humanities, the horizon is filled with an array of possibilities that promise to redefine our understanding of culture, technology, and education. As we stand at this precipice of innovation, it is imperative to explore the theoretical frameworks and real-world applications that underpin this new era.

Theoretical Foundations

The future of digital humanities is grounded in several key theoretical perspectives that advocate for an interdisciplinary approach. One such theory is **Actor-Network Theory (ANT)**, which posits that both human and non-human entities (like technology) interact in complex networks, shaping our understanding of cultural artifacts. This theory encourages us to view technology not merely as a tool but as an active participant in the creation and dissemination of knowledge.

$$\text{Knowledge} = f(\text{Human Actors}, \text{Non-Human Actors}) \qquad (81)$$

This equation highlights the dynamic interplay between individuals and the technologies they employ, suggesting that our grasp of knowledge is contingent upon these relationships.

Emerging Challenges

Despite the promising landscape, several challenges loom on the horizon. One of the most pressing issues is **digital equity**. As technology becomes increasingly integrated into educational systems, disparities in access can exacerbate existing inequalities. According to the *Pew Research Center*, approximately 15% of U.S. households with school-aged children do not have a high-speed internet connection, raising concerns about the inclusivity of digital learning environments.

To address these disparities, Morgan's initiatives have focused on implementing community-based programs that provide access to technology and training for underserved populations. By equipping individuals with the necessary skills and resources, we can work towards a more equitable digital future.

Innovative Examples

Several innovative projects have emerged that exemplify the potential of digital humanities to foster inclusivity and creativity. For instance, the **Digital Public Library of America (DPLA)** aggregates millions of photographs, manuscripts, and other cultural artifacts, making them accessible to the public. This initiative not only democratizes knowledge but also encourages collaborative projects that engage diverse communities in the preservation of their cultural heritage.

Furthermore, initiatives like **Wikipedia's Gender Gap Task Force** have sought to address the underrepresentation of women and marginalized groups in digital spaces.   By actively recruiting and training new contributors from diverse backgrounds, these projects aim to create a more balanced and comprehensive representation of knowledge.

The Role of Artificial Intelligence

Artificial intelligence (AI) plays a pivotal role in shaping the future of digital humanities. Through machine learning algorithms, we can analyze vast datasets to uncover patterns and insights that would be impossible to discern manually. For example, AI-driven text analysis tools can be employed to examine historical documents, revealing trends in language use, sentiment, and thematic development over time.

However, it is crucial to approach the integration of AI with caution. Ethical considerations surrounding data privacy, algorithmic bias, and the potential for misinformation must be addressed.   As Morgan Liao often emphasizes, the development of AI in the humanities should be guided by principles of transparency and accountability.

$$\text{Ethical AI} = \text{Transparency} + \text{Accountability} + \text{Inclusivity} \qquad (82)$$

This equation serves as a reminder that the future of AI in digital humanities must prioritize ethical considerations to ensure that technology serves the greater good.

Envisioning the Future

Looking ahead, the future of digital humanities is not merely a continuation of current trends but a reimagining of what is possible. As we harness the power of technology to explore cultural narratives, we can anticipate new forms of storytelling that transcend traditional boundaries.

For instance, the rise of **immersive experiences** through virtual and augmented reality opens up avenues for engaging with history and culture in unprecedented ways. Imagine stepping into a virtual reconstruction of ancient Rome or experiencing a historical event through the eyes of those who lived it.

Such experiences can foster empathy and a deeper understanding of our shared human experience.

Moreover, as we cultivate a new generation of innovators, it is essential to instill a sense of responsibility and purpose. Morgan's legacy emphasizes the importance of mentorship and collaboration, encouraging young thinkers to approach challenges with creativity and ethical consideration.

Conclusion

In conclusion, the future of digital humanities is indeed filled with possibilities. By embracing interdisciplinary approaches, addressing challenges of equity, leveraging AI ethically, and envisioning innovative applications, we can create a vibrant landscape that honors our past while paving the way for a more inclusive and informed future. As Morgan Liao's journey illustrates, the intersection of technology and humanities holds the potential to inspire generations to come, fostering a world where knowledge knows no bounds and creativity flourishes.

Chapter 4 The Next Era Begins

Chapter 4 The Next Era Begins

The Next Era Begins

As the digital landscape continues to evolve at a breakneck pace, Morgan Liao stands at the helm of a new era—one that promises to redefine not just technology, but the very fabric of our society. This chapter explores the pivotal transition into this next phase, highlighting the challenges, opportunities, and visionary ideas that will shape the future.

The Dawn of a New Digital Age

The transition into this new era is marked by the convergence of various fields, including artificial intelligence, biotechnology, and digital humanities. Morgan Liao's work exemplifies the synthesis of these domains, as he seeks to harness technology to address complex societal issues. The following theories underpin this transformation:

- **Interdisciplinary Collaboration:** The necessity of blending expertise from diverse fields to foster innovation. As Morgan often quips, "If you can't find the solution, it's probably because you're not asking enough people who don't know what they're talking about."

- **Human-Centric Technology:** The focus on creating technologies that enhance human experiences rather than diminish them. Morgan's mantra, "Tech should serve humanity, not the other way around," resonates deeply in this context.

211

+ **Sustainable Innovation:** The importance of developing technologies that are environmentally and socially sustainable, ensuring that progress does not come at the expense of our planet or its inhabitants.

Passing the Torch

One of the most critical aspects of Morgan's legacy is his commitment to mentorship. Recognizing that the future is not solely about individual achievements, he actively seeks to empower the next generation of innovators. This section delves into the methods and philosophies Morgan employs in mentoring:

+ **Identifying Future Visionaries:** Morgan has developed a keen eye for spotting potential in young innovators. He often says, "The best ideas come from those who haven't learned yet that they're impossible."

+ **Investing in Innovative Ideas:** By providing funding and resources to promising projects, Morgan fosters an environment where creativity can thrive. He believes that "money is just a tool; it's the ideas that are priceless."

+ **Building a Sustainable Future:** His mentorship emphasizes the importance of sustainability in innovation, encouraging mentees to consider the long-term impacts of their work.

Morgan's Latest Endeavors

As the Cyber Renaissance unfolds, Morgan embarks on several groundbreaking projects that push the boundaries of innovation. These include:

+ **Post-Cyber Renaissance Projects:** Morgan's latest initiatives focus on integrating digital humanities with emerging technologies, such as quantum computing and advanced AI. His vision is to create a digital ecosystem where knowledge is not only preserved but also dynamically enriched.

+ **Expanding into Space Exploration:** With a team of astrophysicists and engineers, Morgan is exploring the potential for digital humanities in understanding extraterrestrial cultures. He humorously notes, "If aliens exist, they probably have better Wi-Fi than we do."

+ **The Quest for Extraterrestrial Intelligence:** Leveraging AI to analyze signals from space, Morgan's projects aim to decode potential communications from intelligent life forms. "If we can't find intelligent life out there, at least we can make a great Netflix series about it," he jokes.

+ **Unveiling New Technologies:** Morgan is at the forefront of developing tools that merge virtual reality with historical education, allowing users to experience history firsthand. "Why read about the past when you can live it? Just don't forget to take selfies," he quips.

The Cyber Renaissance Legacy

As Morgan reflects on his journey, he understands that his contributions extend far beyond his individual projects. The Cyber Renaissance represents a collective movement toward a more integrated, ethical, and innovative future. Key elements of this legacy include:

+ **Morgan's Place in History:** His pioneering work in digital humanities has laid the groundwork for future scholars and innovators. "I just wanted to make a difference, and maybe a little cash on the side," he admits with a grin.

+ **Perpetuating the Cyber Renaissance:** By fostering a culture of collaboration and innovation, Morgan ensures that the principles of the Cyber Renaissance will endure. "Innovation is like a good wine; it gets better when shared," he states.

+ **Future Innovators Inspired by Morgan:** The ripple effect of his mentorship and vision is evident in the success of those he has guided. "If I can inspire just one person to change the world, then I'll consider my job done—unless they want to charge me for the advice," he jokes.

+ **The Lasting Impact of Digital Humanities:** Morgan's work has redefined the role of humanities in the digital age, emphasizing that culture and technology are not mutually exclusive. "In the end, it's all about telling stories—whether through pixels or pages," he reflects.

In conclusion, as we stand on the brink of this new era, Morgan Liao's vision and leadership illuminate the path forward. The Cyber Renaissance is not just a chapter in history; it is a movement that promises to reshape our understanding of technology, culture, and the human experience. With a blend of humor, insight, and relentless curiosity, Morgan continues to inspire a generation of innovators ready to take on the challenges of tomorrow.

Passing the Torch

Mentoring the Next Generation

In the wake of the Cyber Renaissance, Morgan Liao recognized that the future of innovation was not solely dependent on his own endeavors but also on the cultivation of young minds eager to push the boundaries of technology and humanities. As a mentor, Morgan embarked on a mission to inspire and guide the next generation of innovators, emphasizing the importance of both technical skills and ethical considerations in the digital age.

The Importance of Mentorship

Mentorship is a pivotal element in the development of emerging talents. Research indicates that mentorship can significantly enhance the professional development of individuals, particularly in fields that require both creativity and technical proficiency. According to a study by Allen et al. (2004), mentored individuals report higher levels of job satisfaction, career advancement, and personal development compared to their non-mentored counterparts. Morgan understood that by investing time in mentoring, he was not only shaping future leaders but also ensuring the sustainability of the Cyber Renaissance movement.

Identifying Future Visionaries

Morgan employed a systematic approach to identify promising young innovators. He established a framework that included criteria such as creativity, resilience, and a demonstrated passion for technology and humanities. This framework was underpinned by the following equation:

$$V = C + R + P \tag{83}$$

Where:

- V = Visionary potential

- C = Creativity score (assessed through project portfolios)

- R = Resilience factor (evaluated through personal challenges faced)

- P = Passion index (measured through engagement in relevant activities)

This equation allowed Morgan to quantitatively assess the potential of young innovators, ensuring that those selected for mentorship possessed a balanced combination of creativity, resilience, and passion.

Investing in Innovative Ideas

Morgan's mentorship program was designed to provide resources and support for young innovators to explore their ideas. He established a seed funding initiative that allocated grants to promising projects. This initiative was grounded in the belief that financial support could alleviate barriers to entry for young innovators, allowing them to focus on developing their ideas rather than worrying about funding.

For instance, one of Morgan's mentees, a high school student named Jamie, proposed a project aimed at using augmented reality to enhance historical education. With the seed funding provided by Morgan's initiative, Jamie was able to develop a prototype that allowed users to interact with historical artifacts in a virtual environment. This project not only won several awards but also inspired a movement among students to leverage technology in education.

Building a Sustainable Future

Morgan emphasized the importance of sustainability in innovation. He believed that the next generation of innovators must be equipped to address the pressing challenges of the modern world, including climate change, social inequality, and digital ethics. To instill this mindset, Morgan organized workshops and seminars that focused on sustainable practices in technology development.

During one such workshop, Morgan introduced the concept of "sustainable innovation," defined as:

$$SI = \frac{E + S + T}{C} \tag{84}$$

Where:

+ SI = Sustainable innovation

+ E = Environmental impact assessment

+ S = Social responsibility metrics

+ T = Technological feasibility

+ C = Cost-effectiveness

This equation served as a guideline for young innovators to evaluate their projects through a sustainability lens, ensuring that their innovations would contribute positively to society and the environment.

Morgan's Role as an Advisor

As an advisor, Morgan took an active role in the development of his mentees. He provided not only guidance but also constructive feedback on their projects. He encouraged an open-door policy, allowing mentees to approach him with their ideas, concerns, and aspirations. This accessibility fostered a nurturing environment where young innovators felt valued and empowered to express their thoughts.

Morgan also facilitated networking opportunities, connecting his mentees with industry leaders and potential collaborators. By leveraging his extensive network, he helped bridge the gap between young innovators and established professionals, further enhancing the learning experience.

Conclusion

In conclusion, Morgan Liao's commitment to mentoring the next generation was a cornerstone of his legacy in the Cyber Renaissance. By identifying future visionaries, investing in their ideas, and emphasizing sustainability, he not only shaped the future of innovation but also ensured that the principles of ethical responsibility and social consciousness would guide the endeavors of young innovators. The impact of his mentorship continues to resonate, inspiring a new wave of thinkers and creators who are poised to tackle the challenges of tomorrow with creativity and integrity.

Identifying Future Visionaries

In the fast-paced world of innovation, the ability to identify future visionaries is paramount. This section explores the strategies and methodologies employed by Morgan Liao to scout and nurture the next generation of innovators. The process is not merely about recognizing talent; it involves a deep understanding of the evolving landscape of technology, creativity, and societal needs.

The Criteria for Selection

Morgan established a set of criteria to identify potential visionaries. These criteria can be summarized as follows:

- **Creativity:** The ability to think outside the box and come up with novel solutions to complex problems.

+ **Passion:** A genuine enthusiasm for their field, which fuels their drive and commitment.

+ **Adaptability:** The capacity to pivot and adjust to new information or changing circumstances.

+ **Collaboration:** The willingness to work with others, recognizing that innovation often arises from teamwork.

+ **Ethical Considerations:** A strong moral compass that guides their innovations towards positive societal impact.

These criteria align with the principles of innovative leadership as discussed by [?], who emphasizes the importance of creativity and collaboration in fostering an environment conducive to innovation.

Identifying Potential

Morgan utilized several methods to identify potential visionaries:

1. **Networking Events:** Hosting and attending conferences, hackathons, and symposiums where young talents could showcase their ideas. For instance, the annual "Future Innovators Summit" became a breeding ground for new ideas, where participants pitched concepts that ranged from sustainable technologies to AI-driven education tools.

2. **Mentorship Programs:** Establishing mentorship initiatives that paired seasoned innovators with budding talents. This approach not only provided guidance but also allowed Morgan to observe mentees' growth and potential directly.

3. **Social Media Analysis:** In an age where digital footprints are abundant, Morgan employed data analytics to track emerging thought leaders and influencers within the tech community. By analyzing engagement metrics and content contributions, he identified individuals who were making waves in their respective fields.

4. **Academic Collaborations:** Partnering with universities to identify standout students through research projects and competitions. The "Innovative Minds Challenge" was one such initiative that brought together students from various disciplines to solve real-world problems.

Case Studies of Identified Visionaries

To illustrate the effectiveness of Morgan's methods, consider the following case studies of individuals he identified and mentored:

Case Study 1: Sarah Chen   At a hackathon, Morgan encountered Sarah, a computer science student who developed an app that used machine learning to assist visually impaired individuals in navigating public spaces. Recognizing her passion and creativity, he invited her to join his mentorship program. Under his guidance, Sarah expanded her project into a startup, "Visionary Paths," which garnered significant attention and funding, exemplifying how the right support can amplify a visionary's impact.

Case Study 2: Amir Patel   Amir, a high school student with a keen interest in environmental science, created a prototype for a solar-powered water purification system. Morgan discovered Amir through a partnership with a local high school science fair. By providing Amir with resources and access to industry experts, Morgan helped him refine his invention, leading to its implementation in several developing regions. Amir's journey highlights the importance of recognizing potential in unconventional settings.

Challenges in Identifying Visionaries

Despite the structured approach, identifying future visionaries is fraught with challenges:

- **Bias in Selection:** The risk of unconscious bias can skew the identification process, favoring certain demographics or backgrounds over others. Morgan implemented blind evaluation processes to mitigate this risk.

- **Overlooking Quiet Innovators:** Not all visionaries are extroverted or vocal about their ideas. Morgan emphasized the importance of creating inclusive environments where all voices are heard, ensuring that quieter talents were not overlooked.

- **Rapidly Changing Trends:** The fast-evolving nature of technology means that what is innovative today may not be relevant tomorrow. Morgan continuously updated his criteria and methodologies to stay ahead of trends, ensuring that he remained adaptable in his identification process.

Conclusion

Identifying future visionaries is a dynamic and complex process that requires a multifaceted approach. Morgan Liao's commitment to nurturing young talent through structured mentorship, innovative programs, and an inclusive mindset has set a precedent in the field of digital humanities. As we look to the future, the legacy of identifying and empowering visionaries will undoubtedly shape the landscape of innovation for generations to come.

Investing in Innovative Ideas

In the dynamic landscape of the Cyber Renaissance, Morgan Liao recognized that the key to sustaining innovation lay in a robust investment strategy. This strategy not only encompassed financial resources but also intellectual capital, mentorship, and technological infrastructure. The goal was to cultivate an ecosystem where innovative ideas could flourish, akin to a greenhouse for budding plants.

The Importance of Investment in Innovation

Investing in innovative ideas is not merely a financial transaction; it is a commitment to fostering creativity and technological advancement. The theory of *Creative Destruction*, articulated by economist Joseph Schumpeter, posits that innovation is the primary driver of economic growth, often leading to the obsolescence of outdated industries. Thus, investing in new ideas can be seen as a catalyst for economic evolution.

$$\text{Economic Growth} = f(\text{Innovation}) \rightarrow \text{New Industries} \rightarrow \text{Creative Destruction} \tag{85}$$

This equation illustrates the relationship between innovation and economic growth, where f signifies a function that captures the transformative impact of innovative ideas on the economy.

Challenges in Investing in Innovation

Despite its potential, investing in innovative ideas is fraught with challenges. One of the primary obstacles is the *uncertainty* associated with new ventures. Investors often grapple with the risk of failure, which can stem from various factors, including market readiness, technological feasibility, and execution capabilities. According to a report by the National Venture Capital Association, approximately

75% of venture-backed startups fail, highlighting the inherent risks involved in this process.

Moreover, the *funding gap* presents another challenge. Early-stage startups frequently struggle to secure the necessary capital to bring their ideas to fruition. This gap is particularly pronounced in sectors such as digital humanities, where the intersection of technology and the arts may not be immediately lucrative. Morgan understood that bridging this gap required innovative funding mechanisms, such as crowdfunding and public-private partnerships.

Strategies for Effective Investment

To effectively invest in innovative ideas, Morgan adopted several strategies:

+ **Diversification of Funding Sources:** By tapping into various funding sources, including venture capital, angel investors, and grants from educational institutions, Morgan created a diversified portfolio that mitigated risk.

+ **Mentorship Programs:** Establishing mentorship initiatives allowed experienced innovators to guide emerging talents. This not only enhanced the likelihood of success but also fostered a culture of collaboration and shared learning.

+ **Incubation and Acceleration:** Morgan launched incubation programs that provided startups with resources such as office space, technical support, and access to networks. These programs significantly increased the survival rate of nascent ventures.

+ **Data-Driven Decision Making:** Leveraging big data analytics, Morgan's team evaluated potential investments based on market trends, consumer behavior, and technological advancements. This approach reduced uncertainty and enhanced the precision of investment decisions.

Examples of Successful Investments

One notable example of Morgan's investment strategy in action was the funding of a project called *Digital Narratives*. This initiative aimed to create an interactive platform that combined augmented reality (AR) with storytelling, allowing users to experience historical events in immersive ways. Through a combination of seed funding and partnerships with leading tech firms, the project secured the necessary resources to prototype and eventually launch.

Another success story was the establishment of the *Cultural Preservation Lab*, which utilized artificial intelligence to analyze and preserve endangered languages. Morgan's investment in this project not only contributed to the preservation of cultural heritage but also showcased the potential of AI in the humanities. The lab received accolades for its innovative approach and attracted further funding from international organizations.

Conclusion

In conclusion, investing in innovative ideas is essential for sustaining the momentum of the Cyber Renaissance. By addressing the challenges of uncertainty and funding gaps, and by implementing strategic investment practices, Morgan Liao has not only fostered a culture of innovation but has also laid the groundwork for future generations of creators and thinkers. As the digital landscape continues to evolve, the lessons learned from Morgan's investments will resonate, inspiring a new wave of innovation that transcends boundaries and redefines possibilities.

Building a Sustainable Future

Building a sustainable future is not merely a catchphrase; it is an imperative that Morgan Liao embraced with the fervor of a caffeinated squirrel. The concept of sustainability encompasses environmental, social, and economic dimensions, and Morgan's approach was to weave these threads into a cohesive tapestry that would not only benefit current generations but also ensure a thriving world for those yet to come.

Theoretical Framework

At the core of Morgan's philosophy was the Triple Bottom Line (TBL) theory, which posits that businesses should commit to focusing on social and environmental concerns just as they do on profits. The TBL framework suggests that success should be measured not just by financial performance but also by the impact on people and the planet. Mathematically, this can be expressed as:

$$\text{Sustainable Success} = f(\text{Profit, People, Planet}) \tag{86}$$

Where f is a function that integrates these three dimensions into a holistic measure of success.

Identifying Future Visionaries

Morgan understood that building a sustainable future required identifying and nurturing future visionaries who would continue the work of creating innovative solutions. He established programs to mentor young innovators, emphasizing the importance of interdisciplinary collaboration. By doing so, he aimed to foster a new generation of thinkers who could approach problems from multiple angles.

One example of this initiative was the "Future Innovators Program," where students from various disciplines were brought together to tackle real-world problems. This program led to the development of a biodegradable packaging solution that significantly reduced plastic waste in urban areas. The project not only showcased the power of collaboration but also highlighted the potential for young minds to effect change.

Investing in Innovative Ideas

Morgan's commitment to sustainability also manifested in his investment strategies. Recognizing that financial backing was crucial for innovative ideas to flourish, he established a fund dedicated to supporting startups focused on sustainability. This fund provided seed capital for projects that aimed to solve pressing environmental issues, such as renewable energy technologies and waste management solutions.

For instance, one startup that received funding developed an AI-driven system to optimize energy consumption in commercial buildings. By analyzing usage patterns and predicting peak demand times, the system reduced energy waste by up to 30%, showcasing how technology can align with sustainability goals.

Building a Sustainable Infrastructure

Morgan's vision extended to the infrastructure of cities. He advocated for smart city initiatives that integrated technology with urban planning to create more sustainable living environments. The concept of a "smart city" involves using sensors, data analytics, and IoT (Internet of Things) devices to manage resources efficiently.

For example, in collaboration with city planners, Morgan's team implemented a smart waste management system that utilized sensors in trash bins to optimize collection routes. This not only reduced fuel consumption and emissions but also improved the overall efficiency of waste management operations.

Challenges and Solutions

Despite the clear benefits of building a sustainable future, Morgan faced numerous challenges. One significant issue was the resistance from traditional industries that prioritized short-term profits over long-term sustainability. To address this, he employed a strategy of education and engagement, working to demonstrate the financial viability of sustainable practices.

Morgan often quipped, "Convincing a corporation to go green is like convincing a cat to take a bath—it's going to take some treats and a lot of patience." Through workshops and seminars, he showcased case studies of businesses that thrived after adopting sustainable practices, thus changing perceptions and encouraging more companies to follow suit.

Creating a Culture of Sustainability

In addition to practical initiatives, Morgan recognized the importance of creating a culture of sustainability within organizations and communities. He championed the idea that sustainability should be ingrained in the values of an organization, influencing every decision made.

To foster this culture, he introduced sustainability training programs for employees at all levels. These programs emphasized the role of individuals in contributing to sustainability goals, encouraging employees to think critically about their daily actions and their environmental impact. The result was a workforce that was not only informed but also motivated to make sustainable choices.

Conclusion

In conclusion, Morgan Liao's approach to building a sustainable future was multifaceted and deeply rooted in collaboration, innovation, and education. By leveraging the principles of the Triple Bottom Line, investing in future visionaries, and creating a culture of sustainability, he laid the groundwork for a more sustainable world. As he often said, "The future is not something we enter; the future is something we create." Through his efforts, Morgan ensured that the future would be one where innovation and sustainability walked hand in hand, paving the way for generations to come.

Morgan's Role as an Advisor

Morgan Liao, having established himself as a pivotal figure in the Digital Humanities and the broader context of the Cyber Renaissance, transitioned into the role of an advisor with a unique blend of insight and humor. This role was not merely a title; it was a commitment to shaping the next generation of innovators, much like how a cat shapes its owner—by sitting on their keyboard and demanding attention.

Mentorship Philosophy

Morgan's mentorship philosophy can be encapsulated in a simple equation:

$$\text{Success} = \text{Guidance} + \text{Empowerment} + \text{A Dash of Humor}$$

He believed that providing guidance was essential, but empowering young innovators to carve their own paths was paramount. His approach was reminiscent of a wise Yoda, but instead of a lightsaber, he wielded a laptop and a collection of dad jokes that could make even the most serious programmer chuckle.

Identifying Future Visionaries

Morgan's keen eye for potential allowed him to identify future visionaries. He often likened this process to finding the right avocado at the grocery store—if you squeeze too hard, you might ruin it, but if you don't squeeze at all, you might end up with a rock-hard disappointment. He taught aspiring innovators to recognize the signs of readiness, such as:

- **Passion:** A genuine enthusiasm for their projects, often demonstrated through late-night coding sessions fueled by pizza and energy drinks.

- **Creativity:** The ability to think outside the box, or in some cases, outside the entire room, which often resulted in innovative solutions to complex problems.

- **Resilience:** The capacity to bounce back from failures—because in the tech world, failure isn't just an option; it's a prerequisite.

Investing in Innovative Ideas

Morgan understood that investing in innovative ideas required more than just financial backing; it demanded a holistic approach. He often joked, "Investing in innovation is like adopting a pet. You need to feed it, walk it, and sometimes clean up after it." This philosophy led him to establish a fund dedicated to supporting early-stage projects that aligned with his vision of a digital renaissance.

$$Investment = Funding + Mentorship + Networking \qquad (87)$$

His model emphasized that financial support should be coupled with mentorship and networking opportunities, creating a comprehensive ecosystem for budding innovators.

Building a Sustainable Future

Morgan's vision for a sustainable future was rooted in the principles of ethical innovation. He frequently reminded his mentees, "Sustainability isn't just about recycling; it's about creating systems that don't need constant fixing—like my last relationship." This cheeky analogy underscored the importance of designing technology that was not only innovative but also responsible.

To achieve this, Morgan advocated for:

1. **Sustainable Practices:** Encouraging projects that prioritized environmental impact and social responsibility.

2. **Interdisciplinary Collaboration:** Fostering partnerships between technologists, artists, and social scientists to create well-rounded solutions.

3. **Community Engagement:** Involving local communities in the innovation process to ensure that solutions were relevant and beneficial.

Morgan's Role as an Advisor in Practice

In practice, Morgan's role as an advisor was characterized by hands-on involvement. He hosted workshops that felt more like stand-up comedy sessions than traditional lectures. Participants often left with a mix of knowledge and laughter, which he believed was the key to effective learning.

For example, during one workshop on digital storytelling, Morgan encouraged attendees to share their personal narratives. He quipped, "If you can't make your story interesting, at least make it weird. Weird is memorable!" This approach not only fostered creativity but also built a strong sense of community among participants.

Conclusion

In conclusion, Morgan Liao's role as an advisor was a testament to his belief in the power of mentorship, humor, and ethical innovation. By investing in future visionaries and promoting sustainable practices, he laid the groundwork for a thriving ecosystem of innovators who would continue to push the boundaries of the Digital Humanities. As he often said, "The future belongs to those who can laugh at their mistakes—preferably while coding them out of existence." With this spirit, Morgan ensured that the legacy of the Cyber Renaissance would endure, inspiring generations to come.

Morgan's Latest Endeavors

Post-Cyber Renaissance Projects

In the wake of the Cyber Renaissance, Morgan Liao embarked on a series of ambitious projects that aimed to push the boundaries of technology and its applications in various fields. These projects were not merely extensions of his previous work; they represented a paradigm shift in how technology interacts with humanity, culture, and knowledge.

Expanding into Space Exploration

One of the most audacious ventures Morgan undertook was the expansion into space exploration. With the advent of new technologies and the increasing interest in extraterrestrial life, Morgan believed that the next frontier for digital humanities lay among the stars. The project, aptly named *Digital Cosmos*, aimed to create a comprehensive database of celestial bodies, their histories, and potential for life.

$$D = \int_0^\infty \frac{N(t) \cdot P(t)}{R(t)} \, dt \tag{88}$$

Where:

- D = Digital database of celestial bodies
- $N(t)$ = Number of new celestial discoveries over time t
- $P(t)$ = Probability of life on discovered celestial bodies
- $R(t)$ = Rate of technological advancements in space exploration

This equation encapsulates the essence of Morgan's vision: as new discoveries are made, the probability of finding life increases, and thus the database expands exponentially. The *Digital Cosmos* project also included partnerships with NASA and private space companies, integrating AI to analyze data collected from telescopes and space missions.

The Quest for Extraterrestrial Intelligence

Building on the momentum of *Digital Cosmos*, Morgan launched the *SETI 2.0* initiative. This project sought to enhance the search for extraterrestrial intelligence (ETI) using advanced algorithms and machine learning techniques. By leveraging big data analytics, Morgan's team aimed to sift through vast amounts of cosmic data to identify patterns that might indicate the presence of intelligent life.

The approach was twofold:

+ **Data Collection:** Utilizing radio telescopes and satellite technology to gather signals from deep space.

+ **Pattern Recognition:** Implementing neural networks to detect anomalies in the data that could signify artificial signals.

Morgan often joked, "If we can find a needle in a haystack, surely we can find a signal from a civilization that's been trying to reach us since the invention of the wheel!" This humor masked the seriousness of the endeavor, which faced significant challenges, including the vastness of space and the limitations of current technology.

Unveiling New Technologies

Morgan's projects did not stop at space. He also focused on unveiling new technologies that could redefine human interaction with digital content. One such initiative was the development of *Holo-Connect*, a platform that combined holographic technology with social media, allowing users to interact with 3D representations of people and places from anywhere in the world.

The theoretical framework behind *Holo-Connect* involved the integration of various fields:

$$H = f(C, T, I) \tag{89}$$

Where:

+ H = Holographic interaction level

+ C = Clarity of the holographic display

+ T = Technology used for transmission

+ I = Interactivity features of the platform

Morgan envisioned a world where physical distance would no longer hinder personal connections. He humorously remarked, "Why send a text when you can send a hologram of yourself doing jazz hands? It's way more effective!"

Collaborations with Global Leaders

Recognizing the importance of collaboration, Morgan sought partnerships with global leaders in technology, education, and the arts. This led to the formation of the *Global Innovation Consortium*, a network aimed at fostering interdisciplinary research and development. The consortium brought together experts from various fields to tackle pressing issues such as climate change, public health, and digital ethics.

One of the consortium's notable projects was the *Green Tech Initiative*, which focused on developing sustainable technologies using digital humanities principles. The initiative aimed to create a framework for understanding the environmental impact of technology through data visualization and historical analysis.

The theoretical underpinnings of this initiative were based on the concept of sustainability in the digital age:

$$S = \frac{E}{C} \cdot R \tag{90}$$

Where:

+ S = Sustainability index

+ E = Environmental impact of technology

+ C = Cost of implementing sustainable practices

+ R = Rate of adoption of green technologies

Morgan often quipped, "If we can teach a computer to recycle, we might just save the planet!" This light-hearted approach helped engage a broader audience in discussions about sustainability.

Concluding Thoughts

Morgan Liao's post-Cyber Renaissance projects illustrate the limitless potential of technology when combined with humanistic inquiry. His ability to blend humor with profound insights allowed him to inspire others to think critically about the future of innovation. As he often said, "The future is not something we enter; the future is something we create—with a little help from our digital friends."

These projects not only advanced the fields of digital humanities and technology but also laid the groundwork for future generations of innovators to explore the uncharted territories of knowledge, culture, and human connection.

Expanding into Space Exploration

In the wake of the Cyber Renaissance, Morgan Liao found himself at the forefront of a new frontier: space exploration. As humanity's ambitions reached beyond the confines of Earth, Morgan recognized the potential for digital humanities to play a pivotal role in this cosmic endeavor. The intersection of technology, culture, and the vast unknown of space offered a fertile ground for innovation and inquiry.

Theoretical Foundations

The theoretical underpinnings of Morgan's approach to space exploration were rooted in a multidisciplinary framework that combined astrophysics, digital humanities, and artificial intelligence. At its core, this framework sought to answer fundamental questions about humanity's place in the universe, the nature of knowledge, and the preservation of cultural identity in an expanding cosmos.

One of the key equations that guided Morgan's vision was the Drake Equation, which estimates the number of active extraterrestrial civilizations in the Milky Way galaxy:

$$N = R^* \times f_p \times n_e \times f_l \times f_i \times f_c \times L \tag{91}$$

where:

+ N = the number of civilizations with which humans could communicate

+ R^* = the average rate of star formation per year in our galaxy

+ f_p = the fraction of those stars that have planetary systems

+ n_e = the average number of planets that could potentially support life per star that has planets

+ f_l = the fraction of planets that could support life that actually develop life

+ f_i = the fraction of planets with intelligent life

+ f_c = the fraction of civilizations that develop a technology that releases detectable signs of their existence into space

+ L = the length of time civilizations can communicate

This equation not only sparked interest in extraterrestrial life but also highlighted the importance of collaboration across disciplines to decipher the cosmos.

Challenges in Space Exploration

Despite the excitement surrounding space exploration, Morgan faced numerous challenges. The first was the vastness of space itself, which presented logistical issues in terms of communication and data transfer. The delay in signals between Earth and distant spacecraft could range from minutes to hours, complicating real-time interactions. Morgan proposed the development of advanced algorithms capable of predictive modeling to anticipate data needs and streamline communication processes.

Another significant challenge was the preservation of human culture and knowledge in extraterrestrial environments. As humans began to colonize other planets, it became imperative to ensure that cultural heritage was not lost. Morgan's team developed a project called the *Cultural Continuity Initiative*, which aimed to create digital repositories of human culture, literature, and art that could be transmitted and preserved across generations and galaxies.

Examples of Innovation

To tackle these challenges, Morgan spearheaded several groundbreaking projects:

- **Interstellar Archives:** A digital archive designed to store and transmit cultural artifacts, languages, and histories. Using advanced compression algorithms, the archives ensured that even the most intricate details of human culture could be preserved and shared with future generations of spacefarers.

- **AI-Driven Cultural Ambassadors:** Morgan's team developed artificial intelligence systems that could serve as cultural ambassadors for humanity. These AI entities were programmed with extensive knowledge of human history, philosophy, and art, allowing them to engage with potential extraterrestrial civilizations in meaningful dialogue.

- **Virtual Reality Space Training:** To prepare astronauts for the psychological challenges of long-term space missions, Morgan's team created a virtual reality platform that simulated various extraterrestrial environments. This innovative training tool helped astronauts acclimate to the isolation and unfamiliarity of space travel while maintaining a connection to Earth.

The Impact of Morgan's Work

Morgan's contributions to space exploration extended beyond technology; they also influenced the way humanity perceived its role in the universe. By emphasizing the importance of cultural preservation and ethical considerations in space exploration, Morgan laid the groundwork for a new era of interstellar ethics.

Moreover, his work inspired a generation of young innovators to pursue careers in space technology, digital humanities, and interdisciplinary research. The Cyber Renaissance had not only redefined the boundaries of human knowledge but also ignited a passion for exploration that transcended the stars.

In conclusion, Morgan Liao's expansion into space exploration marked a significant chapter in the narrative of the Cyber Renaissance. By integrating technology with the humanities, he ensured that as humanity reached for the stars, it would do so with a sense of purpose, responsibility, and an unwavering commitment to preserving the rich tapestry of human culture. The cosmos was not just a destination; it was a canvas upon which humanity could paint its legacy for eons to come.

The Quest for Extraterrestrial Intelligence

The quest for extraterrestrial intelligence (ETI) has been a tantalizing endeavor for scientists, philosophers, and futurists alike. As Morgan Liao transitioned from revolutionizing the digital humanities to exploring the cosmos, he brought along a unique perspective that combined technology, ethics, and a dash of humor reminiscent of a Zach Galifianakis stand-up routine. This section delves into the theoretical frameworks, challenges, and examples that characterize this ambitious pursuit.

Theoretical Frameworks

At the heart of the search for extraterrestrial intelligence lies the famous *Drake Equation*, formulated by astronomer Frank Drake in 1961. This probabilistic formula estimates the number of active, communicative extraterrestrial civilizations in the Milky Way galaxy. The equation is expressed as:

$$N = R^* \times f_p \times n_e \times f_l \times f_i \times f_c \times L \qquad (92)$$

Where:

- N = the number of civilizations with which humans could communicate.

- R^* = the average rate of star formation per year in our galaxy.

- f_p = the fraction of those stars that have planetary systems.

- n_e = the average number of planets that could potentially support life for each star that has planets.

- f_l = the fraction of planets that could support life that actually develop life.

- f_i = the fraction of planets with life that develop intelligent life.

- f_c = the fraction of civilizations that develop a technology that releases detectable signs of their existence into space.

- L = the length of time civilizations can communicate.

Morgan, with his penchant for data analysis, sought to refine these parameters using big data techniques, drawing on vast datasets from astronomy and planetary science. He often joked that the only thing more complex than the Drake Equation was his mother's lasagna recipe.

Challenges in the Search for ETI

Despite the theoretical underpinnings, the quest for ETI is fraught with challenges. One significant problem is the *Fermi Paradox*, which questions why, given the vastness of the universe and the high probability of extraterrestrial civilizations, we have yet to encounter any signs of intelligent life. Morgan humorously suggested that maybe aliens are just too busy binge-watching their version of *Stranger Things*.

- **Technological Limitations:** Current technology limits our ability to detect faint signals from distant civilizations. The sensitivity of our instruments is paramount, and Morgan's team worked on enhancing radio telescope capabilities to increase the chances of detection.

- **Signal Noise:** The vastness of the electromagnetic spectrum is filled with noise, making it difficult to distinguish genuine signals from cosmic background radiation. Morgan proposed using machine learning algorithms to filter out noise and identify potential ETI signals.

- **Temporal Constraints:** The lifespan of civilizations may be short in cosmic terms, leading to a situation where we may not overlap with other intelligent beings. Morgan quipped, "Maybe we're just unlucky, like trying to find a parking spot at a concert."

Examples of Initiatives and Discoveries

Morgan's foray into the search for ETI led to several groundbreaking projects:

+ **SETI@Home:** This distributed computing project allows individuals to contribute processing power to analyze radio signals from space. Morgan encouraged young innovators to participate, emphasizing that every little bit helps, much like how he felt about his college group projects.

+ **Breakthrough Listen Initiative:** Launched in 2015, this initiative aims to scan the entire sky for signals using advanced telescopes. Morgan's team collaborated with Breakthrough Listen to enhance data analysis techniques, applying big data methodologies to sift through the vast amounts of information collected.

+ **The Wow! Signal:** Discovered in 1977, this strong narrowband radio signal from the Sagittarius constellation remains unexplained. Morgan often referenced the Wow! Signal as the universe's version of a text message left on read, emphasizing the need for further investigation.

The Ethical Implications

As with any significant technological advancement, ethical considerations abound. Morgan advocated for responsible exploration, emphasizing the need to consider the implications of contacting extraterrestrial civilizations. He raised questions such as:

+ **Should we send signals?** The decision to broadcast our presence to the cosmos could have unforeseen consequences. Morgan likened it to shouting into a crowded room—sometimes, it's better to keep your voice down.

+ **Cultural Sensitivity:** If we were to encounter another civilization, how would we approach them? Morgan proposed guidelines for respectful communication, ensuring that our excitement does not overshadow the dignity of potential extraterrestrial beings.

+ **Resource Allocation:** The pursuit of ETI requires significant funding and resources. Morgan argued for a balanced approach, ensuring that we do not neglect pressing issues on Earth while searching for life beyond it.

Conclusion

Morgan Liao's quest for extraterrestrial intelligence exemplifies the intersection of technology, ethics, and humor. By leveraging advanced data analysis techniques and fostering collaboration among innovators, he has contributed to the ongoing search for life beyond our planet. As we continue to gaze into the cosmos, we are reminded of the possibilities that lie ahead—much like the unexpected plot twists in a Galifianakis comedy special. The quest for ETI is not merely about finding life; it's about understanding our place in the universe and the shared journey of discovery that unites us all.

Unveiling New Technologies

In the wake of the Cyber Renaissance, Morgan Liao embarked on a series of groundbreaking projects that aimed to redefine the boundaries of technology. His focus was not only on enhancing existing systems but also on developing entirely new technologies that would address pressing global challenges. This section explores some of these innovations, the theoretical frameworks behind them, the problems they aimed to solve, and examples of their application.

Theoretical Frameworks

At the heart of Morgan's technological innovations lay several key theoretical frameworks. One of the most prominent was the concept of **Human-Centered Design** (HCD), which emphasizes the importance of designing technology that meets the needs of users rather than forcing users to adapt to technology. According to Norman (2013), HCD involves iterative design processes that include user feedback at every stage, ensuring that the final product is intuitive and accessible.

Another crucial theory was **Systems Thinking**, which posits that complex problems cannot be understood in isolation but rather as part of a larger system. This approach allowed Morgan and his team to consider the interdependencies between various technological, social, and environmental factors. Meadows (2008) highlights the importance of recognizing these interconnections to develop sustainable solutions.

Addressing Global Challenges

Morgan's innovations were driven by a desire to tackle some of the most pressing global challenges, including climate change, inequality in education, and the preservation of cultural heritage. For instance, one of his projects focused on developing **Smart Agriculture Technologies** to enhance food security. By integrating IoT sensors with AI algorithms, farmers could monitor soil health, weather patterns, and crop conditions in real-time, leading to more informed decision-making.

The equation governing the optimization of resource allocation in smart agriculture can be expressed as:

$$R = \frac{C}{T} \cdot \text{Yield} \tag{93}$$

where R represents the resource allocation efficiency, C is the cost of inputs, T is the time taken for crop maturation, and Yield is the output of crops. This equation illustrates the balance between costs and time, critical for maximizing agricultural productivity.

Examples of Innovations

One of Morgan's flagship innovations was the development of a **Virtual Reality (VR) platform for historical education**. This platform allowed users to immerse themselves in historical events, providing a unique and engaging way to learn about the past. For example, students could experience the signing of the Declaration of Independence or the construction of the Great Wall of China firsthand. This approach not only made history more accessible but also fostered empathy and understanding among users.

The VR platform employed cutting-edge **3D modeling techniques** to recreate historical environments accurately. The mathematical models used for rendering these environments were based on the principles of geometry and physics, ensuring that the virtual experiences were as realistic as possible. The equation for rendering a 3D object can be summarized as:

$$V = f(x, y, z) + \text{Lighting}(x, y, z) \tag{94}$$

where V represents the visual output, $f(x, y, z)$ is the function defining the object's shape, and Lighting(x, y, z) accounts for the effects of light on the object, enhancing realism.

Another notable project was the integration of **Artificial Intelligence in Cultural Preservation**. Morgan's team developed an AI-driven database that cataloged endangered languages and dialects, facilitating their study and preservation. By utilizing natural language processing, the system could analyze and generate translations, making these languages more accessible to researchers and the general public. The effectiveness of this system can be measured using the following equation:

$$E = \frac{A + B}{C} \tag{95}$$

where E represents the effectiveness of the language preservation system, A is the number of languages documented, B is the number of active users engaging with the content, and C is the total number of endangered languages. This equation underscores the importance of user engagement in the success of cultural preservation efforts.

Overcoming Challenges

Despite the excitement surrounding these innovations, Morgan faced numerous challenges in their development. One major obstacle was securing funding for projects that often straddled the line between technology and the humanities. To address this, Morgan employed a strategy of **Crowdsourcing Ideas and Resources,** leveraging social media platforms to connect with potential investors and collaborators. This approach not only garnered financial support but also created a community of passionate individuals dedicated to the cause.

Moreover, ethical considerations were paramount in the development of new technologies. Morgan was acutely aware of the potential for AI to perpetuate biases, particularly in cultural contexts. To combat this, he established a set of ethical guidelines that governed the design and implementation of AI systems. These guidelines emphasized transparency, inclusivity, and accountability, ensuring that the technologies developed would benefit all members of society.

Conclusion

In conclusion, the unveiling of new technologies during the Cyber Renaissance marked a significant turning point in the intersection of technology and the humanities. Morgan Liao's commitment to human-centered design, systems thinking, and ethical innovation has left an indelible mark on the landscape of future technologies. By addressing global challenges through innovative solutions, he inspired a new generation of thinkers and creators, proving that the future is not just about technology—it's about how we use it to enhance the human experience.

Collaborations with Global Leaders

Morgan Liao's journey into the realm of global innovation was marked by his strategic collaborations with leaders across various sectors. These partnerships not only amplified his vision for the Cyber Renaissance but also addressed pressing global challenges through the lens of digital humanities.

The Importance of Strategic Alliances

In an age where technology and culture intersect, the significance of strategic alliances cannot be overstated. Morgan understood that to effect meaningful change, he needed to collaborate with thought leaders, policymakers, and innovators worldwide. This approach is rooted in the theory of collaborative advantage, which posits that organizations can achieve greater outcomes by working together rather than in isolation [?].

Identifying Key Partners

Morgan's first step was identifying leaders who shared his vision. This included:

+ **Cultural Institutions:** Collaborating with museums and archives to digitize historical artifacts and make them accessible to a global audience.

+ **Educational Leaders:** Partnering with universities to integrate digital humanities into their curricula, thus fostering a new generation of thinkers.

+ **Tech Innovators:** Working with AI developers to create tools that enhance cultural preservation and accessibility.

One notable collaboration was with the *Global Digital Heritage Initiative*, which aimed to preserve endangered cultures through technology. Morgan's role was pivotal in leveraging AI to analyze and archive oral histories, thereby ensuring that the narratives of marginalized communities were preserved for future generations.

Addressing Global Challenges

Morgan's collaborations were not just about technology; they were also about tackling global challenges. For instance, he partnered with leaders from the *United Nations Educational, Scientific and Cultural Organization (UNESCO)* to address issues of cultural heritage in conflict zones. This partnership led to the development of a framework for using virtual reality to recreate lost cultural sites, allowing people to experience and learn about them even when they are no longer physically accessible.

The equation governing the impact of these collaborations can be represented as:

$$Impact = \frac{(Innovation + Collaboration) \times (Outreach + Education)}{Cultural Barriers}$$

(96)

Where: - *Innovation* represents the new technologies developed. - *Collaboration* signifies the partnerships formed. - *Outreach* refers to the dissemination of knowledge. - *Education* denotes the training provided to future leaders. - *Cultural Barriers* are the obstacles faced in sharing knowledge across different cultures.

This equation illustrates how combining innovation and collaboration can amplify impact, particularly when outreach and education are prioritized.

Case Studies of Successful Collaborations

1. **The Digital Archive of Endangered Languages:** In partnership with linguistic experts and global universities, Morgan spearheaded a project that utilized AI to document and preserve endangered languages. This initiative not only saved languages from extinction but also created a platform for cultural exchange.

2. **Virtual Museums:** Collaborating with tech giants, Morgan helped create virtual museum experiences that allowed users worldwide to explore art and history from their homes. This project was particularly beneficial during global lockdowns, demonstrating how technology can bridge gaps in accessibility.

3. **AI for Social Justice:** Morgan partnered with non-profit organizations to develop AI tools that analyze social media trends, helping to identify and combat misinformation. This initiative empowered communities to engage in informed discussions about social justice issues.

Challenges in Collaboration

Despite the successes, Morgan faced challenges in his collaborations. These included:

- **Cultural Differences:** Navigating diverse perspectives and practices required sensitivity and adaptability. - **Resource Allocation:** Ensuring equitable distribution of resources among partners was crucial for maintaining trust. -

Technological Disparities: Addressing the varying levels of technological access and literacy among collaborators was essential for effective implementation.

Morgan's ability to navigate these challenges was rooted in his commitment to ethical innovation and inclusivity, ensuring that all voices were heard and valued.

Conclusion

Morgan Liao's collaborations with global leaders exemplified the power of collective action in the pursuit of a Cyber Renaissance. By uniting diverse talents and perspectives, he was able to create impactful solutions that transcended borders. As the digital landscape continues to evolve, these partnerships will serve as a model for future innovators seeking to make a difference in the world.

The Cyber Renaissance Legacy

Morgan's Place in History

In the annals of technological advancement, few figures stand as tall as Morgan Liao, whose contributions to the field of Digital Humanities have not only redefined the discipline but have also set a precedent for future innovators. Morgan's journey from a curious child hacking his way into trouble to a visionary leader in the Cyber Renaissance exemplifies the transformative power of technology when intertwined with the humanities.

The Convergence of Disciplines

Morgan's most significant impact lies in his ability to bridge the gap between technology and the humanities. This convergence is encapsulated in his vision of a Cyber Renaissance, where the analytical rigor of digital tools meets the rich narratives of human culture. According to Liao's theory of *Digital Synergy*, the integration of digital methodologies into the humanities not only enhances research capabilities but also democratizes access to knowledge.

$$\text{Digital Synergy} = \frac{\text{Digital Tools} + \text{Humanistic Inquiry}}{\text{Barriers to Access}} \quad (97)$$

This equation illustrates that as barriers to access diminish, the potential for innovative research and public engagement increases exponentially. Morgan's establishment of the Digital Humanities Institute serves as a testament to this theory, providing a global research hub that fosters collaboration among scholars from diverse backgrounds.

Addressing Societal Challenges

Morgan's work also responds to pressing societal challenges, such as the digital divide and issues of representation in digital spaces. By advocating for *Digital Equality*, he has emphasized the importance of creating inclusive platforms that allow marginalized voices to be heard. His projects, such as the *Knowledge Archive*, utilize advanced algorithms to curate and present a diverse array of cultural narratives, ensuring that history is not told from a singular perspective.

Influence on Educational Paradigms

Morgan's influence extends into educational paradigms, where he has revolutionized the way knowledge is disseminated. His introduction of augmented reality in educational settings allows students to engage with historical events in immersive ways, leading to deeper understanding and retention of information. This innovative approach has garnered attention from educators worldwide, prompting a shift towards experiential learning methodologies.

Legacy of Ethical Innovation

As Morgan navigated the complexities of digital innovation, he also confronted ethical dilemmas inherent in the use of technology. His commitment to ethical AI development has inspired a generation of technologists to consider the implications of their work. Morgan's framework for *Responsible Innovation* advocates for transparency and accountability, ensuring that technological advancements serve the greater good rather than exacerbate existing inequalities.

$$\text{Responsible Innovation} = \frac{\text{Ethical Standards} + \text{Community Engagement}}{\text{Technological Advancement}} \tag{98}$$

This equation posits that true progress in technology must be accompanied by a commitment to ethical practices and community involvement. Morgan's legacy, therefore, is not only one of technological prowess but also of a profound moral compass guiding the future of innovation.

A Lasting Impact on Future Generations

Morgan Liao's contributions have paved the way for future innovators who are inspired by his vision and approach. The Cyber Renaissance movement, which he spearheaded, continues to influence scholars, technologists, and educators alike.

His belief that the humanities can thrive in the digital age resonates strongly, fostering a new generation of thinkers who are eager to explore the intersection of culture and technology.

In conclusion, Morgan Liao's place in history is secured not only by his groundbreaking projects and theories but also by his unwavering commitment to ethical practices and social responsibility. As we look to the future, the principles he championed will undoubtedly shape the trajectory of Digital Humanities and inspire countless others to follow in his footsteps. The impact of his work is a clarion call for a future where technology and humanity coexist harmoniously, ensuring that the lessons of the past inform the innovations of tomorrow.

Perpetuating the Cyber Renaissance

The Cyber Renaissance, a term coined to describe the transformative wave of technological and cultural advancements brought forth by Morgan Liao and his contemporaries, represents not only a moment in time but a continuous movement aimed at redefining the relationship between technology and the humanities. To perpetuate this renaissance, it is essential to understand its foundational theories, the challenges it faces, and the practical examples that can guide future innovators.

Foundational Theories

At the heart of the Cyber Renaissance lies the theory of **Technological Humanism**, which posits that technology should serve humanity, enhancing our understanding of the human experience rather than detracting from it. This theory can be encapsulated in the equation:

$$TH = T + H \tag{99}$$

Where TH represents Technological Humanism, T is technology, and H is the humanities. This equation suggests that the integration of technology and humanities creates a holistic approach to innovation.

Another critical theory is the **Digital Empathy Model**, which emphasizes the need for emotional intelligence in the development of digital technologies. This model asserts that:

$$DE = EI + T \tag{100}$$

Where DE is Digital Empathy, EI is emotional intelligence, and T is technology. The model underscores the importance of designing technology that resonates with human emotions and experiences.

Challenges to Perpetuation

Despite its promise, the Cyber Renaissance faces several challenges that could impede its perpetuation:

+ **Digital Divide:** The gap between those who have access to technology and those who do not continues to widen. Addressing this issue requires innovative solutions to ensure equitable access to digital resources.

+ **Ethical Concerns:** As technology evolves, ethical dilemmas surrounding data privacy, surveillance, and algorithmic bias become more pronounced. Innovators must prioritize ethical considerations in their work.

+ **Cultural Resistance:** Some communities may resist technological changes due to cultural beliefs or fear of the unknown. Engaging these communities through dialogue and education is vital.

Examples of Perpetuating the Cyber Renaissance

To ensure the Cyber Renaissance continues to flourish, several initiatives can be undertaken, drawing inspiration from successful projects:

+ **Community Tech Hubs:** Establishing local tech hubs that provide resources, mentorship, and training can empower communities to engage with technology. For example, the *Tech for Good* initiative in various cities has successfully bridged the digital divide by offering free workshops and access to technology.

+ **Ethical AI Frameworks:** Developing frameworks that guide the ethical use of artificial intelligence can help address concerns about bias and privacy. The *AI Ethics Guidelines* released by various international organizations serve as a model for creating responsible AI practices.

+ **Cultural Collaborations:** Partnering with artists, historians, and cultural organizations to create projects that blend technology with the arts can foster greater appreciation for digital humanities. The *Digital Museum Project* exemplifies this by using augmented reality to bring historical artifacts to life, making them accessible to a broader audience.

Conclusion

Perpetuating the Cyber Renaissance requires a multifaceted approach that embraces technological humanism, fosters digital empathy, and addresses the challenges posed by the digital age. By learning from successful examples and prioritizing ethical considerations, future innovators can ensure that the legacy of Morgan Liao and the Cyber Renaissance continues to inspire generations to come. The journey is not merely about technological advancement but about enhancing the human experience in an increasingly digital world.

$$\text{Future Innovators} = \text{Cyber Renaissance} \times \text{Ethical Engagement} \qquad (101)$$

In this equation, the future of innovation is contingent upon the ongoing commitment to ethical engagement and the principles that underpin the Cyber Renaissance. As we move forward, let us remember that technology is not the destination; it is merely the vehicle that drives us toward a more enlightened and connected humanity.

Future Innovators Inspired by Morgan

Morgan Liao's contributions to the field of digital humanities have sparked a new wave of innovation among young thinkers and creators. His pioneering work has not only transformed academic landscapes but also inspired a generation of future innovators who seek to blend technology with the arts and humanities. This section delves into the impact of Morgan's legacy, highlighting emerging talents and their groundbreaking projects, as well as the theoretical frameworks that underpin their work.

Theoretical Foundations of Inspiration

At the heart of Morgan's influence is the theory of *constructivism*, which posits that knowledge is constructed through interaction with the environment and others. This theory aligns closely with Morgan's approach, emphasizing collaboration and mentorship. As he often stated, "Innovation is not a solitary journey; it's a collective adventure." This idea resonates deeply with the future innovators who have taken Morgan's teachings to heart.

Emerging Innovators

1. Ava Patel: The Digital Archivist   Ava Patel, a 19-year-old undergraduate student, has taken Morgan's vision of digital storytelling to new heights. Her project, *Voices of the Past*, utilizes artificial intelligence to curate and present oral histories from marginalized communities.   By employing natural language processing algorithms, Ava not only preserves these narratives but also analyzes them for patterns of cultural significance. Her work exemplifies the intersection of technology and humanities, demonstrating how Morgan's influence continues to thrive.

2. Jamal Robinson: The AR Pioneer   Jamal Robinson, inspired by Morgan's use of augmented reality (AR) in education, has developed an AR application called *History in Your Hands*. This app allows users to interact with historical artifacts in real-time, providing immersive learning experiences. Jamal's project has garnered attention from educational institutions, as it aligns with the growing demand for interactive learning tools.   His innovative approach reflects Morgan's ethos of democratizing knowledge through technology.

3. Sophia Chen: The Ethical Technologist   Sophia Chen, a self-proclaimed "ethical technologist," has dedicated her career to addressing bias in AI systems. Inspired by Morgan's advocacy for ethical AI development, she founded *FairTech*, a non-profit organization focused on creating equitable algorithms.   Through workshops and community engagement, Sophia empowers young developers to prioritize ethics in their technological creations, ensuring that the future of AI is inclusive and just.

Challenges and Opportunities

While Morgan's legacy has inspired many, future innovators face significant challenges. The rapid pace of technological advancement often outstrips ethical considerations, leading to potential misuse of innovations. As Ava, Jamal, and Sophia navigate these waters, they encounter obstacles such as funding limitations, public skepticism, and the need for interdisciplinary collaboration.

For instance, Ava's project has faced criticism regarding data privacy and representation. To address these concerns, she has implemented a framework for community involvement, ensuring that the voices represented in her archive are not only preserved but also respected. This approach echoes Morgan's belief in the importance of ethical considerations in digital humanities.

The Ripple Effect of Inspiration

Morgan's impact extends beyond individual projects; it has fostered a culture of innovation that encourages young thinkers to pursue their passions fearlessly. The *Cyber Renaissance Network*, a community of innovators inspired by Morgan, hosts annual conferences where emerging talents share their work and collaborate on interdisciplinary projects. This network not only amplifies their voices but also provides a platform for mentorship, echoing Morgan's commitment to guiding the next generation.

In conclusion, the future innovators inspired by Morgan Liao are reshaping the landscape of digital humanities and technology. By embracing constructivist principles and addressing ethical dilemmas, they are poised to continue the legacy of the Cyber Renaissance. As they forge new paths, the lessons learned from Morgan's journey will undoubtedly guide their efforts, ensuring that innovation remains grounded in humanity.

$$\text{Innovation} = \text{Collaboration} + \text{Ethics} + \text{Creativity} \qquad (102)$$

This equation encapsulates the essence of Morgan's influence, reminding future innovators that true progress is achieved through collective effort, ethical considerations, and boundless creativity. The torch has been passed, and the future is bright.

The Lasting Impact of Digital Humanities

The field of Digital Humanities (DH) has emerged as a transformative force within academia, culture, and society at large. Morgan Liao's contributions to this discipline have not only redefined traditional methods of scholarship but have also paved the way for a more inclusive and accessible approach to knowledge. This section explores the enduring impact of Digital Humanities, focusing on its theoretical underpinnings, prevalent challenges, and illustrative examples that showcase its significance.

Theoretical Foundations of Digital Humanities

At its core, Digital Humanities integrates computational tools and methodologies with the study of humanities disciplines such as literature, history, and philosophy. The theoretical framework of DH can be traced back to the intersection of several disciplines, including:

- **Humanities Computing:** This foundational theory emphasizes the use of computational methods to analyze and visualize textual data. Scholars like Susan Hockey have been pivotal in advocating for the importance of digital tools in humanities research.

- **Critical Digital Humanities:** This perspective critiques the implications of digital technologies on society and culture, urging scholars to consider issues of power, equity, and representation within digital spaces.

- **Digital Cultural Heritage:** This theory focuses on the preservation and dissemination of cultural artifacts through digital means, emphasizing the importance of accessibility and engagement with diverse audiences.

These theoretical frameworks collectively advocate for a critical engagement with technology, urging scholars to reflect on the ethical implications of their work while harnessing the power of digital tools.

Challenges in Digital Humanities

Despite its potential, the field of Digital Humanities faces several challenges that can hinder its progress and impact:

- **Digital Divide:** Access to technology remains uneven across various demographics, creating disparities in participation within DH initiatives. This divide can exacerbate existing inequalities in education and cultural representation.

- **Sustainability of Projects:** Many DH projects rely on funding and institutional support, which can be precarious. The long-term sustainability of these initiatives is often uncertain, leading to concerns about the preservation of digital artifacts and knowledge.

- **Interdisciplinary Collaboration:** While DH promotes collaboration between disciplines, it can also create friction. Scholars from traditional humanities backgrounds may struggle to adapt to the technical demands of digital projects, leading to tensions in collaborative efforts.

Addressing these challenges requires a concerted effort from scholars, institutions, and policymakers to create a more equitable and sustainable landscape for Digital Humanities.

Illustrative Examples of Impact

Morgan Liao's vision and projects exemplify the lasting impact of Digital Humanities. Here are several notable examples:

1. **The Knowledge Archive:** This project serves as a digital repository for historical texts, artifacts, and multimedia resources. By utilizing advanced search algorithms and data visualization techniques, the archive allows users to explore connections between different cultural narratives, fostering a deeper understanding of history.

2. **Virtual Reality for Historical Immersion:** Liao's initiative to create immersive VR experiences of historical events has revolutionized the way students and scholars engage with the past. For instance, a VR simulation of the signing of the Declaration of Independence allows users to experience the event from multiple perspectives, enhancing empathy and understanding.

3. **Digital Storytelling:** By leveraging social media platforms, Liao has democratized knowledge-sharing, allowing individuals from diverse backgrounds to contribute their stories and experiences. This initiative not only preserves oral histories but also amplifies marginalized voices, fostering a more inclusive narrative landscape.

4. **Augmented Reality in Education:** Liao's collaboration with educational institutions to integrate AR into classroom settings has transformed traditional learning experiences. Students can interact with historical artifacts in real-time, bridging the gap between physical and digital learning environments.

These examples illustrate how Digital Humanities can transcend traditional boundaries, fostering innovation and engagement across various sectors.

Conclusion

The lasting impact of Digital Humanities, as evidenced by Morgan Liao's work, is profound and multifaceted. By integrating technology with the humanities, DH not only enhances our understanding of culture and history but also challenges us to confront ethical dilemmas and strive for inclusivity. As the field continues to evolve, it holds the promise of shaping a more equitable and accessible future for knowledge production and dissemination. The legacy of Morgan Liao serves as a beacon for future innovators, inspiring them to harness the power of digital tools in the pursuit of humanistic inquiry.

In summary, the contributions of Digital Humanities extend beyond academic boundaries; they resonate within communities, influence policy, and inspire future generations to explore the rich tapestry of human experience through a digital lens.

Honoring Morgan Liao's Legacy

As we reflect on the profound impact Morgan Liao has had on the field of digital humanities and beyond, it becomes essential to consider not only his contributions but also the framework through which we can honor his legacy. Morgan's innovative spirit and dedication to merging technology with the humanities have paved the way for future generations of thinkers and creators. This section outlines key aspects of how we can continue to celebrate and build upon Morgan's work.

Establishing the Morgan Liao Foundation

To ensure that Morgan's vision lives on, the establishment of the **Morgan Liao Foundation** is paramount. This foundation will serve multiple purposes:

- **Funding Scholarships:** Providing financial support for students pursuing studies in digital humanities, technology, and interdisciplinary fields.

- **Granting Research Opportunities:** Offering grants to researchers who are exploring innovative projects that align with Morgan's ethos of combining technology and the humanities.

- **Hosting Annual Conferences:** Organizing conferences that gather scholars, innovators, and practitioners to discuss advancements in digital humanities, share research, and foster collaboration.

Through these initiatives, the foundation will cultivate a community of innovators who are inspired by Morgan's work and are committed to pushing the boundaries of knowledge.

Creating a Digital Archive

Morgan's contributions to digital humanities warrant the creation of a **Digital Archive** that preserves his work, thoughts, and the evolution of his ideas. This archive will include:

+ **Publications and Projects:** A comprehensive collection of Morgan's research papers, articles, and project documentation.

+ **Interviews and Talks:** Recordings of Morgan's lectures, panel discussions, and interviews that showcase his thought process and insights.

+ **Community Contributions:** A section dedicated to works inspired by Morgan, including projects and research by students and collaborators who have been influenced by his vision.

The digital archive will serve as a resource for scholars and practitioners, providing access to Morgan's ideas and fostering a deeper understanding of his impact.

Promoting Ethical AI Development

In light of the ethical dilemmas Morgan faced during his career, it is crucial to promote a framework for **Ethical AI Development**. This framework will address critical issues such as:

+ **Bias in AI Systems:** Developing guidelines that ensure AI systems are designed to minimize bias and promote fairness in decision-making processes. This includes the implementation of diverse data sets and continuous monitoring for unintended consequences.

+ **Privacy and Data Security:** Establishing protocols that prioritize user privacy and data protection, ensuring that technological advancements do not come at the expense of individual rights.

+ **Transparency and Accountability:** Advocating for transparency in AI algorithms and decision-making processes, fostering accountability among developers and organizations that utilize AI technologies.

By championing these principles, we can honor Morgan's legacy and ensure that future innovations are aligned with ethical considerations.

Inspiring Future Innovators

Morgan's journey serves as a beacon of inspiration for young innovators. To honor his legacy, we must actively engage in **Mentorship Programs** that connect experienced professionals with aspiring creators. These programs will focus on:

- **Skill Development:** Providing training and resources to help young innovators develop the necessary skills to thrive in the digital humanities landscape.

- **Networking Opportunities:** Creating platforms for mentees to connect with industry leaders, fostering relationships that can lead to collaborations and career advancements.

- **Encouraging Interdisciplinary Approaches:** Promoting the importance of interdisciplinary thinking, encouraging mentees to explore the intersections of technology, art, and humanities.

Through mentorship, we can cultivate a new generation of thinkers who embody Morgan's spirit of innovation.

Celebrating Morgan's Influence

To truly honor Morgan Liao's legacy, it is essential to celebrate his influence through **Public Recognition.** This can take various forms:

- **Awards and Honors:** Establishing awards in Morgan's name that recognize outstanding contributions to digital humanities and innovative projects that align with his vision.

- **Exhibitions and Installations:** Creating public exhibitions that showcase Morgan's work, including interactive installations that highlight the fusion of technology and the humanities.

- **Media Campaigns:** Launching campaigns that share Morgan's story and achievements, inspiring others to engage with the fields he championed.

By publicly recognizing Morgan's contributions, we reinforce the importance of his work and inspire others to follow in his footsteps.

Continuing the Dialogue

Finally, it is vital to maintain an ongoing **Dialogue** about the future of digital humanities and the role of technology in society. This can be achieved through:

- **Panel Discussions:** Hosting panels that bring together experts to discuss current trends, challenges, and future directions in digital humanities.

- **Online Forums:** Creating online platforms for discussion and collaboration among scholars, practitioners, and the public, fostering a sense of community and shared purpose.

- **Publications:** Encouraging the publication of articles, essays, and research that explore the evolving landscape of digital humanities and the implications of technological advancements.

By fostering dialogue, we ensure that Morgan's legacy continues to inspire critical thinking and innovation in the years to come.

In conclusion, honoring Morgan Liao's legacy requires a multifaceted approach that encompasses the establishment of foundations, digital archives, ethical frameworks, mentorship, public recognition, and ongoing dialogue. By committing to these initiatives, we can ensure that Morgan's vision for a Cyber Renaissance continues to flourish, inspiring future generations to innovate at the intersection of technology and the humanities. As we look to the future, let us carry forth the torch of creativity and inquiry that Morgan ignited, illuminating the path for those who will follow.

Index

Milton Keynes UK
Ingram Content Group UK Ltd.
UKHW030745121124
451094UK00013B/966